Making Mark Twain Work in the Classroom

Making Mark Twain Work in the Classroom

Edited by James S. Leonard

Duke University Press   *Durham & London 1999*

© 1999 by Duke University Press
All rights reserved
Printed in the United States of America on acid-free paper ∞
Typeset in Trump Mediaeval by Keystone Typesetting, Inc.
Library of Congress Cataloging-in-Publication Data appear
on the last printed page of this book.

This volume is dedicated to the memory of two stalwart friends

of Twain Studies and of Twainians:

James D. Wilson (1946–1996) and Pascal Covici Jr. (1930–1997)

Contents

Acknowledgments

The editor gratefully acknowledges the assistance of the Citadel Development Foundation, which provided funding for research and manuscript preparation for this volume. Thanks, too, to Citadel Vice President for Academic Affairs R. Clifton Poole for his unflagging support of Mark Twain and other research at The Citadel and to Christine E. Wharton for her invariably (and invaluably) insightful comments on the manuscript. I am also indebted to student assistants Giselle Cheeseman and Truyen Nguyen for their help in preparing the manuscript, and to the following libraries for access to relevant materials: The Citadel's Daniel Library, the College of Charleston's Robert Scott Small Library, Elmira College's Gannett-Tripp Library, and Duke University's Perkins Library.

And thanks to the following Twainians for their thoughtful and thorough responses to the questionnaire on teaching *Huckleberry Finn* and other works by Twain, which formed the basis for the introductory essay, "Who's Teaching Mark Twain, and How": Joseph Alvarez, Anthony Berret, Earl Briden, Wesley Britton, Stanley Brodwin, Christina Bucher, Louis Budd, Everett Carter, Joseph Church, Pascal Covici, Jr., James Cox, Richard Cracroft, Victor Doyno, Dennis Eddings, E. N. Feltskog, Janet Gabler-Hover, Susan Harris, Kay House, Goldena Howard, Lawrence Howe, David Ketterer, Michael Kiskis, Richard Kopley, Charles Leech, J. R. LeMaster, Jay Martin, Charlotte McClure, Joseph McCullough, Jim McWilliams, Jeffrey Melton, Linda Morris, Ed Piacentino, Grace Polivka, Stan Poole, Robert Regan, Herbert Risley, Robert Sattelmeyer, David Sloane, Gayle Smith, Rich Stonum, Thomas Tenney, David Tomlinson, Richard Tuerk.

Who's Teaching Mark Twain, and How?

James S. Leonard

Mark Twain's novel *Adventures of Huckleberry Finn* is generally acknowledged as the literary work most frequently taught in U.S. colleges and high schools—and is, no doubt, one of the American texts most frequently taught in other countries as well, since among American writers Twain ranks behind only Jack London in international popularity. Considering the attention the novel has received from such twentieth-century luminaries as Ernest Hemingway ("All modern American literature comes from one book by Mark Twain called *Huckleberry Finn*"), T. S. Eliot ("a masterpiece"), and Lionel Trilling ("one of the world's great books and one of the central documents of American culture"), the novel must be regarded as a cultural monument that cannot reasonably be ignored; and ongoing controversies over the book's racial implications indicate the degree to which it remains significant in our contemporary climate. Other Twain works often taught are *The Innocents Abroad, A Connecticut Yankee in King Arthur's Court, Pudd'nhead Wilson,* various short tales and sketches, and (mainly at the more advanced levels) assorted unfinished fragments from the "later" Twain.

Teaching Twain's works can involve some formidable pedagogical questions:

1. How can a teacher successfully deal with the more than two hundred occurrences of various forms of the word "nigger" in *Huckleberry Finn* and with Twain's portrayal of the slave Jim (at times) in accordance with some of the most demeaning of nineteenth-century stereotypes for African Americans? Should these aspects of the novel disqualify it from being taught? Or can they be turned to pedagogical advantage?

2. How can a teacher cope with the curious structural and the-

matic dislocations of *Huckleberry Finn*'s last twelve chapters, sometimes known as the "evasion" section? Can, and should, the ending be justified?

3. Do *Huckleberry Finn* and Twain's other "boy books" inappropriately valorize adolescent attitudes and values to the detriment of more responsible, adult attitudes and values?

4. How should a teacher approach the casual violence that such works as *A Connecticut Yankee in King Arthur's Court* seem indifferent—or even approving—toward?

5. How can the role of women in Twain's works, now mostly submerged, be made more visible? What can we learn from Twain's works about nineteenth-century attitudes toward women?

6. What is the thematic result in Twain's works of the internal conflict between his championing of the "common man" (vis-à-vis the aristocracy) and his frequent recourse to misanthropic views?

7. How do Twain's roles as a public figure and an entrepreneur enter into the fabric of his fiction? What are the significances of these penetrations of fictional text by "nonliterary" elements?

To try to answer these questions and, more generally, the two questions posed in my title, I sent out a questionnaire to members of the Mark Twain Circle of America in 1993 asking what Mark Twain works are taught, in what contexts, and by what methods. The studious statistician will, of course, immediately note that my statistical profile can tell little about what the *average* teacher is doing since members of the Mark Twain Circle are representative of that part of the scholarly community most committed to teaching Mark Twain and most likely to be expert at it. This is no random sample. On the other hand, there is a case to be made for expertise vis-à-vis representativeness. What I will try to present here, then, is a picture of how those most conversant with Mark Twain use his works in the classroom.

I began with an assumption already mentioned: that *Adventures of Huckleberry Finn* is the most widely taught of Mark Twain's works and the one in which most people are interested. Thus, I divided the questionnaire into two sections, the first half dealing entirely with *Huckleberry Finn* and the second devoted to other works by Twain. The responses seem to have justified my assumption, in that virtually all those responding indicated that they have taught *Huckleberry Finn*, usually often and in various contexts. The only two exceptions were middle-school teachers—one of whom uses *The Adventures of Tom Sawyer* and the other teaches mainly Twain's biography, using Twain and his family to represent nineteenth-century domestic life in New England. The total number of responses was sixty-three.

Teaching Huckleberry Finn

HUCK'S PLACE IN THE CURRICULUM

The questionnaire first asked, *In what courses have you used "Adventures of Huckleberry Finn" as a text? (Please give descriptive title of course and level—e.g., freshman, sophomore, upper-division, graduate.)* As expected, the novel is taught at all levels from high school through graduate programs and in continuing education courses. It apparently is not commonly taught—and the consensus of scholarly opinion is that it *should* not be taught—at the junior high or middle-school level. The two reasons for avoiding the novel at this level are that (1) it is difficult, so students do not adequately appreciate its subtleties, and (2) the violence and racial issues might be too disturbing to younger students. This attitude toward the novel is generally consistent with judgments expressed in the essay collection *Satire or Evasion? Black Perspectives on "Huckleberry Finn"* (1992), where several African American scholars suggested that students below the high school level are likely to take the novel's racism literally (i.e., nonironically) and thus miss what is normally perceived by more sophisticated readers as Twain's antiracism theme in the novel. On the other hand, three high school teachers who responded indicated that they do teach *Huckleberry Finn*—one to juniors, one to seniors, and the other at an unspecified high school level.

In colleges and universities *Huckleberry Finn* is regularly taught at both introductory and advanced levels. The courses in which it is used fall roughly into the following categories:

1. About 25 percent of the respondents reported teaching the novel in freshman composition and introduction to literature courses, where it was deemed useful as both a stylistic example and a stimulus to thematic discussion. Themes discussed included race relations, bases for moral judgments, and censorship.

2. Approximately 40 percent of respondents reported teaching *Huck Finn* in sophomore surveys. Most commonly, this was an American literature survey, with the syllabus usually limited to a specific period

in American literature that Twain would fit into (nineteenth century, late nineteenth century, American Realism, etc.). Two respondents reported teaching the novel in American humor courses at the sophomore level, and one teaches it in a sophomore course devoted exclusively to Mark Twain.

3. Nearly all the respondents have taught *Huck Finn* in upper-division courses. Again, period courses were the most common (about 32 percent). About 20 percent have used *Huck Finn* in upper-division novel courses, and 9 percent in American humor courses. Upper-division courses devoted entirely to Twain and that use *Huckleberry Finn* have been taught by 16 percent of those responding, and 5 percent have used the novel in courses focusing on Twain and other specific writers (Henry James, Stephen Crane, Sarah Orne Jewett, and Sigmund Freud were mentioned).

4. *Huckleberry Finn* also does well at the graduate level, where 66 percent of respondents reported teaching it. Here the largest groups (23 percent each) were period courses and courses focusing specifically on Twain. Other groups represented were Twain and other specified writers (9 percent; Herman Melville and Edgar Allan Poe were mentioned), the American novel (7 percent), American humor (4 percent), and race in American literature (2 percent).

5. One respondent reported teaching *Huckleberry Finn* in a continuing education course titled "Mark Twain: His Life and Works."

From the above we can arrive at the not surprising conclusion that Twain's widely acknowledged masterpiece *Huckleberry Finn* is a very popular text among Twain specialists. More interestingly, we see that nearly everyone in the sample is finding some opportunity to teach *Huckleberry Finn* in upper-division courses and that a majority also teach the novel at the graduate level, with much of that teaching occurring in courses devoted largely or exclusively to Twain's works.

WHICH EDITION TO USE

Editions of *Adventures of Huckleberry Finn* are so numerous as to be bewildering to someone not familiar with their relative virtues. However, the questionnaire responses showed a high degree of agreement among Twain specialists as to the appropriateness of particular editions for specific teaching situations. Here is how the editions for teaching sort out:

1. *Works of Mark Twain Edition* (University of California Press). This is clearly the definitive edition of *Huckleberry Finn* at the present time. It gives the best available text of the novel, including restoration of the raftsmen episode to Chapter 16—a textual situation currently preferred by most Twain scholars. The *Works of Mark Twain* also includes the complete original illustrations by Edward Windsor Kemble (a big textual bonus) as well as extensive discussion of the text and its history. It thus provides the logical starting point for serious study of the novel. The big problem in using this edition is cost. In most cases the expense is justified only for graduate or upper-division courses in which the novel plays an unusually large role. Nonetheless, 21 percent of those responding to the questionnaire indicated that they had used the *Works of Mark Twain* edition as a classroom text.

2. *Norton Critical Edition.* Historically, this has been the most popular text for upper-division courses and is often used at other levels as well; 30 percent of respondents reported having used it for teaching. It provides a soundly established text (with the raftsmen episode included as an appendix) and adds to that a judiciously chosen selection of textual background and representative critical essays. The text has the editorial integrity characteristic of Norton Critical Editions, and the attached essays and background materials provide a solid beginning for student research. This is a versatile and modestly priced text; it is intended for use in college courses, and it serves that purpose well. Its one major defect is the lack of illustrations.

3. *Mark Twain Library Edition.* This is the same as the *Works of Mark Twain* edition, but without the extensive discussion of textual methods and issues. It is available in paperback at a price low enough to make it a reasonable choice in any situation where the novel is being taken fairly seriously (as it always should be, of course). This edition has all the textual virtues of the *Works of Mark Twain* edition, including complete illustrations. In the relatively brief time that it has been available, it has become the principal rival to the Norton Critical Edition as the most popular text of the novel for college courses; 20 percent of respondents reported having used it. The illustrations are especially useful (became some of them picture Jim in accordance with popular racial stereotypes of Twain's era) for helping to establish a sense of the racial climate in the nineteenth-century United States.

4. *American Literature Anthologies.* Versions of *Huckleberry Finn*

included in anthologies have been used by 16 percent of the question-naire respondents. This obviously occurs mainly in American litera-ture survey courses. The anthology mentioned most often was Nor-ton (12 percent of respondents). Others were Heath, Prentice-Hall, and Macmillan.

5. *Facsimile Editions.* One respondent mentioned having used a fac-simile reproduction of the first edition of *Huckleberry Finn* which is no longer available; two others said that they would use such an edi-tion if it were currently obtainable. Harper a few years ago took the curious step of sending out copies of a paperback version (the Harper Centennial Edition) of the novel free to selected college faculty, but then did not make it available for sale to students. However, a cloth version of the Harper Centennial Edition can be purchased at a higher (but not prohibitively high) price. This is a useful option for giving a sense of the novel's original character and impact, and it includes Kem-ble's illustrations.

6. *Cheaper Editions.* In many contexts, teachers find that the least expensive edition of *Huckleberry Finn* is the appropriate one. The ones mentioned most frequently were Signet (11 percent), Riverside (7 per-cent), Penguin (5 percent), Rinehart (4 percent), and Bantam (4 percent). The Riverside edition (published by Houghton Mifflin) was singled out as especially respected because of the excellent editorial work of Henry Nash Smith. Dover markets a nicely produced, inexpensive (only $2.00) edition that appeared too recently to be included in the survey. For courses in which other Twain works are being taught along with *Huck Finn*, one respondent recommended *The Viking Portable Mark Twain*. And Signet, in addition to its separate edition of *Huckleberry Finn*, has a joint edition of *Huckleberry Finn* and *Tom Sawyer*; Signet also includes it (along with *The Scarlet Letter*, *Billy Budd*, and *The Red Badge of Courage*) in a modestly priced volume titled *Four Classic American Novels*.

7. *Other Editions.* Bedford Books publishes a reasonably priced edi-tion of *Adventures of Huckleberry Finn* (subtitle: *A Case Study in Critical Controversy*), edited by Gerald Graff and James Phelan. The text is accompanied by selected illustrations and by critical essays intended to support Graff's well-known teaching-the-controversies ap-proach. This should be especially useful within a context interested in critical approaches.

8. *No Specified Edition.* A few respondents indicated that in some

contexts they have allowed students to use any edition that is available. I have done this, for example, in a graduate-level Principles of Literary Criticism course in which *Huckleberry Finn* was used as an application text for the various critical methods that were studied but was not itself a part of the course's subject matter.

9. *Two Further Choices.* The following important editions, both moderately priced, appeared in 1996, after the "Teaching Twain" survey was conducted:

–The Random House edition of *Adventures of Huckleberry Finn* contains material included in the first-half manuscript of *Huckleberry Finn*, discovered in 1990, but not published in the novel. Victor Doyno, a recognized authority on the *Huck Finn* manuscript, has selected the textual additions and provided commentary on their significance. There is also an introduction by Twain biographer Justin Kaplan. This volume makes new sorts of classroom exploration of the novel possible.

–The Oxford Mark Twain edition of *Huckleberry Finn* offers a facsimile reproduction of the first American edition, including illustrations, with a foreword by Nobel Prize-winner Toni Morrison and an afterword by Victor Doyno. Although the Oxford Mark Twain has been marketed mainly as a 29-volume set, individual volumes are available for separate purchase and are suitable (indeed, excellent) for classroom use.

HOW WELL DOES "HUCKLEBERRY FINN" WORK?

In reply to the question, *In which course(s) has "Huckleberry Finn" worked well for you, and what aspect [of the novel] do you think was most responsible for its success?*, the overwhelming majority of questionnaire respondents answered with something like, "*Huckleberry Finn* always works well!!" Why?

1. The reason most frequently cited for the novel's pedagogical success was its thematic potency. Respondents found it intriguing to students and a strong basis for discussions of race, hypocrisy, class differences, societal corruption, and individual responsibility. The character of Huck himself often figures prominently in such discussions. Most readers immediately like and respect Huck and readily become concerned with his problems.

2. Next after theme was the novel's humor. Although one respon-

dent felt that the humor in *Huckleberry Finn* does not play well today, many others specified the novel's comic success as the most important reason why students are interested in it and enjoy it.

3. Narrative technique was another frequently mentioned strength of the novel. Here the sense of modernity was cited as especially important. In period courses, students who have read such predecessors as James Fenimore Cooper (the eternal victim of comparisons to Twain), Nathaniel Hawthorne, and Melville find Twain refreshingly readable and full of positive energy. They can easily sympathize with Hemingway's often-quoted judgment about *Huckleberry Finn*'s seminal relation to "modern American literature."

One respondent noted that *Huckleberry Finn* "is never a teaching disaster," which certainly is a comforting thought for even the most battle-hardened pedagogue.

In reply to the counter-question, *In which course(s) has "Huckleberry Finn" not worked well, and what do you see as the reason for its lesser effectiveness?*, about one-third of the respondents gave no response at all—which in most cases was probably intended to convey that they had encountered no problems whatever in teaching the novel. Most of those who did give responses likewise indicated that problems in teaching *Huckleberry Finn* constitute a null set. But there are, of course, some problems:

1. Many college students have read—or think they have read—*Huckleberry Finn* and may therefore be reluctant to read it (again). But this negative can also have its positive aspects. Some respondents indicated that prior familiarity can be helpful because the experience of rereading with greater sophistication may reveal something about levels and varieties of possible response to the text.

2. The novel's racial implications can be unsettling. I find this aspect most difficult when there are only a few African American students in the class. Those students may feel that they have to bear the psychological burden of "representing," even if not explicitly asked to do so, the attitudes and sensitivities of African Americans in the face of a racially charged text and in the presence of a perhaps monolithic, perhaps hostile white majority.

3. The nineteenth-century setting can seem too remote from the students' own experience.

4. Students may find the dialect, especially Jim's, difficult to understand. An obvious solution is to read passages aloud and have students

do the same. But one has to be cautious here because many otherwise delightful passages contain racial slurs that cannot be allowed to pass without careful comment. And many of Jim's speeches, when lifted from their context in the novel, play into racial stereotyping.

HOW TO DEAL WITH THE RACIAL ISSUES

In terms of the life that a text lives within a particular culture at a particular time, the history of *Huckleberry Finn* has from the beginning been instructive. Twain's novel has weathered controversies related to good taste, proper decorum, literary merit, societal values, and philosophical soundness, but only in recent years, near the centennial of its 1884–85 publication, have the racial questions that now seem so prominent in the novel been widely perceived as a major issue. The psychological result for teachers was predictable. What had been seen as a solid, uplifting presentation of right instincts triumphing over meretricious training was now seen by some as being itself an instrument for maintaining prejudice. What had been a fairly straightforward pedagogical task—exposing positive thematic turns and helping students to fully experience the novel's humorous and thematic impact—now became a situation fraught with danger.

The reasons for the timing of this change are obvious. The civil rights movement of the 1950s and 1960s brought about an increased consciousness not only of the unfairness of legal barriers that African Americans faced but also of the psychological harm that could result from European American insensitivity to racial insults like those present in *Huckleberry Finn*. More specifically, the integration of schools in the South, along with less extreme but nonetheless often turbulent remixing of student populations in the North, created a fundamental change in the audience to whom the teacher must play. This change had to do not only with the number of African Americans in a given classroom but with the teacher's perception of the nature of his/her primary constituency. In short, the teaching of *Huckleberry Finn* had become problematized.

How to deal with the problematization? In response to the question, *To what degree do you dwell on racial questions, and how do you handle them?*, nearly everyone indicated that this issue was a crucial consideration; in fact, I received lengthier responses to this question than to any other. Some see their task as trying to justify Sam Clemens as a nonracist in order to build a base of credibility for *Huckleberry*

Finn; others show Twain as struggling against racism but often drawn into racial offensiveness despite good intentions. A few simply declare that *Huckleberry Finn* does present a racist point of view, and they have either given up teaching it (very few have chosen this option) or now teach it as an example of the prevailing racist views of the late nineteenth century. Whatever one's position within that spectrum (assuming only that she or he has not stopped teaching the novel altogether), the available means for dealing with racial issues in *Huckleberry Finn* fall mainly into the categories of (1) close textual analysis and (2) background information. Textual analysis emphasizing the text's ironies, voicing, assignment of narrative responsibility, and patterns of imagery, incident, and language can sharpen the students' vague impressions and help them confront the issues more directly. Helpful background reading can include biographical information on Twain to try to establish the author's relation to his text, or it can focus more broadly on the nineteenth-century sociopolitical climate both before and after the Civil War. (See the Reference Resources section below for some recommended readings.)

OTHER THEMES

Although attention to racial issues in recent years has tended to overshadow everything else, *Adventures of Huckleberry Finn* offers rich opportunities for other thematic explorations. In this regard, the novel's somewhat episodic structure is a virtue since it presents a wide variety of situations; but as with the racial questions, this variety can also make thematic contradictions more likely. Some of the most commonly taught themes:

1. parent-child relationships,
2. relation to literary tradition (both reliance and hostility),
3. freedom vs. responsibility,
4. realism vs. romance,
5. mythological motifs,
6. the function of humor,
7. religious belief, skepticism, hypocrisy,
8. critique of Southern culture or American culture in general,
9. the worthiness or unworthiness of the average person,
10. the role of women in *Huckleberry Finn*.

Item 10, the role of women, has not been a major subject of discussion until the later 1980s, but even a cursory review of topics for books, articles, and conference presentations in recent years will confirm that it is an area of growing interest.

STRUCTURAL MATTERS

The most common topic for structural analysis is the appropriateness or inappropriateness of the "evasion" section—the novel's last twelve chapters. In these chapters, Tom Sawyer reappears after being absent since the early chapters and turns the serious relationship between Jim and Huck into a burlesque in which the two boys execute an elaborate scheme to "free" Jim—who, as it turns out and as Tom already knew, has already been freed by his now-deceased owner, Miss Watson, in her will. The trend in discussing this part of the novel seems to be toward justifying it in terms of thematic appropriateness and a logical working out of various linguistic and imagaic motifs, but many still regard the "evasion" as a major weakness in the novel's structure.

Other structural matters often discussed are Twain's methods for achieving humor and irony, his use of dialect and other "realistic" devices, his reliance on motifs such as the number "forty," and the novel as an example of Southwestern humor, the tall tale, or the picaresque adventure. A major topic, of course, is how the various episodes and characters fit together.

INTERTEXTUAL COMPARISONS

Huckleberry Finn is a novel in which books are frequently mentioned, parodied, and otherwise alluded to. In answer to the question, *What comparisons to works by other authors do you find most useful?*, the greatest frequency of responses indicated works related to the racial context: *Uncle Tom's Cabin, Narrative of the Life of Frederick Douglass*, other slave narratives, Charles Chesnutt's short story "The Goophered Grapevine," and Joel Chandler Harris's "Free Joe and the Rest of the World." Other categories frequently mentioned were bad-boy stories and Southwestern humor stories. Other authors and books mentioned more than once were Cervantes's *Don Quixote*, J. D. Salinger's *The Catcher in the Rye*, Henry James (*Daisy Miller* and *The American*), William Dean Howells, Herman Melville, Walt Whitman, George Washington Cable (*The Grandissimes*), James Fenimore Cooper's *The Last of the Mohicans*, Stephen Crane's *Maggie*, Kate Chopin's *The Awakening*, Ernest Hemingway, *Gil Blas*, and Thomas Bailey Aldrich's *Story of a Bad Boy*.

AUDIOVISUAL RESOURCES

In answer to the question, *What audiovisuals do you find most useful?*, the most frequent response was "none." Not much help there. But for those of a less morose disposition, there are some possibilities.

The most highly regarded audiovisual resources are the recordings of Hal Holbrook's Mark Twain impersonations, which continue to be popular and therefore readily available. One of the continuing despairs (perhaps a source of the moroseness alluded to above) of teachers of Mark Twain and other Mark Twain enthusiasts is that Holbrook's excellent performances have not been made available on videotape. A useful survey of other audio materials pertinent to teaching Twain can be found in Wesley Britton's "Mark Twain on Tape" in the August 1987 issue of the *Mark Twain Circular*.

Video representations of *Huckleberry Finn* have met with considerably less approbation than Holbrook's recording. Many movie and television versions of the book have appeared, but most Twain fanciers find all of them seriously flawed. The two which currently are of most interest are the 1993 Walt Disney Company's *The Adventures of Huck Finn*, principally because it is the most recent, and the 1985 PBS four-part version. The worst adaptation of Twain's novel in my view (with apologies to Mickey Rooney fans) is the 1939 movie starring Rooney, which ends with Huck piloting a steamboat upriver to save Jim from a lynch mob in St. Petersburg. Lots of action, but . . . Others, of course, have their own nominees for worst video version; there are many solid candidates for the title.

One old-style visual aid that works well and is being newly rediscovered by many teachers is the original set of illustrations by E. W. Kemble. These are not available in the cheap editions or the anthology versions of *Huckleberry Finn*, and, as I indicated above, they are also missing from the Norton Critical Edition, but they can be found in the University of California's *Works of Mark Twain*, its more modestly priced Mark Twain Library edition, the Harper Centennial edition, the Oxford Mark Twain edition, and the 1996 Random House "Comprehensive Edition." The illustrations are useful for evoking the nineteenth-century context, for noting the representation of racial characteristics, and for understanding the original impact of the book when it was published fully illustrated. This also can lead to a discussion of the relation of the author (who in this case "authorized" the illustrations) to his text and to the demands of subscription publishing.

A valuable addition to the portfolio of Mark Twain video resources is a fifty-minute video simply titled *Huckleberry Finn* (available from Films for the Humanities and Sciences) that features analysis by scholars Victor Doyno, Justin Kaplan, and David Smith, and a very creditable impersonation of Mark Twain by McEvoy Layne. Current price: $149.

For high school teachers, the Thomas Kleist video *Uncle Mark*, which is also available as a filmstrip and as a CD-ROM, contains some interesting pictures as well as a mostly solid introduction to the biography of Mark Twain; my review of this resource appears in the July-September 1994 *Mark Twain Circular*.

For the more technologically adventurous, the CD-ROM disk *Twain's World* offers a wealth of visual materials. This extraordinary resource is further discussed below under Reference Resources and was reviewed by Joseph Towson in the *Mark Twain Circular*'s July-September 1994 issue.

REFERENCE RESOURCES

The body of available reference resources for teaching Mark Twain in general and *Huckleberry Finn* in particular can be formidable (to say the least) for the nonspecialist; even the moderately well-informed Twainian may find it a bit daunting at times. My survey on teaching *Huckleberry Finn* included the question, *"What reference resources (biographical, critical, or other) do you find most useful to yourself and your students?"* The following summarizes the responses, with the addition of some excellent resources that have become available since the survey was done:

1. *All-Purpose Reference*

Clearly the best resource for studying Mark Twain at any level is *The Mark Twain Encyclopedia*, edited by J. R. LeMaster and James D. Wilson (Garland, 1993). This volume offers information on virtually any topic relating to Twain's life or writings. The encyclopedia is the work of leading Twain scholars and is highly authoritative as well as comprehensive—though the large number of contributors inevitably results in some unevenness in the quality of the entries.

Alan Gribben's *Mark Twain's Library: A Reconstruction* (G. K. Hall, 1980), besides being the definitive source of information about what books Twain owned and read, is encyclopedic in its coverage of topics related to Twain's life. In short, it offers much more than its title implies; and because it is the work of a single author who is meticulous and knowledgeable about his subject matter, there is no problem of unevenness.

R. Kent Rasmussen's *Mark Twain A to Z* (Facts on File, 1995) is another useful encyclopedic treatment of Twain and his works. It is especially well-suited to the nonspecialist because it gives such basic details as plot summaries and character identifications without assuming that the reader is already well-acquainted with the works being discussed. This approach, of course, can also be helpful as a quick reference even for those who teach Twain regularly.

Thomas A. Tenney's *Mark Twain: A Reference Guide* (G. K. Hall, 1977) provides a comprehensive annotated bibliography of Twain scholarship. This work is used by Twain scholars as a starting point for research. Tenney has provided annual supplements, first in *American Literary Realism* (1977–83), then in the *Mark Twain Circular* (1987–96). The supplements are indexed in the *Circular*, but are nonetheless unwieldy to use. An up-to-date second edition is currently under way to supersede the supplements.

American Literary Scholarship, published annually by Duke University Press, is another valuable resource for keeping up to date on what's happening in Twain studies. Here a leading Twain scholar gives a capsule summary and evaluation of the year's events in biography, criticism, new editions, etc. It can also be useful for a quick review of a particular book or article from a past year. The summary evaluation in *American Literary Scholarship* is consistently of high quality, although the Twain reviewer usually changes every few years.

For information specifically about *Adventures of Huckleberry Finn*, the *Works of Mark Twain* (University of California Press, 1985) contains extensive scholarly material that is well worth perusing by anyone who has even a moderately serious interest in the novel.

For those with a bit of high-tech capability, the CD-ROM *Twain's World* offers electronic texts of most Twain's works and, in addition, some interesting audiovisuals and background materials. For the adept user, the material is easily accessible.

Also in the high-tech area, excellent web sources are available for teaching Mark Twain. For a start, try one of these sites:

Twain Web (Mark Twain Forum home page) (http://web.mit.edu/ linguistics/www/forum/twainweb.html)

The Mark Twain Papers and Project (Bancroft Library) (http:// library.berkeley.edu/BANC/MTP)

Mark Twain, from the Mining Company (by Jim Zwick) (http:/ /marktwain.miningco.com)

Mark Twain in His Times (by Stephen Railton, University of Virginia) (http://etext.virginia.edu/railton/index2.html)

2. *Biography*

The standard work on Clemens's life remains Justin Kaplan's *Mr. Clemens and Mark Twain* (Simon and Schuster, 1966), which was cited by nearly 20 percent of the questionnaire respondents. Some later biographical works that have made significant contributions:

Andrews, Kenneth. *Nook Farm: Mark Twain's Hartford Circle.* Archon, 1967.

Budd, Louis J. *Our Mark Twain.* University of Pennsylvania Press, 1983.

Cardwell, Guy. *The Man Who Was Mark Twain.* Yale University Press, 1991.

Dolmetsch, Carl. *"Our Famous Guest": Mark Twain in Vienna.* University of Georgia Press, 1992.

Emerson, Everett. *The Authentic Mark Twain.* University of Pennsylvania Press, 1984.

Skandera-Trombley, Laura. *Mark Twain in the Company of Women.* University of Pennsylvania Press, 1995.

Steinbrink, Jeffrey. *Getting to Be Mark Twain.* University of California Press, 1991.

In addition, the following works predating Kaplan's continue to have vitality wth respect to the Twain biography:

Brooks, Van Wyck. *The Ordeal of Mark Twain.* Dutton, 1920.

De Voto, Bernard. *Mark Twain at Work.* Harvard University Press, 1942.

———. *Mark Twain's America.* Little, Brown, 1932.

Hill, Hamlin. *Mark Twain: God's Fool.* Harper and Row, 1973.

Paine, Albert Bigelow. *Mark Twain: A Biography.* 3 vols. Harper, 1912.

Smith, Henry Nash. *Mark Twain: The Development of a Writer.* Belknap Press of Harvard University Press, 1962.

The best chronologies of Clemens's life can be found in *Mark Twain: Collected Tales, Sketches, Speeches, and Essays* (2 vols.), edited by Louis J. Budd (Library of America, 1992), and *The Mark Twain Encyclopedia.*

There are three major versions of Mark Twain's autobiography:

Clemens, Samuel L. *Mark Twain's Autobiography.* Ed. Albert Bigelow Paine. 2 vols. Harper, 1924.

———. *The Autobiography of Mark Twain.* Ed. Charles Neider. Harper, 1959.

———. *Mark Twain's Own Autobiography: The Chapters from the "North American Review."* Ed. Michael J. Kiskis. University of Wisconsin Press, 1990.

Each of these versions has its own virtues and adherents. Paine's has the authority of being close to the source since Paine actually took Sam Clemens's dictation of the material, but Twain scholars sometimes question how much of the material is Twain's and how much is Paine's. Neider's version, being later, has the advantage of being able to build on the strengths of Paine's work; however, Neider plays to a general readership more than a scholarly one. Kiskis's book is less extensive than the other two; but it has the clear authority of Twain himself since it contains only material that Twain published, and it includes an introduction that gives an excellent overview of the autobiographical writings. Also of some interest is *Papa,* by Clemens's daughter Susy (ed. Charles Neider; Doubleday, 1985).

3. *Genesis of "Huckleberry Finn"*

There are three major sources:

Walter Blair's *Mark Twain and Huck Finn* (University of California Press, 1960) has enjoyed the status of a standard work on this subject.

Victor A. Doyno's *Writing Huck Finn* uses the last half of the *Huckleberry Finn* manuscript (held by the Buffalo-Erie County Library) to analyze Twain's composition methods, concentrating especially on the significance of revisions. Doyno is currently at work on another book that will analyze the first half of the *Huckleberry Finn* manuscript discovered in 1990.

The *Works of Mark Twain* edition of *Huckleberry Finn* contains a description and analysis of the original versions of *Huckleberry Finn* and provides a rationale for assigning authority to one textual possibility rather than another.

Shelley Fisher Fishkin's *Was Huck Black? Mark Twain and African-American Voices*, cited below, is also of interest with respect to genesis, since it discusses the influence of African American speech on Twain's portrayal of characters in *Huckleberry Finn*.

4. *Critical Works*

Here, as with the biographies, the choices are difficult. Mark Twain is an extremely popular subject for literary criticism, and much first-rate work has been done. I will indicate some useful critical works in the following categories, with apologies for the many worthy ones that I fail to mention:

Twain's Humor. This has been a particularly fertile area of Twain criticism. Some of the most outstanding:

> Covici, Pascal, Jr. *Mark Twain's Humor: The Image of a World.* Southern Methodist University Press, 1962.
> Cox, James M. *Mark Twain: The Fate of Humor.* Princeton University Press, 1966.
> Sloane, David E. E. *"Adventures of Huckleberry Finn": American Comic Vision.* Twayne, 1988.
> ———. *Mark Twain as a Literary Comedian.* Louisiana State University Press, 1979.
> ———, ed. *Mark Twain's Humor: Critical Essays.* Garland, 1993.

Racial Issues. The standard resource here is *Satire or Evasion? Black Perspectives on Huckleberry Finn*, edited by James S. Leonard, Thomas A. Tenney, and Thadious M. Davis (Duke University Press, 1992). This collection contains fifteen essays by African American scholars on *Adventures of Huckleberry Finn*, some approbative and some attacking the novel as racist. It also contains an extensive annotated bibliography (by Tenney) on the subject of *Huckleberry Finn* and race.

Shelley Fisher Fishkin's *Was Huck Black? Mark Twain and African-*

American Voices (Oxford University Press, 1993) adds a new dimension to the discussion of racial issues. It makes the argument that the voicing of characters in *Huckleberry Finn* and other works by Twain was significantly influenced by African American speech that Twain had been exposed to. Arthur Petit's *Mark Twain and the South* and Kenneth Lynn's *Mark Twain and Southwestern Humor*, cited below, are useful additional sources on the subject of Twain's relation to the racial climate of the late nineteenth century.

Some of Twain's own short works and biographical/autobiographical fragments can be of use here as well. "A True Story" and the newspaper piece "Sociable Jimmy" are deemed particularly pertinent; both are discussed at length in Fishkin's book.

Essay Collections. Besides those indicated above, the following essay collections on *Adventures of Huckleberry Finn* were mentioned by questionnaire respondents as useful:

> Budd, Louis J., ed. *New Essays on Adventures of Huckleberry Finn.* Cambridge University Press, 1985.
>
> Inge, M. Thomas, ed. *Huck Finn Among the Critics: A Centennial Selection.* University Publications of America, 1985.
>
> Sattelmeyer, Robert, and J. Donald Crowley, eds. *One Hundred Years of Huckleberry Finn: The Boy, His Book, and American Culture.* University of Missouri Press, 1985.
>
> Smith, Henry Nash, ed. *Mark Twain: A Collection of Critical Essays.* Prentice-Hall, 1963.

Other. One convenient source of standard critical essays, along with some source material, is the Norton Critical Edition of *Huckleberry Finn* (ed. Sculley Bradley, Richmond Croom Beatty, E. Hudson Long, and Thomas Cooley; 2nd ed.; Norton, 1977). Another is the Bedford Books *Adventures of Huckleberry Finn: A Case Study in Critical Controversy* (ed. Gerald Graff and James Phelan, 1995). In addition, the following critical works were mentioned by respondents to the questionnaire:

> Budd, Louis J. *Mark Twain: Social Philosopher.* Indiana University Press, 1962.
>
> Lynn, Kenneth. *Mark Twain and the Southwestern Humor.* Little, Brown, 1960.

Pettit, Arthur G. *Mark Twain and the South.* University Press of Kentucky, 1974.

Teaching Other Works by Mark Twain

COURSES ON MARK TWAIN

In response to the question, *Have you taught any course(s) wholly or largely devoted to Mark Twain?*, about 85 percent of respondents indicated they had. Although these were mainly at the graduate and advanced undergraduate levels, one junior high school teacher (Grace Polivka, Northford, Connecticut) reported teaching a course called "Growing up Victorian: Papa Clemens and His Brood," in which she used the Clemens family as a focal point for exploring life (in polite society, obviously) in the late nineteenth century. Courses devoted entirely to Mark Twain tend to fall under the rubric of graduate seminar, senior seminar, or "major literary figures." Two variations reported were "The Literary Personae of Mark Twain" and "Mark Twain and His Circle." Among those frequently teamed with Twain in advanced courses are Henry James, William Dean Howells, Edith Wharton, Stephen Crane, Bret Harte, George Washington Cable, and Joel Chandler Harris.

WORKS MOST FREQUENTLY TAUGHT

In response to the question, *What works by Mark Twain other than "Huckleberry Finn" have you used as texts?*, the lineup was for the most part unsurprising. Here is a list of those mentioned in more than one response (with percentages):

A Connecticut Yankee in King Arthur's Court 56
The Tragedy of Pudd'nhead Wilson 37
The Adventures of Tom Sawyer 32
Roughing It 24
The Innocents Abroad 17
"The Man That Corrupted Hadleyburg" 17
The Mysterious Stranger 15
"The Notorious Jumping Frog of Calaveras County" 14
Life on the Mississippi 12
Selected Short Stories 10

HOW TO MAKE THEM WORK

Four questions invited analysis of the teachability of individual works:

1. *With what works have you had most success? (Please indicate the pedagogical situation and the nature of the success.)*
2. *Which works have you found less successful? What do you think was the problem?*
3. *What themes and issues do you emphasize for particular works?*
4. *What contextual or intertextual aspects do you find most useful in teaching Mark Twain?*

Responses to these questions yielded the following conclusions:

A Connecticut Yankee in King Arthur's Court ranks high as a teachable text because it tells a good story and seems applicable to the present. Respondents found it effective as satire and as devastating social criticism. Its particular currency has to do with the ambivalences that Twain exhibits in the novel. His vacillations with respect to technology, modernity, romanticism, and the fundamental goodness or badness of humanity, combined with the novel's surprising, seemingly illogical alternations between high-spirited comedy and brutal violence, give *Connecticut Yankee* what can readily be perceived as a postmodern ambience and establish fertile ground for classroom discussion and individual interpretation. The connections to historical context also create worthwhile pedagogical possibilities. *A Connecticut Yankee* occupies a peculiar place in the American consciousness in that, in spite of the fact that the main character slaughters more than 24,000 people and expresses little remorse for having done so, it is often regarded as a children's novel and is taught or assigned for individual reading at the junior high or high school level. It seems that the comedy overshadows the violence to such a degree that readers are able simply to ignore the violence. And as with *Huckleberry Finn*, this also leads to interesting possibilities for reexperiencing the novel at more advanced stages where the violence and other disjunctions of style and theme are not ignored, but emphasized. These same disjunctions, however, were indicated by some respondents as an objectionable aspect of the novel since students may be confused or annoyed by thematic contradictions and a plot that does not yield the sort of conclusion it seemed to promise. *A Connecticut Yankee* is often taught in conjunction with Utopian literature, with historical documentation relating to societies of the nineteenth century and the medieval period, and with versions of the story of King Arthur. I have found it very successful in an honors course, "The Arthurian Legend," in which it serves to deflate many of the pretensions of the narratives of Malory and Tennyson, while at the same time finding some of the values of those tellings, especially Malory's, not so deflatable as Twain's first-person narrator would have us believe.

The Tragedy of Pudd'nhead Wilson has in the last few years shared to some extent in the controversy over *Adventures of Huckleberry Finn*'s racial depictions. Although it has often been used as high school or even junior high school reading, it now tends to be viewed as suitable for more mature audiences who are better able to grapple with the complexities of the depiction of race, not to mention a bit of sex and violence. It can be taught alongside *Huckleberry Finn* to deepen the consideration of racial representation still further. In addition to racial aspects, the humor, the narrative style, and the theme of heredity vs. environment are worthy of attention. The book can also be taught as a detective story, and in this connection it can be studied in combination with other detective stories—for example, those of Arthur Conan Doyle or Edgar Allan Poe.

The Adventures of Tom Sawyer is Twain's most popular book for high school and junior high school, yet it is often taught at more advanced levels, too. It works very well as a genre novel—the genre being the bad-boy book, which creates an opportunity for discussing bad-boy books in general, idylls of childhood, rebellion vs. conformity, and childhood vs. adulthood. It is often taught in combination with *Huckleberry Finn*, both to provide background for Huck's narrative and to highlight differences that reflect interestingly on both novels. For other intertextual comparisons, some useful possibilities are Thomas Bailey Aldrich's *The Story of a Bad Boy*, George W. Peck's *Peck's Bad Boy*, Louisa Mae Alcott's *Little Women* and *Little Men*, and Booth Tarkington's "Penrod and Sam" books (although racial stereotyping is a problem in Tarkington's books).

Roughing It is useful as an introduction to Mark Twain as a personality and storyteller, and in this respect it can serve the secondary function of background for *Huckleberry Finn* or other works by Twain. The chief complaints about *Roughing It* relate to its length, slow movement, and digressive style, which suggests that in many situations selections should be read rather than the entire work. In advanced or specialized situations it might be read in combination with the writings of other western humorists and travel writers, especially Bret Harte and Twain's Nevada cohorts Dan De Quille and Joe Goodman.

The Innocents Abroad is of interest for its humor, its social commentary, and its highlighting of vernacular vs. standard speech. It is a good text for study of the variety of Mark Twain's writing styles. Complaints, as with *Roughing It*, relate mainly to length and plotlessness, so again excerpts are probably the right approach in most cases. For intertextual comparison, it can be set against Henry James's and Edith Wharton's "international theme" novels and Henry Adams's *Mont-Saint-Michel and Chartres*.

"The Man That Corrupted Hadleyburg" is the most popular shorter work for classroom use. It works well because the plot structure is suspenseful and somewhat surprising, and its irony, dark humor, and themes of hypocrisy, hidden sin, and illusion vs. reality remain as current as ever. On the other hand, it sometimes strikes students as repetitious and a bit slow in getting to the climax. Contextual explorations often emphasize Puritanism vs. transcendentalism with "Hadleyburg" showing an inclination toward the former.

The Mysterious Stranger is a controversial entry in the Mark Twain pedagogical canon. Like "Hadleyburg," it represents Twain's later, "dark" period and is thus interesting for comparison to earlier works, especially *Tom Sawyer* and *Huckleberry Finn*. Major themes are "the damned human race" and problems of identity. The big problem with *The Mysterious Stranger* is that it exists in no definitive version since Twain not only did not publish it but left behind multiple versions of the manuscript, which were then synthesized, in what Twain scholars sometimes refer to as an "editorial fraud," by Albert Bigelow Paine and Frederick Duneka. Some readers also find its condemnation of humanity too simplistic and simply too dark. However, these problems can also be sources of interest, especially at the graduate level. The version currently preferred among serious Twainians is *No. 44: The Mysterious Stranger*.

"The Notorious Jumping Frog of Calaveras County" works well as an example of the tall tale and Southwestern humor and as a showcase for narrative technique in general and manipulation of point of view in particular. It is especially amenable to close analysis because its structure seems so loose but is, in fact, so thoroughly logical. A drawback is that students sometimes fail to appreciate the humor. Themes include gullibility, truth vs. lie, and genteel civilized values vs. the freedom and expression of the frontier. It provides a useful context for Twain's later, much longer works, and can be profitably read in combination with other examples of Southwestern humor.

Life on the Mississippi is often taught as an introduction to Mark Twain as narrator, as background for other works, especially *Huckleberry Finn*, and as a piece of social history. Except at the graduate level, excerpts are probably best in view of the book's length and unevenness. Within the corpus of Twain's works, *Life on the Mississippi* helps to show, as one respondent said, "Twain's recovery of his boyhood life and his developing sophistication in treating it."

Letters from the Earth falls generally into the same categories as *The Mysterious Stranger*. Both are posthumous publications reworked by editors (and therefore somewhat questionable as "works" of Mark Twain), and both exemplify the later, darker Twain. Some students find this aspect of Twain the most intriguing, but many either are offended or fail to make a meaningful connection with such writings. *Letters from the Earth*'s version of Adam and Eve obviously works best in the context of comparison to their originals in Genesis and the formidable retelling of their story in *Paradise Lost*.

The Gilded Age, coauthored with Charles Dudley Warner, is of interest as Twain's first novel, as an example of his work as a collaborator, and for its connection to its era. However, it is long and clearly not Twain's best work, as students tend to notice. Themes include political corruption and individual responsibility. Relevant contextual readings would be primarily historical works on the sociopolitical climate of the United States in the middle to late nineteenth century.

The *Autobiography* of Mark Twain is usable in writing courses and in comprehensive treatments of Twain, but it is stylistically uneven, factually unreliable, and uncertain with respect to textual authority. It can be studied as context for Twain's other works, but in most cases it is more appropriate for reading by the teacher (who can take it with the necessary grains of salt) than by students.

The Prince and the Pauper is a Twain novel that gets little serious attention from scholars but is often read at the high school and junior high levels. This is Twain in his less difficult, less problematic mode; it can be appealing for its humor, the reasonably well constructed and suspenseful plot, and its amusingly audacious premise about the interchangeability of royalty and street urchins. The principal contexts here are the history of the period (early sixteenth century) and adolescent literature.

WHAT TEXTS TO USE

The standard editions of Twain's works are the Works of Mark Twain series, published by the University of California Press. *The Adventures of Tom Sawyer / Tom Sawyer Abroad / Tom Sawyer, Detective; A Connecticut Yankee in King Arthur's Court; What Is Man? and Other Philosophical Writings; The Prince and the Pauper; Early Tales and Sketches, Vol. 1 (1851–1864); Early Tales and Sketches, Vol. 2 (1864–1865)*, and *Roughing It* are now available. However, for most teaching situations, the Mark Twain Library editions, which offer the same texts as the Works of Mark Twain, but without the scholarly extras, are a better choice because they offer textual authority, and often original illustrations, at a reasonable price. Titles include *A Connecticut Yankee; Roughing It; The Adventures of Tom Sawyer; The Prince and the Pauper; Tom Sawyer Abroad / Tom Sawyer, Detective*; and *No. 44: The Mysterious Stranger.*

Norton Critical Editions of *A Connecticut Yankee* and *Pudd'nhead Wilson* are available. These have good textual authority and a useful sampling of background material and critical essays, but few illustrations. Like the Mark Twain Library editions, they are reasonably priced.

The 29-volume Oxford Mark Twain, which appeared in late 1996, republishes each of the volumes published by Mark Twain during his lifetime. These, as I have indicated above, are facsimile reproductions of the first editions and include the original illustrations as well as commentary by recognized scholars and current major fiction writers. These volumes, which can be purchased individually as well as in the complete set, should prove strong contenders in the competition for course adoption.

For shorter works, the Riverside *Selected Shorter Writings of Mark Twain*, edited by Walter Blair, is frequently used. Another good choice is the *Viking Portable Mark Twain*, edited by Bernard De Voto. "The Notorious Jumping Frog," "Jim Baker's Blue-Jay Yarn," "The Man That Corrupted Hadleyburg," and various other short works by Twain are often included in American literature anthologies, and sometimes in introduction to literature and freshman composition readers.

In the realm of the super-cheap, the current champion is the $1.00 Dover edition titled *The Mysterious Stranger and Other Stories*. However, the Signet editions are also inexpensive. Signet titles are *Tom Sawyer, Connecticut Yankee, Innocents Abroad, Life on the Mississippi, The Mysterious Stranger and Other Stories, The Prince and the Pauper, Pudd'nhead Wilson, Roughing It, The Gilded Age*, and *The Wit and Wisdom of Mark Twain*. Penguin offers *Tom Sawyer, Connecticut Yankee, Life on the Mississippi, The Prince and the Pauper, Pudd'nhead Wilson, Roughing It*, and *Tales, Speeches, Essays, and Sketches* (ed. Tom Quirk). Bantam has editions of *Tom Sawyer, Connecticut Yankee, Life on the Mississippi, The Prince and the Pauper, Pudd'nhead Wilson*, and *The Complete Short Stories of Mark Twain* (ed. Charles Neider).

The Library of America's clothbound American writers series includes some excellent editions of Twain's works:

1. *Mississippi Writings* (1982; contents: *The Adventures of Tom Sawyer, Life on the Mississippi, Adventures of Huckleberry Finn*, and *Pudd'nhead Wilson*).
2. *The Innocents Abroad, Roughing It* (1984).
3. *Collected Tales, Sketches, Speeches, and Essays, 1852–1890* (1992).
4. *Collected Tales, Sketches, Speeches, and Essays, 1891–1910* (1992).
5. *Historical Romances* (1994; contents: *The Prince and the Pauper, A Connecticut Yankee in King Arthur's Court, Personal Recollections of Joan of Arc*).

These are fairly expensive volumes, but because each volume contains so much, they can be practical in courses where more than one Twain work is being studied. The two-volume *Collected Tales, Sketches, Speeches, and Essays*, superbly edited by Louis J. Budd, is especially valuable since it brings together in reliable form such a vast array of Twain's work.

The Library of America also publishes paperback editions of *Tom*

Sawyer and *Life on the Mississippi* that are reasonably priced for use at any level.

AUDIOVISUALS

In answer to the question, *What audiovisual aids do you find most useful?*, many respondents again said they have found none that are worthwhile. However, the following items received some positive mention:

1. Audio recordings of Hal Holbrook's Mark Twain impersonations. Again, this is the most popular audiovisual item, with complaints because no video version is available.
2. The original illustrations, when available, especially Daniel Carter Beard's illustrations for *A Connecticut Yankee*.
3. Maps of the settings for various works.
4. *Mark Twain's America*. This is an excellent black-and-white film (vintage 1960) that includes a remarkable collection of nineteenth-century photographs and can be purchased rather cheaply (for example, for $19.95 from the Mark Twain House in Hartford).
5. The American Short Story (PBS) version of "The Man That Corrupted Hadleyburg." But there were also some negative comments about this production.
6. The PBS version of *The Innocents Abroad*, noting changes in emphasis from the original.
7. Claymation *Adventures of Mark Twain*.
8. Photographs and slides of Twain-related sites. These can now be found on the Internet at various locations.

REFERENCE RESOURCES

In response to the question, *What reference resources (biographical, critical, or other) do you find most useful to yourself and your students?*, many of the items mentioned were the same as those listed above for *Huckleberry Finn*. However, there were a few additional entries:

1. Works of Mark Twain Edition. For the works included in this series (University of California Press), each individual volume gives a wealth of textual and other introductory information on the subject

text. See "What Texts to Use," above, for a list of works published to date.

2. *The Mark Twain Papers Series.* This ongoing series of University of California Press publications of previously unpublished writings of Mark Twain provides biographical and other genetic materials that can be of great interest, especially in dealing with a writer mythologized to the extent that Mark Twain continues to be. Some important titles to date: *Notebooks and Journals*, volumes I–III; *Letters*, vols. I–V; *Letters to His Publishers, 1867–1894; Satires and Burlesques; Which Was the Dream: and Other Symbolic Writings of the Later Years; Hannibal, Huck and Tom; Mysterious Stranger Manuscripts; Correspondence with Henry Huddleston Rogers, 1893–1909;* and *Fables of Man.*

3. Budd, Louis J., and Edwin H. Cady, eds. *The Best from American Literature: On Mark Twain.* Duke University Press, 1987.

4. Wilson, James D. *A Reader's Guide to the Short Stories of Mark Twain.* G. K. Hall, 1987.

5. Gillman, Susan, and Forrest G. Robinson, eds. *Mark Twain's "Pudd'nhead Wilson." Race, Conflict, and Culture.* Duke University Press, 1990.

6. Ketterer, David, ed. *The Science Fiction of Mark Twain.* Archon, 1984.

7. David, Beverly. *Mark Twain and His Illustrators.* Whitston, 1986.

8. Machlis, Paul, ed. *Union Catalog of Clemens Letters.* University of California Press, 1986.

9. Machlis, Paul, ed. *Union Catalog of Letters to Clemens.* University of California Press, 1992.

10. *Mark Twain Journal.* A semiannual journal devoted exclusively to Mark Twain scholarship, especially to biographical articles, edited by Thomas A. Tenney.

11. *Mark Twain Circular.* The quarterly newsletter of the Mark Twain Circle of America; contains news of Mark Twain events, bibliography of current scholarship, and short articles on Twain's life and work, edited by James S. Leonard.

12. *The Oxford Mark Twain.* A 29-volume facsimile reproduction (edited by Shelley Fisher Fishkin) of everything that Twain published in book form during his lifetime. In addition to showing the original publication format, with illustrations, each volume includes a general introduction by Fishkin, a foreword by a currently prominent fiction

writer, and an afterword by a Twain scholar; there are also essays (by Beverly David and Ray Sapirstein) on the illustrations in various volumes.

Overall—and I did not need to send out a questionnaire to make this discovery—the teaching of Mark Twain in graduate schools, colleges and universities, and high schools is a thriving enterprise. That is because of the one resource that really counts: Mark Twain himself.

I Discovering Mark Twain

From Innocence to Death:
An Approach to Teaching Twain
Dennis W. Eddings

A course in Mark Twain, especially on the undergraduate level, presents an instructor with a decided problem. Cantankerously messy, Twain refuses tidy pigeonholing or typecasting. Thus the problem: while a specific thesis approach tends to reduce Twain's richness, some organizing principle beyond mere chronology is needed to help illuminate that richness. One resolution that I have found effective involves tracing the development of what I see as the four major stages of Twain's career through the correlative themes of freedom and the search for a place where such freedom may be realized. While this approach obviously requires selectivity in the works considered and a bit of juggling to make everything fit together, it nonetheless provides a flexible framework that establishes an opening for discussion of Twain's major works as well as helping students see the continuity and development of his career. I emphasize that this approach provides a frame for discussion, not the entire focus of the class. I identify works that are not part of the syllabus, including ones that do not fit neatly into this scheme, and encourage students to examine these on their own (term papers abet that encouragement). Using this frame as a starting point, consideration then ranges freely over many other issues and concerns that make up Twain's complex art.

The first stage of this remarkable career involves creating and exploring the thematic and comic possibilities of the Innocent, the authorial persona of the youthful Mark Twain, and the search for a place capable of providing the necessary freedom to realize that character. I begin with *Roughing It*, primarily because it treats the Innocent more complexly than does *Innocents Abroad*, but also because students, especially in the Western states, tend to respond to it more favorably. Twain's removal to Nevada enables him to sample many roles and characters, including timber entrepreneur (and inadvertent arsonist), miner, and reporter. No such choices exist in Missouri. The closing of the Mississippi by Union forces during the Civil War represents a closing off of the freedom to enjoy the role that Twain appears to have found in "Old Times on the Mississippi." Moving west, away from the constraints of the world he has known, liberates him, accounting for the lyric description of the crossing of the plains.

In Nevada, the Innocent apparently finds a world of possibility—thus the many roles he tests. Yet even this early in Twain's career we encounter a duality that haunts his work—the positive assertion of the necessity of freedom and the negative assertion that nowhere on earth does such freedom exist. Individual episodes in the book, as well as its overall structure, reveal this duality. For example, the Innocent moves constantly westward, even to the apparent island paradise of Hawaii. But even there we see the pattern of disillusionment so prevalent in the book. Eden once again proves illusory. Belying the tropical beauty of the Hawaiian Islands' physical setting, Hawaiian history presents an ancient, vast panorama of pagan superstition and bloody butchery.

From this perspective, *Roughing It* becomes very important in any consideration of Twain's career. Thirteen years before the appearance of *Huckleberry Finn*, the book insinuates that, despite Huck's assertion, there really is no territory to light out to. That realization, however, presented a problem for Twain. In *Roughing It* he had found his authorial persona and the character through which that persona could be explored and developed. Yet that character had no place to go after Hawaii; Twain had run out of frontier. His solution to this dilemma takes him to the close of his first stage while opening the door to the second.

In "Old Times on the Mississippi," Twain responds to the knowledge gained in the end of *Roughing It* by traveling backward through memory rather than forward through space. Going back into the past enables him to retain a type of prelapsarian world that negates the lessons of his Western tour, evidenced by the transformation of the Innocent into the Cub. In that world, the creation of "Mark Twain" continues, exaggerating even more that persona's innocence and the inevitable humiliation arising from it.

Despite their widely different subject matter, "Old Times" resonates with echoes of *Roughing It*. At the beginning of the work, Twain again finds himself deprived of one role and in search of another. He transforms the plains into the river and the stagecoach into the boat, creating another fluid world of apparent possibility and freedom. In that world, he again attempts to assume a specific role, this time that of the magisterial pilot, the one (not insignificantly) in control. And again, naïve expectations clash with harsh reality, leading to laughter for the reader and, gradually, knowledge for the Cub.

As with the knowledge inherent in *Roughing It*, the knowledge in "Old Times" contains a dark implication that Twain refuses to acknowledge overtly. No one, it appears, enjoys such freedom as a riverboat pilot—he commands all, subject to neither captain nor owner. Such freedom from authority, however, exists only in the tiny confines of the pilot house. Outside, the river rules. The pilot, confronted with a constantly changing river, must always relearn lessons, only to discard them and start over. Apparently a place where freedom exists, the river actually represents a world of reality that must be conformed to. The justly famous passage where Twain comments on his two views of the river—pre-knowledge and post-knowledge—reflects a loss of innocence totally lacking in any Emersonian compensation.

The Cub's aspiration to join the grand fraternity of pilots mirrors the Innocent's desire to become one of the "boys" in *Roughing It*. In "Old Times," however, the Cub achieves his goal. He (finally) learns the river; he becomes a pilot; he joins the elite group. The very fact of his success, however, creates a major problem for Twain, for the Innocent's character is predicated upon failure. Twain's solution is to go even further backward in time and memory, and, in doing so, he enters the second stage of his career.

"The idyll of boyhood" best summarizes this stage, and it involves two works that most students are familiar with. Putting *Tom Sawyer* and *Huckleberry Finn* into the context of Twain's overall career enables these students to view them from a new perspective. The eight years separating these two books saw, of course, the appearance of several works, such as *A Tramp Abroad*, *The Prince and the Pauper*, and *Life on the Mississippi*, that do not seem to fit into this scheme. While some ingenious arguments in student papers suggest that even these works are not totally incompatible with the progression being traced, I review these three books in a way which shows students that we are tracing an overall progression in Twain's career rather than developing a definitive reading of it. If nothing else, this caveat helps students see that critical pronouncements need themselves to be taken warily and tested thoroughly.

In *Tom Sawyer*, whose writing overlaps "Old Times," Twain completes his backward journey, creating a nostalgic never-never land free of adult concerns. Tom never becomes concerned about his role, never worries about where he can fulfill that role, for he inhabits a world of play. Magnificently sure of himself and his imaginative ability to make the world conform to that self, Tom appears to be the one Twain character who controls his world. Setbacks in Tom's world are only temporary, sure preludes to even greater triumphs. Remarkably resilient, Tom simply refuses to let any aspect of the outside world impinge too directly on his created reality. *Tom Sawyer*, then, apparently presents us with a free character who inhabits an unfettered place where his freedom enjoys full reign. It thus seems to present the Eden that Twain failed to find in his journey west and in his trek backward through time and memory. But the imagined Eden of St. Petersburg turns out to be just as illusory as Hawaii.

Tom's play world derives more from his reading than from his imagination, and his inability to go beyond the book suggests the limits on his freedom. We see those limits even more clearly when the adult world impinges on his play world. Stated simply, Tom cannot avoid the adult reality of consequences. Tom's role as star attraction and central amusement of St. Petersburg requires him to conform to the very St. Petersburg values he apparently (and only apparently) rebels against. His socially trained conscience impels him to come forth to testify for Muff Potter, a courageous act that shows Tom is willing to put conscience and responsibility ahead of his own well-being—an adult perspective, indeed.

In the cave episode, Tom faces yet another situation where his play world offers no help, and he again behaves in a manner that adults would approve of, protecting and comforting Becky and engaging in the sentimental rhetoric that Twain so often ridiculed. The end of his book finds Tom still at play in the fields of summer, but his "respectability" speech to Huck makes him the spokesman for the very world that Twain has been making fun of. Tom's accommodation to St. Petersburg reveals a truth hidden in much of Twain's work: responsibility costs us our personal freedom, the unavoidable price of our inescapable adulthood. Awareness of this truth leads Twain into an evasion so he can avoid directly confronting it in a book intended to celebrate a child's world of freedom.

In *Tom Sawyer*, Twain abandons the Mark Twain persona of the

Innocent. His presentation of Tom's adventures in the third person gives the book a detached objectivity appropriate to a fairy tale. The transformation from participant to puppeteer enables Twain to draw the curtain before anything really painful occurs, maintaining the illusion of boys forever young in a summer that will never end. Consequently, we do not laugh at Tom as we do the Innocent, where painful occurrences create the humor. The point of view, accordingly, represents a type of evasion, a Tom Sawyer-like reaction that allows Twain to look the other way before a truth he knows but wishes not to acknowledge. But those facts refuse to go away, resurfacing with a vengeance in *Huckleberry Finn*.

The inescapable reality of the world in *Huckleberry Finn* belies the never-never land of *Tom Sawyer*. Huck's desperate attempts to evade responsibility and maintain a world of Tom Sawyer play prove futile, for unlike Tom's escapades in the earlier book, all of Huck's actions have consequences. Trying to remain in Tom's play world requires sacrificing his comfort and freedom in an accommodation with St. Petersburg. Returning to his former "comfortable" ways with Pap on the Illinois side involves imprisonment and the very real possibility of physical harm during one of Pap's drunken tirades. "Foolin' Jim" with a dead snake backfires when its mate bites Jim. Playing Tom on the *Walter Scott* jeopardizes Huck and Jim and quite likely kills the crooks on board. And so the pattern goes throughout the book. Huck, being the boy he is, wants to play, but the world, being the way it is, refuses to accommodate that play in the way St. Petersburg accommodates Tom. The first-person narration, furthermore, prevents any evasion, any merciful drawing of the curtain, before this truth. The realism of *Huckleberry Finn* presents a world fraught with unavoidable responsibilities and the inevitable consequences that spring from them. The only way to avoid them, the only way to remain a boy and free, is to be totally alone. And Huck cannot stand loneliness.

Huckleberry Finn arrives at the same conclusion as *Roughing It*. Like the Innocent in the earlier book, Huck leaves a world of compromise and enters a fluid world where he appears to have the freedom to play and have grand adventures. Reality belies that appearance, however. External realities that Huck cannot control keep intruding—steamboats, feuds, the King and the Duke. His internal conflict over Jim adds to those external realities, all of them combining to deny the existence of a world of freedom devoid of consequences. The disturbing evasion in the last quarter of *Huckleberry Finn* can well be read as Huck's (and Twain's) desperate attempt to turn his back on the knowledge gained during the journey downriver, the mature knowledge that all of life is a compromise. But the attempt to remain Peter Pan fails when the pattern repeats itself on the Phelps farm. Consequences again occur. Tom's wounding echoes the more dire shooting of Buck Grangerford. And while Jim has his freedom, he appears to have sacrificed it because he could not let Tom die, proof again that involvement in humanity carries a heavy price tag.

So Huck decides to light out for the territory, away from the spurious civilization of St. Petersburg, away from the false values that the book has exposed. Huck's flight represents yet another evasion rather than the grand assertion of freedom many would make of it. Huck, after all, lights out for the territory "ahead of the rest" to continue his adventures "amongst the Injuns"—to remain, in other words, a boy. Besides, the lark is intended to last only a few weeks. But, at this point, Twain himself must acknowledge the uselessness of Huck's flight, regardless of duration, for it duplicates Twain's own. The description of "howling adventures amongst the Injuns" echoes the opening of *Roughing It*: "Pretty soon he [Orion] would . . . see buffaloes and Indians, and prairie dogs, and antelopes, and have all kinds of adventures, and maybe get hanged or scalped. . . ." Just as *Huckleberry Finn* begins where *Tom Sawyer* ends, so *Huckleberry Finn* ends where *Roughing It* begins.

That ending, consequently, marks the end of the second stage of Twain's career. His exploration of freedom and his search for a place that allows for such freedom led him to the knowledge that no such place exists, that freedom itself is an illusion. Attempts to remain innocent of that reality, to remain boyishly free of consequences, lead nowhere, for the intrusion of reality is inescapable. Twain consequently turned away from the memory of his own adventures, real and imaginary, and entered into a fictional world that would transform Tom and Huck into adults. This third stage of Twain's career, much darker and more pessimistic in tone than the earlier two, affirms what Twain learned at the end of *Roughing It* and tried to evade in the works that followed. Seeing this type of continuity enables students, especially those who think of Twain primarily as a humorist, to come to some understanding of Twain's dark side.

A Connecticut Yankee is another journey book, but now the trip goes far back through time rather than forward in space. Hank's journey thus subtly suggests Twain's own in the first two stages of his career. His adventures vary from the wildly burlesque to the deadly serious. Hank tries to play Tom Sawyer in Arthurian Britain, but he cannot escape the Huckleberry Finn reality of the consequences of those games. Furthermore, Hank's adventures demonstrate with crushing finality both the illusory nature of human freedom and the bleak reality that human history has never offered a place where freedom could be realized. We as humans are mere creations of the world that makes us, and no place provides escape from that world, for we carry it within us. Hank demonstrates this truth when he tries to transform sixth-century Britain into nineteenth-century America. The failure of that attempt, and Hank's apocalyptic response, emphasizes just how trapped we are. Unable to maintain a boylike innocence, Hank plunges into a world of adult consequences that he does not want and cannot avoid by fleeing through space, or memory, or time.

No wonder, then, that Twain caps this third stage by grounding its final expression in the concrete world of Dawson's Landing. *Pudd'nhead Wilson* creates no myth of childhood innocence, of eternal summer, of human freedom. All the inhabitants of Dawson's Landing are slaves, regardless of color. The grown-up world contains no redeeming values. Innocent babes get shuffled about as a direct result of the threats that the grown-up world presents, only to grow up, in turn, reflecting its warped perspective. Only Wilson triumphs. Dubbed a "pudd'nhead" because of an innocent (and funny) remark, he endures his imposed role with almost Faulknerian persistence. His triumph lies in forcing the good citizens of Dawson's Landing to see him as he wishes them to, converting their judgment of "pudd'nhead" into his own view of his true character. Wilson's is a Pyrrhic victory, however, given the reality of Dawson's Landing. The fickleness of the villagers makes one wonder how long that triumph will last, while the very nature of the village makes one wonder if conquering it was worth twenty years of exile and ridicule. (And, as one student sagely suggested, Pudd'nhead's dogged determination to remain in Dawson's Landing may be the final ironic twist of Twain's dark tale, for it implies that Pudd'nhead is indeed a pudd'nhead.)

Pudd'nhead Wilson directly presents the truth that many of Twain's earlier works had masked through their humor or through Twain's own evasions—the adult world enslaves us all and we cannot escape that enslavement. The third-person narrative, the very perspective that enabled Twain to avoid the truths which *Tom Sawyer* threatened to reveal, makes those truths overt in *Pudd'nhead Wilson*. Even more telling, Twain's ironic commentary forces us to see the reality of Dawson's Landing from a detached perspective that mirrors Twain's own Olympian detachment. Twain's narrative separation from his world marks the end of his third stage, signaling a final separation from a world that denied what he so profoundly wished for—a world of freedom.

Twain's fourth stage consequently turns its back on physical reality and enters the world of dream. Typical of an actual dream, this stage gives us fragments full of disconnected hopes and fears. Furthermore, the dream keeps recurring, as "The Mysterious Stranger" manuscripts reveal. But just as dreams have no resolution, no resolution steps forth in the dream fragments. The unconscious desires and suppressed knowledge that drove the other stages of Twain's career resurface in the warped metaphors of his dream tales. "Extracts from Adam's Diary" and "Eve's Diary" prove again that Eden never existed. Satan makes a wonderful playmate, but his games lead to adult knowledge about the world and the consequences resulting from that knowledge. Humans find themselves trapped in this reality. Only Satan, separated from it, can laughingly call everything a dream, a detached laughter that one suspects Twain wished to duplicate but could not, being himself all too human.

This final phase of Twain's career presents students with the most difficulty. The dark brooding of the dream tales, the damning of the human race, and the veneration of death as the great liberator run counter to the Twain that most students carry in their minds and hearts. Recognizing that this last phase results from the failure of life to meet Twain's desires enables students to see the true poignancy of his last years. Death alone, as Twain well knew, provides the final separation from the human within us. No wonder, then, that the last fifteen years of his life, in many respects, echo Keats's "and, for many a time / I have been half in love with easeful Death." Perhaps this love, half-ironically stated in some of the entries of Pudd'nhead Wilson's Calendar, more vociferously uttered in many of the entries of Pudd'nhead Wilson's New Calendar, and finally relentlessly reiterated in Twain's letters and many of the fragments of his final years, forms the inevitable and appropriate coda to the four stages of Twain's career. When students can couple the personal and emotional disasters of those final years with the disheartening acknowledgment that the human desire for freedom represents nothing more than a cruel hoax, then Twain's veneration of death is understandable. It is the only place where we can be free.

Race and Mark Twain

S. D. Kapoor

The race concept has never been an innocuous one, ever since the time of the Greeks, who regarded all those who did not belong to their race as barbarians. The Greeks had their own reason for considering other races as "inferior," but the fact remains that such categorization of races between "inferior" and "superior" has persisted through the centuries, although racial myths, and therefore the race concept itself, have changed. In our own century the issues concerning race have become more acute both in the United States and in countries where apartheid is still practiced. W. E. B. Du Bois was not wide of the mark when he said early in this century that the problem of the twentieth century is the problem of the color line. Since other issues have got mixed up with it, issues of race require much more careful and serious thought than has ever been given to them. New areas of inquiry have been opened, and scholars have gone to the extent of questioning the racial bias in the interpretation of knowledge and literature. (Toni Morrison and Edward Said are two such interpreters.)

During the Civil War and the period of Reconstruction, the issues were simpler, and the answers, though not completely satisfying, were less ambiguous. "Social uniformity" in the United States was remarkable—no titles and no social status supported by law. "There was only one great division in society, that between the slave and the free. But among the free, according to most observers—it would, of course, hardly seem so to us after two hundred years of further progress in our expectations of, and the reality of, equality—a remarkable equality and uniformity prevailed. . . . The chasm between white and black, slave and free, seemed too great for any ideal of fraternity to bridge."[1] Some kind of accommodation was on the minds of the white people after the Civil War, despite the fact that the South was nursing the wound of defeat. Frederick Douglass, who struggled to become a free black American, ended his autobiography *My Bondage and My Freedom* on a note of optimism. He hoped to work, in collaboration with those whites who saw no distinction between the two races, to elevate the moral and intellectual status of his people. However, in the twentieth century, issues like "black consciousness," "civil rights," "human rights," and "cultural nationalism" have replaced simple issues of equality and liberty, even of fraternity—so much so that blacks and whites seem to be engaged in a war over the nature of reality.

Today the discussion of race cannot be confined to its primary sense in which certain homogeneous groups belong to the same stock, whose distinguishing characteristics are biologically determined, allowing for some variation. It cannot be separated from the cluster of attitudes that have gathered round it over the centuries—so much so that even those who do not believe in racism and caste discrimination unconsciously become its carriers. Such attitudes are largely governed by religious, political, or economic reasons, depending on the ruling ideas of the age. Thus it is difficult to think of race without racism and racial myths, even when there is no scientific basis for believing in the inequality of human groups. In the words of Juan Comas: "Racism involved the assertion that inequality is absolute and unconditional, i.e., that a race is inherently and by its very nature inferior or superior to others quite independently of the physical conditions of its habitat and of social factors."[2]

Color, which was already accepted as synonymous with inferiority, has now acquired a new framework of class, culture, and nation. James Baldwin put it succinctly when he wrote in *The Fire Next Time* that color is not a human or personal reality; it is a political reality, and unless this is accepted, the problem cannot be solved. According to Toni Morrison, "Race in fact now functions as a metaphor so necessary to the construction of Americanness that it rivals the old pseudoscientific and class-informed racism whose dynamics we are never used to deciphering."[3]

If the race concept were confined only to physical traits and genetically determined characteristics, it would not pose so difficult a problem. But the moment that it is taken to the level of intelligence and culture (determined by one's own yardsticks) and economic status, the problem arises. The imperialist justified his rule over the native on the ground that the native was at a low level of cultural and intellectual development. The racists justified their superior existence on the basis of purity of blood. It is a paradox of the twentieth century that human races are no longer isolated, confined to geographical territories, but, at the same time, no wholesale fusion has taken place. The immediate fusion and the distant fusion are avoided in the name of color, caste, and superior existence. This situation becomes all the more complicated when divisions and hierarchies appear within one racial type. We saw this development occur during World War II when millions of Jews were exterminated in the name of caste based on the supposed purity of "German blood." As for the Indian caste system, it is as firmly entrenched as ever, zealously preserved by those who want to retain their privileged status.

As Fredric Jameson wrote in *The Political Unconscious*, our readings of the past are vitally dependent on our experience of the present. But such readings should not lead us to obliterate the past and impose on it modern categories of thought. In the postmodernist period the fixity of any test—historical or literary—has become difficult to establish. The problem is compounded when the belief exists that the past cannot be captured in its totality because the remains of the past not only are incomplete but are also part of the present. However, I think some form of objectivity is possible. Since we have the advantage of hindsight, we might look for questions that were never raised, issues that were relegated to the background, and roads not taken. "The most illuminating questions might be, what were people not talking and thinking about which perhaps they should have been. The details of the past should be listened to with an ear attuned to silence."[4] The issues that the present century has helped crystallize may enable us to give meaning to silence. "Since the race war goes on as fiercely as ever in this country," Gore Vidal writes in *At Home*, "I think candor about blacks and whites is necessary." He adds that it was Abraham Lincoln who "foresaw the long and ugly confrontation and tried to spare the future generations by geographically separating the races."[5]

Even when one goes back to the past with certain issues in mind, one cannot disregard the levels of existence of the two races and the extremes to which they could go during earlier periods. Since it is impossible to escape the "coercion of the times" (Cox), it is necessary to create a framework to understand the question of race during the nineteenth century. I found such a framework available in the last article by that reclusive scholar James M. Cox before he retired to his ancestral land in the South and chose the "freedom not to write." The framework is constructed around two incidents that he highlights in his article and that might suggest the range and level of relationship of the two races. One incident is from the autobiography of Frederick Douglass, where Douglass has a fight with the slave supervisor Covey. Cox writes: "In the great moment of the book, when Douglass fights with the slave-breaker Covey, the two figures seize each other and cannot let go. That interlocked struggle could stand for Douglass's rhetorical situation. He has taken hold of slavery and cannot let it go."[6] This fight should be seen in the context of the all-pervading terror of slavery, the fear of being condemned to lifelong drudgery and hard labor, and the determination to come out of it and to breathe the air of freedom. Douglass's entire life after he became a spokesman for his people was devoted to helping his people gain freedom and, after the Civil War, to rehabilitating them in a new social and political order. Yet, although Douglass resisted the restrictions placed on him by the Garrisonians when he was asked to narrate his experiences, it was obvious that he and the Garrisonians were working within the framework prescribed by the liberal whites.

The other incident refers to a Baptist churchyard for which Cox's grandfather, his father, and later Cox himself gave land, reserving one block for themselves and their descendants. Cox could see his grand-father's marble gravestone from the kitchen window of his house. On his return, when he went to look at the graves more closely, he noticed that "the slaves are buried in the graveyard with uninscribed fieldstone to mark their graves with a single exception, Edmund Cox, who died a free man in 1883."[7] The segregation was carried to the graveyard to the extent that one could not know their identity. Their bones might have mingled with those of the whites under the earth, but on its surface discrimination seemed eternal. The unbridled joy and excitement that blacks displayed on becoming free was caught by Du Bois in the following words: "Shout, O Children: Shout, you're free. For God has brought you liberty."[8] They had crossed the first hurdle and were now free, it seemed, to do whatever they liked with their lives. Thus one cannot disregard their status and their aspirations while considering the question of race during that period. It is apparent that both blacks and liberal whites were concerned about the question of minimum rights and did not have the time to examine the complex issue of race relations. It was the question of freedom at the basic level that was being debated. The questions of identity, double consciousness, and manhood would come later.

In the nineteenth century, apart from a small minority, whites were still not clear about the level of relationship they should have with blacks. The attitudes and prejudices that had been formed over the decades came into play the moment the question of equality came up. William Faulkner has shown this dilemma cogently in the characters of McEachern, Joanna Burden, Percy Grimm, and Doc Hines in *Light in August*. Since the level of relationship that the Southerners had taken for granted was suddenly disturbed, they could not return to "a little democracy" except in their memory, with the aristocratic taint in which lines were clearly drawn. And, as Mark Twain says, "It was there and nobody found fault with the fact or ever stopped to reflect that its presence was an inconsistency."[9]

Twain says that when he was a child, he had no aversion to slavery. In fact, he did not realize that there was anything wrong about it. "No one arraigned it in my hearing; the local papers said nothing against it; the local pulpit taught us that God approved it, that it was a holy thing and the doubter need only look in the Bible if he wished to settle his mind— and then the texts were read aloud to us to make the matter sure; if the slaves themselves had an aversion to slavery they were nice and said nothing."[10] Not that everything inhuman was kept out of Twain's ken, but the dominant attitude toward slavery did not allow him to react to it as he did later. At an early age he saw an overseer crush a slave's skull and saw another slave, accused of raping a white woman, lynched in full view of a crowd. Once when a white man killed a black man for a trifling offense, people were not bothered about the slave but sympathized with the owner for having lost his property. And, "I vividly remember seeing a dozen black men and women chained to one another once and lying in a group on the pavement awaiting shipment to the Southern slave market. These were the saddest faces I have ever seen."[11]

Twain's views on race took shape only gradually, although his sympathies for the black race were evident from the beginning. Until the 1880s—that is, until the time he met Frederick Douglass and Booker T. Washington—he did not identify himself openly with the cause of blacks. Shelley Fisher Fishkin has discovered a letter from Twain which revealed that he financed at least one black student at Yale Law School.

According to Arthur G. Pettit, Twain's career moved from a "segregationist and Negrophobe" to a "self-professed reconstructed Yankee" to a "champion of interracial brotherhood in *Huckleberry Finn*."[12]

It is true that the fight for the institution of slavery and its assumptions about race relations was also a fight for the retention of a certain economic order, but the Southerners had realized that the forces released by industrialism could no longer be ignored. The social, political, and moral loss that the South suffered with defeat was a consequence of its perception being countered by a new one. The defiance and resistance that one finds in Southerners during this period resulted from this loss. These are complex issues and cannot be simplified. "Since the society became increasingly predicated on slavery, and since slavery became increasingly the moral and political issue dividing the nation, the South became more and more a fixed image in the Northern mind, and subsequently in the national mind, of a society divided into planters and slaves, with a middle class refuse of illiterate whites making up the remainder."[13]

But one must not forget that slavery was only one aspect of race relations, although it became a dominant metaphor as it involved the entire range of racial relationships—human, inhuman, and paternal. The dominant thinking was that "Negroes" belonged to an inferior race and their status in America was in fact an elevation. On the basis of this justification, the majority of white people wanted to maintain the status quo. The earliest defense of white biological superiority came from preachers. In 1772 the Reverend Thomas Thompson published *The Trade in Negro slaves on the African Coast in Accordance with Humane Principles and with the Laws of Revealed Religion*. In 1852 the Reverend Josiah Priest wrote *A Bible Defense of Slavery*. But a sounder theoretical framework for white racial superiority was provided by J. H. Hammond and J. H. Evrie. Hammond, a successful plantation owner from South Carolina, in a Senate speech on 4 March 1858 propounded what he characteristically called the "mudsill" theory based on a division of society into two clearly defined groups, one performing superior functions, and the other performing inferior ones, very much like the "caste" system in India. "All social systems need a class to do the menial duties, perform the drudgery of life. There must be such a class so that the other class can make progress, refinement and civilization. The white Americans found such a class in Negroes who, they thought, were eminently qualified in temper, rigor and docility to perform such a function. The whites have given them a better existence by making them their slaves."[14]

John H. Van Evrie was equally vigorous in his defense of the existing division between the two races. He considered the Negro as belonging to a lower order of man, and, in fact, to a different species from whites. He propounded the "plurality" theory, which meant that every man did not originate in a single center of creation. "The Negro is a man but a different species of man who would no more originate from the same source as ourselves, than the owl could from the eagle, or the shad from the salmon, or the cat from the tiger; and who can no more be forced by human power to manifest the faculties, or perform the purposes assigned by the Almighty creator to the Caucasian man, than can either of these forms of life be made to manifest faculties other than inherent, specified and eternally impressed upon their organization" (60). Evrie believed that the Negro race never passed beyond the hunter conditions that still prevailed in Africa.

Mark Twain comprehended the issue imaginatively in *Pudd'nhead Wilson*, where he converted it into an issue of inherited versus acquired traits. By swapping the two boys, Driscoll's and Roxy's, he made his countrymen look at the question of race from the point of view of nature and nurture. Were the defects in Roxy's son the consequence of upbringing and environment or the manifestation of inherent traits? Similarly, could the defects put into Driscoll's son by upbringing and environment be corrected? The theorists did not admit of any questioning on the neat categorization of races, but Twain made the issue open-ended.

To believe that the problem of race would suddenly disappear after the Civil War was to evade the issue. The new Southern governments enacted what were called the Black Codes, defining the new status of the Negro. Although these codes were different in different states, it was evident that Negroes were to have a subordinate status even in the post-Civil War period. Some people considered these codes a continuation of the conditions of slavery; those defending them argued that the codes were being enacted to instill discipline among the newly freed slaves. The Radicals wanted drastic conditions to be imposed on the states, and under their pressure Negro suffrage was made part of the U.S. Constitution, but even this right did not bring any radical change in blacks' status. Through various strategems—poll taxes and literacy tests, for example—they were prevented from casting votes for the Reconstruction governments.

But slaveocracy and race theories never went uncontested. Always there existed a strong lobby advocating equality of men and races in the United States. As early as 1791, Benjamin Banneker brought out a series of almanacs that became household reading. He convincingly argued that the talents of black brethren were equal to those of men of other colors and that mental powers were not the exclusive preserve of white people. The same idea was strengthened through the abolitionist movement, which gained momentum in the early part of the nineteenth century. Despite stiff opposition, abolitionism did succeed in inculcating a questioning attitude in the people of the North. The most radical among such groups was the one led by William Lloyd Garrison, who went to the extent of demanding separation of the North from the South.

Since the defense of slavery related to the question of race inequality, Southerners feared that abolition would lead to free mixing of the two races, which they abhorred. But even in the North, where the movement of racial equality was marked, there was discrimination to the extent that Negroes were totally segregated. Richard Wright writes in *American Hunger*, a sequel to his autobiography *Black Boy*, of his frustration in the North. In Chicago, the city perennially controlled by the political machine, things were different only in form, and the relationship between the two races was lined with fright and hatred. Wright symbolized the suffering of blacks by the image of devocalized dogs gaping in the void in a soundless wail.

To understand the intricate and complex problem of race relations in the second half of the nineteenth century, one should listen to the black man's version of himself and of white people. Who could be a better person for this expression than Frederick Douglass, who first as a slave and later as a free black lived through the most turbulent period in American history. In fact, his life reflects the changing phases of American society. It was in the 1840s that he began talking about his experiences from the platform provided by the Garrisonians and later by the English. In England he discovered that his skin did not define his identity. Some of the speeches that he made there and the letter that he wrote to his former master are included in the second version of his autobiography (he wrote three versions), which he called *My Bondage and My Freedom*.

All eight extracts that he included in this book deal with the evil system of slavery and its effects on blacks and, to some extent, on whites. In a speech that he made at Finbury Chapel in 1846, he examined the question of the Negro as property. A slave is a marketable property, to be bought and sold at the caprice of the master. The slave's human qualities, his intellect and emotions, have no place in such a scheme. The limits of his existence are prescribed by the wishes of his master. "If he is fed, he is fed because he is property. If he is clothed, it is with a view to the increase of his value as property. Whatever of comfort is necessary to him for his body and soul that is inconsistent with his being property is carefully wrested from him, not only by public opinion, but by the law of the country. He is carefully deprived of everything that tends in the slightest degree to detract from his value as property."[15]

In order that he remain a property, strict laws are made. If he runs away, the law enjoins other whites to return him to his lawful owner. His existence becomes more miserable once he is caught and returned to his owner, for no one trusts a "runaway nigger." Even religion is enlisted in slavery's support. Douglass accepted only that religion which is based upon gracious principles of love to God and to man. "It is because I love this religion that I hate the slaveholding, the woman-whipping, the mind-darkening, the soul-destroying religion that exists in the southern states of America."[16]

Since he is a property, as a horse is property, he is exploited by the master to the master's advantage. The fruits of his labor are collected by the master. "He is industrious that another may live in idleness; he eats bolted meal that another may eat the bread of fine flour; he labors in chains at home, under a burning sun and biting lash, that another may ride in ease and splendor abroad; he lives in ignorance that another may be educated."[17]

What Douglass suggested through these speeches was that this anomaly would persist as long as slavery remained a permanent and hereditary condition of a class of human beings in the United States. The principles of natural justice and political freedom did not apply in their case. Douglass brought out these anomalies in an 1852 lecture in Rochester, New York, entitled, "What to the Slave Is the Fourth of July?" "To drag a man in fetters into the grand illuminated temple of liberty, and call upon him to join you in joyous anthems were inhuman mockery and sacrilegious irony."[18] According to Douglass, the United

States was being false to the past as well as to the present, and if the country did not accept the equal manhood of another race, it would continue to be false to the future. He wanted to arouse the conscience of the nation, expose its hypocrisy, and proclaim its crime against God and man. "To him [the slave] your celebration is a sham; your boasted liberty, an unholy license; your national greatness, swelling vanity; your sounds of rejoicing are empty and heartless; your denunciations of tyrants, brass-fronted impudence; your shouts of liberty and equality, hollow mockery; your prayers and hymns, your sermons and thanks-giving with all your religious parade and solemnity are to him mere bombast, fraud, deception, impiety, and hypocrisy, a thin veil to cover up crime which would disgrace a nation of savages."[19]

These contradictions should be seen in relation to the question of human dignity that Douglass raised in his letter to his former master, Thomas Auld. Even when he was a slave, the question "Why am I a slave?" always troubled him. He was not willing to accept the stock answer that God wanted some people to be slaves and others masters. Besides, he had heard old slaves talking of their parents having been stolen from Africa and sold in North America. Apart from that, not all Negroes were slaves, and black color was not necessarily a thing to be despised. By the time he decided to write a letter to his master, Douglass had a status in society and was listened to with respect and interest. Thus, he wrote the letter from a position of equality: "I am myself; you are yourself; we are two distinct persons, equal persons. What you are, I am. You are a man, and so am I. God created both, and made us separate beings. I am not by nature bond to you, or you to me."[20] But Auld, and other masters like him, denied him this basic human right. What pained Douglass was that his brothers and sisters were still in captivity and he did not even know where they were. But the most disturbing part of the letter is where Douglass poses the question in human terms, imagining the reversal of roles of the master and the slave. "How, let me ask, would you look upon me were I, some dark night in company with a band of hardened villains, to enter the precincts of your elegant dwelling, and seize the person of your own lovely daughter, Amanda, and carry her off from your family, friends and all the loved ones of her youth—make her my slave—compel her to work, and I take her wages—place her name on my ledger as property—disregard her personal rights—fetter the powers of her immortal soul by denying her the right and privilege of learning to read and write—feed her coarsely—clothe her scantily, and whip her on the naked back occasionally, more, and still more horrible, leave her unprotected—a degraded victim of the brutal lust of fiendish overseers who would pollute, blight and blast her fair soul."[21]

It goes to Douglass's credit that he raised the right issues concerning the question of race and the plight of his people. But what he could not achieve, despite his rhetorical skill and passionate indignation, Mark Twain did achieve imaginatively by conceiving situations that credibly revealed the human aspect of the relationship of the two races. It is true that although Twain was much ahead of his time in his antiracist stance, he was not entirely untouched by the ruling ideas of his age. The weakening of the radical Republican idea of Reconstruction as represented by the compromise of 1877 was reflected in him and his imaginative creations. The conflict between the liberal or human and the conservative idea was taken right to the end of *Adventures of Huckleberry Finn*. At the same time, one cannot deny that the questions of man as property vs. freedom and human dignity that Douglass so forcefully raised were given a human dimension through Twain's characters. And in doing so, he revealed the irony inherent in such a treatment. When Roxy in *Pudd'nhead Wilson* tells Tom that he was in fact a "nigger" and her son and not Driscoll's son, his entire perception about life and its possibilities changes. He cries, "Why were niggers and whites made? What crime did the unwretched first nigger commit that the course of birth was decreed for him? And why this awful difference made between white and black?" (53). By placing two contradictory attitudes in one character, Twain brings out the latent irony in the human situation.

Twain represented the white liberal view of race and race relations. What distinguishes him from Douglass is his representation of the ideological shift in American society. This enables him to examine the white man's changing attitudes toward blacks. The liberals wanted to grant freedom to blacks on their own terms, not freedom from all kinds of restraint, as Julius Lester calls it, but a kind of freedom in which limits are fixed by the whites. They did not want to replace the stereotyped image of the black as a docile, grateful, and dependent "nigger," always ready to serve his master, by a human image. But unlike other liberals, Twain gets inside the skin of "nigger Jim" and questions this limited attitude toward freedom. Still, even he cannot escape the moral responsibility of helping, in Huck Finn's words, "a nigger to get his freedom; and if I was ever to see anybody from that town again, I'd be ready to get down and lick his boots for shame" (chapter 31). This coexistence of differing attitudes can be seen by comparing the central part of the novel, in which Jim is the moral center, with the beginning and the end, in which he is a "comic butt" or a "stage prop." In the novel's last chapters the image that Jim has acquired as a loving human being becomes almost meaningless. It is saved somewhat when Jim decides to risk his own freedom to save the life, not of Huck, but of Tom. But in spite of this depicted gesture, the stereotyped image of the black is reestablished. For this reason, critics have reacted sharply to the ending; the conflict between the antiracist stance and the racist attitude cannot be resolved. In this unresolved opposition, Twain dramatizes the dilemma of the Northern middle class. According to Carrington, *Adventures of Huckleberry Finn* is a great but sadly typical drama of race: not a stark, black tragedy of black suffering, but a complex tragicomedy of white weakness and indifference.[22] In other words, it is the weakening of the liberal idea.

Twain catches the central conflict of the age, of which his compatriots were only dimly aware. The community suppressed the conflict by giving plausible explanations. Jim's predicament, his terror of being dragged back into bondage if he could not reach a free state, his tension, and his unbridled joy at the very thought of freedom give him stature in the novel. The irony of his being so close to freedom and the fear that he might never get it is brought out tellingly by Twain. One has to compare Jim's dilemma with a similar episode in Douglass's autobiography to realize the superiority of Twain's treatment. Douglass writes, "The border lines between slavery and freedom were the dangerous ones for the fugitives. The heart of no fox or deer, with hungry hounds on his trail, could have beaten more anxiously or noisily than did mine from the time I left Baltimore till I reached Philadelphia."[23]

Another aspect in which Twain excels is his treatment of white characters whose perceptions are distorted by racism. In fact, he shows the full range of "what racial ideology does to the mind, imagination, and behavior of masters" (Morrison, *Playing in the Dark*, 12). Toni Morrison argues that Jim is indispensable for Huck's moral growth. Twain catches the conflict in the mind of Huck, who is divided between "the human claims of friendship and the impersonal but compelling values of property."[24] The human values and property values are placed squarely in Huck's consciousness, and despite the fact that he finally rejects property values, he is not completely free. He can be fully free only when he is part of a loving family and a community that makes him grow along with it. He has a cruel father, and the community wants him to live according to their mores without disturbing the status quo. At one point in the novel Jim is greatly excited about the prospect of reaching a free state and expresses himself openly in the presence of Huck, a white boy. He shares his hidden aspirations with Huck, who is surprised that Jim cares so much for his family and their freedom when Huck knows that own father not only ill-treats him but lives off him.

While Jim's character acquires a human dimension, Huck becomes a symbol of moral questioning. The revelation of Jim's authentic self causes a crisis of conscience in Huck:

> Every time he danced around and says, "Dah's Cairo!" it went through me like a shot, and I thought that if it *was* Cairo I reckoned I would die of miserableness.
>
> Jim talked out loud all the time while I was talking to myself. He was saying how the first thing he would do when he got to a free state he would go to saving up money and never spend a single cent, and when he got enough he would buy his wife, which was owned on a farm close to where Miss Watson lived; and then they would both work to buy the two children, and if their master wouldn't sell them, they'd get an Ab'litionist to go and steal them.

Twain here uncovers the stark truth about the black man's existence. No white man could imagine that a black man felt so strongly about the members of his family and would be willing to go to any extent to obtain their freedom. What troubles Huck is his willing or unwilling complicity in this design, and here racial attitudes come into operation. On the one hand, he shows that Jim is an exemplary freeman, on the other, how the white man denies him this freedom. By dramatizing the conflict in Huck's mind, and by showing the consequences of it, Twain indicts the very functioning of American society. Through Jim's character he "brings into intense focus the contradiction between human views of the whole self and the market society view that part of the self can be alienated and as a commodity can be sold for what it will command as labor. The irony is that Jim is whole, Huck and the dominant society are divided."[25]

Despite the somewhat racially ambivalent close of the book, it is difficult to accept the charge that Twain was against racial equality. After all, he does convincingly show that there is no innate racial inferiority in the black race. Jim is capable of full human development, and in this respect he is no different from whites. In fact, in one way he is superior. He is willing to do anything to win freedom for his wife and children. Twain shows that feelings are not distributed along race lines. The relationship that Jim develops with Huck is an extension of the feelings that he shows for his family. The story Huck makes up to mislead the slave-catchers coming to the raft and Jim's overwhelming response combine to show that a deeper bond can be established between the black and the white communities in spite of the ruling ideology of separation.

The remarkable thing about Twain was that he took the entire issue of race relations to a human level and made people see the dangers if relations at this level were ignored. He would have agreed with Richard Wright when Wright wrote in *American Hunger* that the race problem would be solved only after the deeper problems of American society had been faced and solved. And if those deeper problems continued to be ignored, they would come back with redoubled force, turning people to cynicism and despair.

Notes

1 "Nathan Glazer: Liberty, Equality, Fraternity, and Ethnicity," *Daedalus* 105, 4 (Fall 1976): 116.
2 Juan Comas, *Racial Myths* (Paris: Ionesco, 1953), 49.
3 Toni Morrison, *Playing in the Dark* (Cambridge, Mass.: Harvard University Press, 1992), 47.
4 M. Andrew Scott, "Henry George, Henry Adams, and the Dominant American Ideology," *SAQ* 76 (1977): 237.
5 Gore Vidal, *At Home* (New York: Random House, 1988), 286.
6 James M. Cox, "Trial for a Southern Life," *Sewanee Review* (Spring 1989): 251.
7 Ibid.
8 Quoted by Rajmohan Gandhi, "Shame, Pain, and Freedom," *Hindustan Times*, 11 July 1993, 4.
9 *The Autobiography of Mark Twain*, ed. Charles Neider (New York: Harper, 1959), 30.
10 Ibid., 59.
11 Ibid., 33.
12 Arthur G. Pettit, "Mark Twain in Our Times," in *Huck Finn Among the Critics*, ed. M. Thomas Inge (Frederick, Md.: University Publications of America, 1985), 5.
13 Cox, "Trial for a Southern Life," 251.

14 Leslie Fishel, Jr., and Benjamin Quarles, *The Black American: A Documentary History* (Glenview, Ill.: Scott Foresman, 1970), 59.

15 Frederick Douglass, *My Bondage and My Freedom* (New York: Arno Press, 1968), 408.

16 Ibid., 416.

17 Ibid., 430.

18 Ibid., 441.

19 Ibid., 445.

20 Ibid., 423.

21 Ibid., 427–28.

22 Quoted by Wayne Booth, *The Company We Keep* (Berkeley: University of California Press, 1988), 471.

23 Frederick Douglass, *Life and Times of Frederick Douglass* (New York: Collier Books, 1962), 200.

24 Robert Shulman, "Fathers, Brothers, and the Diseased," in *One Hundred Years of "Huckleberry Finn": Centennial Essays*, ed. Robert Sattlemeyer and J. Donald Crowley (Columbia: University of Missouri Press, 1985), 333.

25 Shulman, "Fathers, Brothers, and the Diseased," 335.

Personal Recollections of Joan of Arc
in Today's Classroom
Victoria Thorpe Miller

At a time when little in education seems to be standing still, Mark
Twain's place in the American literary canon seems assured. However,
the universal appeal of his writing, translated as it has been into more
than seventy languages, has never extended to include his *Personal
Recollections of Joan of Arc*. Long derided by virtually all critics, *Joan*
has been read only by the most ardent Twain fans; it has rarely been
taught, and then only with limited success. This is unfortunate, for it
contains a wealth of possibilities for today's classroom.

The story of Joan of Arc as told in the book by her page and secretary,
Sieur Louis de Conte, to his great-great-grand-nephews and -nieces met
with a generally favorable reception when in was published in 1896
(Budd, 140). Not only were Victorians fascinated by the Middle Ages,
but the historical Joan was currently undergoing sanctification, prior
to her canonization by the Roman Catholic Church. Critics have not
been so kind, however. Thought to be Clemens's desperate effort to
ward off his deepening despair, *Joan* has been considered Victorian
sentimentalism at its worst, a mixture of medievalism and Southwestern humor that was little more than, as Bernard De Voto put it, a
"capitulation to romance" written by a "Missouri democrat on leave
from his trade" (280, 282).

In recent years, however, this work has received more careful scholarly attention. J. D. Stahl, for example, profitably examined the fusion
of Joan and the narrator. More recently, Bruce Michelson considered
the work in the light of Mark Twain's rebellion against consistency,
reminding us that Twain's late works often "turn against themselves,
subverting the very themes they champion at the start" (175). Studies
like these serve to broaden our perspective on *Joan*, and they often
reveal a previously undiscovered richness.

Elsewhere I have argued that a reading unhampered by expectations generated in earlier scholarship can reveal Twain's novel to be not an aberration in the Twain canon but a work that is characteristically ironic. Read this way, *Joan* is very much in line with other late fiction by Twain: it is an expression of, not a failed attempt to counteract, Clemens's growing pessimism. Certainly, what critics have seen is literally there, but the story de Conte tells and the implications created by the way he tells it are markedly different. In this, it is not unlike Twain's *Adventures of Huckleberry Finn*. In her pathbreaking work *Was Huck Black? Mark Twain and African-American Voices*, Shelley Fisher Fishkin explores the doubleness of Huck's story, reminding us that "Twain devoted a major portion of his writing to the project of helping his reader learn to avoid the sin of literalness" (61). We cannot take seriously Twain's admonition that the reader not seek a moral in *Huckleberry Finn*; by the same token, I would argue, we are naïve to assume that *Joan* is merely another record of the exploits of the Maid of Orleans.

This doubleness in *Joan*, which goes well beyond the dual narrative voices of the young and the old de Conte noted by previous scholars, is a feature of the work that makes it especially useful in the classroom. Undergraduate students are often inclined to read literally, and their study of this work will give them opportunities to gain experience with ironic discourse. For example, although scholars have generally found the attitude of the narrator de Conte to be uncritically worshipful of Joan, students—perhaps especially female students—will be able to see that de Conte is surprisingly unable to accommodate his heroine's non-traditional perspective: while telling a story that is clearly intended to be a paean to Joan, his uncritical praise of her has the ironic effect of diminishing both her character and her mission. Such a collision of male and female views rarely fails to interest students, as it yields the pedagogical bonus of raising the question of male vs. female perspectives.

A second reason for using this text in the classroom is its fascinating critical history in which both its genre and its value as literature have been called into question. While many literary works have been the subjects of such critical discussion, undergraduate students, aware of their own lack of expertise, often take the easy way out and select one critic with whom to agree. *Joan*, however, is another matter. Seldom has there been a work about which opinion was so universally negative but that nonetheless managed to remain in print. Unless they, too, want to dismiss *Joan* out of hand (and most will not), students cannot simply parrot the words of someone else but must construct their own arguments. Consequently, working with this particular text encourages student participation in the critical discourse of literary study.

My belief in the work's effectiveness as a teaching tool stems in part from the changing nature of the classroom, where more and more of us are finding that we must rethink the way we teach our students. In the literature classroom the emphasis is shifting gradually but inexorably away from the traditional exposure to "great works," with the teacher presenting background information and modeling a literary analysis that students will learn to emulate, toward an active, collaborative learning that takes place as the student confronts the text directly. My conviction that *Joan* can be used to foster this learning process grows out of my experience at Alverno College, a four-year liberal arts college for women and a pioneer in teaching abilities that students need for lifelong learning. I designed my unit on *Joan* for junior and senior English majors and minors with an eye toward strengthening their abilities to analyze, respond to aesthetically, and communicate about a literary work. *Joan*, one of Twain's longest—and, I would argue, more complex—works, might prove daunting to students less experienced and thus less prepared for the demands of this particular text. The student with limited analytic ability, for instance, might pay little attention to de Conte's descriptions of the military incidents. Reasoning that this is a story about Joan of Arc, she might focus only on what de Conte says about Joan, thus missing much of the work's irony. Similarly, the student less used to responding aesthetically to a literary work might simply decide that de Conte is too long-winded to suit her and thus fail altogether to respond. A student more advanced in these abilities, however, should not only be able to make connections among her responses to other works, but should be considering literary works as expressions of values, those of the writer and his or her society. That is, like the beginning student, she might find deficiencies in de Conte's ability to tell his story, but she should be able to explore and articulate more clearly the implications of this shortcoming. The advanced student might also be more attuned to the values inherent in de Conte's curious attitudes toward the war in which he finds himself a participant.

Because this is a long work, I planned a relatively long unit, designed around five two-hour classes. My own undergraduate experience of sometimes having to read twelve to fifteen novels in a semester-long course convinced me that one may learn plot summaries that way, but not necessarily how to read literature. More time spent on an individual work, with a variety of classroom experiences to accommodate students' different learning styles, does far more to prepare students to become effective readers.

Students' initial responses to *Joan*, perhaps shared first in small groups, lead into a preliminary discussion of the work during the first class. Invariably, questions arise about matters that puzzle the students. Many are historical. Did Joan of Arc really exist? Why didn't anyone from France save her? Some concern the author. How did Mark Twain get interested in Joan of Arc? I thought he wrote books that children could read, but what kid could read this one? At this point, I refrain from attempting to answer any of their questions, for I would rather have students view me as another kind of student, one perhaps more experienced than they are, but one who does not necessarily have all the answers. Rather than let all questions drop unanswered, however, I do make an effort to see what another student may think or know about the matter. Active, collaborative learning engages students in the discussion; lecturing from one to whom they feel inferior often shuts them down. Moreover, I never fail to be surprised about what this or that student has seen in a literary text or knows about a writer's life and works. Such a gathering of information can be rich. So the questions I use to guide discussion are these: What do you know about Twain? About his works? About this work? And what might it help you to know about Twain? About his works? About this work? Only after I have exhausted the students' store of information and suggestions do I provide any of my own, and even then I try to limit myself to that which is pertinent to our study and which they could not quickly or easily obtain for themselves. I try to avoid saying anything that they might regard as dictating what should be their ultimate response to the work.

At some point in this first class, students do some close reading of particular pages. With *Joan*, the pretextual matter is a valuable place to start. When asked to consider the title, for instance, students are reminded that these are not Joan's recollections, but recollections *about* Joan by Sieur Louis de Conte, her page and secretary. Students first observe the layers of opacity through which we receive this tale: Clemens's sources; Clemens himself; de Conte's manuscript, designated

"unpublished" on the title page; and, finally, the manuscript's translation by one Jean François Alden. They then note the repeated insistence on historical truth, with a curious disclaimer at the end of the
translator's note. By this time they begin to wonder what sort of story
they are being told. I have noted elsewhere how this opening material
induces skepticism, especially when it is immediately followed by the
first lines of the text itself, where we learn that de Conte is writing
at the age of eighty-two, when events that he witnessed have "receded
deeper and deeper into the past and [grown] ever more strange and
wonderful and divine and pathetic" (2). Students, in the course of careful reading, observe their own growing skepticism.

In the second class, analysis is preeminent as we apply frameworks
with which students are already familiar. These might be the always
useful New Critical, or formalist, framework, or it might be one that
asks them to consider literature as a message from author to reader,
with possible areas of "noise," or "static," in both text and reader.
Taking this perspective of literature as communication reveals that de
Conte's narration is problematic, for his limited and possibly unreliable abilities as a storyteller serve to muddle his message. Another
perspective might be an approach that asks them to regard literature as
a protest against, or affirmation of, the society it depicts—in this case,
that of fifteenth-century France. Application of this framework also
discloses confusion in de Conte's tale; although the narrator's praises
of Joan seem effusive, he manages at the same time to undercut the
very qualities that he praises.

As part of the activities in the third class, students are asked to
stretch their analytic abilities still further as we discuss a topic or
question of critical interest. For instance, we might profitably take up
the question of genre. Is this work biography? History? Romance? Some
combination of these? Sharing some early reviews with the students
assures them that the book's genre has indeed been a matter of some
debate. Students should see that de Conte's claims that his tale is "true"
history are called into question by his own assertion that history is
"second-hand information that we get from our fathers" (11). Moreover,
his habit of lying, altering his story as he tells it—and telling us he is
doing so—only increases our skepticism about the "history" that he is
giving us. Further muddling the issue is the fact that de Conte applies
the "historian" to the Paladin, a teller of blatantly outrageous stories
(117). Students who say this work is not exactly history are tempted to

conclude that its genre is biography until they consider how much of the time Joan completely disappears from the text, while the narrator pops in and out with dizzying frequency. Is it a romance? De Conte scoffs at the romanticizing of events, as when he speaks dismissively of an old fan and rusty sword discovered in a castle wall as "pathetic relics" (189). No one, however, could be more of a romantic than the narrator when he speaks with reverence of the power of Joan's sword, also found, rusty and in need of cleaning, buried in a wall.

Another fertile area of discussion is whether de Conte and Clemens are one and the same. Most critics, perhaps relying on the identical initials of Sieur Louis de Conte and Samuel Langhorne Clemens, along with their professed admiration of Joan, have suggested that they are. I believe that the relationship is far more complex. For example, while de Conte may share Clemens's enthusiasm for Joan, he possesses many other characteristics that are completely his own, traits that Mark Twain parodies elsewhere. And, although de Conte and Clemens seem to share a deepening cynicism about human nature, de Conte is never aware that he himself exemplifies the very qualities of human nature that fill him with such despair. Because grounds exist for disagreement as to the relationship between Clemens and de Conte, the subject can produce lively class discussion. Some of de Conte's ambivalences are like Twain's own: on the one hand, the narrator can scorn the ceremonies of the court, "this cheap spectacle, this tinsel show, with its small King and his butterfly dukelets"; and, on the other, he can admire the "long and imposing" coronation of that same king, a coronation that has "everything that is right for such occasions" (108, 109). (Students might enjoy seeing photographs indicating a similar duality in Clemens—for example, one showing him bare-chested on his fiftieth birthday, and another wearing the academic regalia in which he received his honorary doctorate from Oxford.) Evidence against their being one and the same, however, lies in de Conte's reaction to events of the war. He regards it as theater, a spectacle in which he is privileged to participate. He uses adjectives like "gorgeous," "splendid," "fine," and "pleasant" without irony; yet to the reader, they can seem heavily ironic in the context of the human slaughter he describes. While de Conte's view of war as adventure does mimic that of many Victorian and Edwardian males (Adams, 73–84), his enthusiastic commentary on the bloodshed is not consistent with other of Twain's writings on war, writings that more obviously expose war's savagery and idiocy. ("The

War Prayer" works well in this context, and students rarely miss the irony there.) The ultimate effect of the gusto with which de Conte details the human destruction resulting from Joan's military battles is to undercut his heroine; the reader begins to question her military mission, as well as her heart, which, as de Conte rhapsodizes, is "overflowing with the joys and enthusiasms of war" (184).

Thorough discussion of such issues will inform students' work on panel presentations that I assign for the next class, and I leave the second part of the present class for students to prepare in small groups. At some time before the next class I will have supplied each group of four students with one or two short articles summarizing one of the more accessible current critical theories, asking them to read the articles before the next meeting. For example, I may ask a group to explain a theoretical framework (feminist, psychoanalytic, reader-response, or speech-act, for instance) and discuss its applicability to *Joan*, making it clear that I do not expect that they will be experts. During this class time, each group works through the new framework, while I move among them to clarify points, answer questions, and so on.

In the fourth class, the student panels present their findings. On this day the focus is on analysis and communication. Students' applications of the assigned critical theories vary according to the complexity of the framework and to the level of their own skills of analysis, but most enjoy the challenge and are able to make cogent observations about the text. A group working with feminist criticism, for example, may observe the maudlin sentimentality and uncritical admiration with which the narrator seems to view Joan, impeding his observation of her real strengths. Perceptive students may notice, in addition, that while de Conte is relating the story of his heroine, he is also very busy telling us about himself. And isn't he, then, telling us about ourselves as well? A panel covering psychoanalytic criticism will have much to work with here, for de Conte's attitudes toward Joan are complex and bound up with his own psychological makeup. Even without knowledge of Victorian attitudes toward women, students will be able to link de Conte's having been raised in the company of males to his sometimes ambivalent attitudes toward his heroine, and, in fact, toward his experiences in general. Students applying a reader-response framework to this text can focus on how much of each student's response to the text is a product of her own culture.

Finally, an examination of de Conte's story from the perspective of speech-act theory is extremely fruitful. No matter how limited their experience with direct literary analysis, students all know what they expect from a good storyteller; they find it easy to create their own criteria for narration and then to judge de Conte's performance as narrator. A reader usually expects a narrator-biographer in a published text to be, at the very least, reliable, honest, and competent; de Conte has deficiencies in all of these areas. In many ways, he seems the ultimately unreliable narrator: he is prejudiced, superstitious, credulous, garrulous, hyperbolic, and sentimental. He is also dishonest. Even when he vows to avoid further deception, he falls into his habit of protecting Joan from the truth when he incorporates verbatim into the text of *Joan* what appears as an epigraph to chapter 6 of *Pudd'nhead Wilson* (ostensibly from Pudd'nhead Wilson's calendar): de Conte finds himself "opening up with a small lie, of course, for habit is habit, and not to be flung out of the window by any man, but coaxed downstairs a step at a time" (*Joan*, 49). His deceptions are numerous enough that his repeated claims to be telling a "true" history merely increase our skepticism. In addition, he admits to a failing memory, reminding us that "one's mind wanders around here and there and yonder, when one is old" (290). Finally, while at times he irritates his readers with rambling digressions, elsewhere he casually dismisses events that the reader finds significant.

The group presentations prepare students for the final activity of this unit, a consideration of the work's literary merit and the creation of a new aesthetic response. To focus discussion, I prepare and bring to class a series of overhead transparencies containing some of the more entertaining paragraphs to be found in the criticism on *Joan*. Given the students' now fairly comprehensive work with the text, they may be even more surprised that criticism has found so little of value in it. If students have read other works by Twain—*Huckleberry Finn*, for instance—interesting comparisons are possible. John Seelye has written of a structural similarity between the two works ([xiii–xiv]) noting that the first two-thirds of both works are "loose and rambling," with a severely restricted focus in the final third. *Huck Finn* lapses into "farcical fantasy," while in *Joan*, "Innocence . . . is put on trial by Evil incarnate" ([xiv]). Other correspondences exist as well, especially if, as I do, you regard the narrator, and not Joan, as the main character. Both Huck and de Conte, for example, are naïve narrators who seem to have difficulty applying what they have learned from past experience to new situations. And, just as Huck will not be able to escape civilization by lighting out for the Territory, de Conte cannot escape into mythmaking, for he has mythologized Joan out of his own values, the very values he wishes to flee. Inevitably, de Conte, like Huck, must take his own "civilization" with him.

With a new and more complex awareness of *Joan*, students now write aesthetic responses to bring to the unit's fifth and final class. They may or may not have revised their original opinions of the work, but they are now able to write out of a context that has been made considerably richer. My experience is that now the students are able to demonstrate awareness of the connections between their work in the course and their own lives, addressing this question: What has Twain revealed to you about what it is to be human?

In this final class I assess students' individual learning, creating a context in which the students are able to demonstrate their command of this literary work. For instance, I may set up the situation in which it has been announced that because of funding difficulties, the Mark Twain Project is considering the cancellation of its projected publication of the California Edition of *Joan*, reasoning that it is one of Twain's least-known and least-valued works. I would ask the students to write a letter to the Project arguing for or against its retention in the publication schedule. Such a letter would assess each student's knowledge of *Joan*, her ability to construct a coherent argument, and her competence in managing the conventions of writing.

Use of Twain's *Joan* in a variety of activities that focus on developing students' abilities makes the classroom an exciting place as students are empowered to take an active role in the discourse of literary studies. Robert Scholes has pointed out that "reading and writing are important because we read and write our world as well as our texts, and are read and written by them in turn" (xi). Given that both our world and our classrooms are changing, we need to consider using Twain's works in new ways. In my students' exploration of *Personal Recollections of Joan of Arc*, I find that, above all, they come away with a sense of the complexity not only of that particular work, but of the writer who called himself Mark Twain. In making that discovery, they have learned more about the extraordinary complexity of their own world. Perhaps that, after all, is the most important lesson we teach.

Works Cited

Adams, Michael C. C. *The Great Adventure: Male Desire and the Coming of World War I.* Bloomington: Indiana University Press, 1990.

Budd, Louis. *Our Mark Twain: The Making of His Public Personality.* Philadelphia: University of Pennsylvania Press, 1983.

De Voto, Bernard. *Mark Twain's America.* Rev. ed. Boston: Little, Brown, 1935.

Fishkin, Shelley Fisher. *Was Huck Black? Mark Twain and African-American Voices.* New York: Oxford University Press, 1993.

Michelson, Bruce. *Mark Twain on the Loose: A Comic Writer and the American Self.* Amherst: University of Massachusetts Press, 1995.

Miller, Victoria Thorpe. "Truth No One Would Believe: Ironic Discourse in Twain's *Personal Recollections of Joan of Arc.*" Paper given at the MLA convention, New York, 30 December 1992.

Scholes, Robert. *Textual Power: Literary Theory and the Teaching of English.* New Haven, Conn.: Yale University Press, 1985.

Seelye, John. Introduction to Mark Twain, *Personal Recollections of Joan of Arc.* Hartford, Conn.: Stowe-Day Foundation, 1980. [i–xiv.]

Stahl, J. D. *Mark Twain: Culture and Gender.* Athens: University of Georgia Press, 1994.

Twain, Mark. *Personal Recollections of Joan of Arc.* Hartford, Conn.: Stowe-Day Foundation, 1980.

Parody and Satire as Explorations of
Culture in *The Innocents Abroad*
James E. Caron

Of Mark Twain's major work before *Adventures of Huckleberry Finn*
(1885), *The Innocents Abroad* (1869) may be the least well-known.
Students have heard of *The Adventures of Tom Sawyer* (1876), and they
may have heard about *The Gilded Age* (1873), or at least have a sense of
its subject matter, since its title is now used to designate a whole era of
post-Civil War corruption in big business and national politics. And
even if the stories are unread, the subjects of "Old Times on the Mississippi" (1874) and *Roughing It* (1872)—steamboat piloting and the Far
West—are commonly associated with Mark Twain. But Sam Clemens's
reporting of and commenting on one of the first American pleasure
cruises to Europe and the Middle East is obscured by those later efforts.
That it should be so is an irony because *The Innocents Abroad* in a very
real way cleared the path for what followed by becoming a bestseller
and making Clemens famous and rich enough to be a (more or less)
respectable suitor to the daughter of a New York coal merchant. It is
thus not too much to say that *The Innocents Abroad* was the making of
Sam Clemens and Mark Twain.

If one is teaching a course on Mark Twain, such credentials alone
may be enough for inclusion in the syllabus, though other reasons
exist. To begin with, *The Innocents Abroad* is still entertaining. Moreover, the text provides an excellent opportunity to highlight Twain as a
comic character and to discuss Clemens as a satirist. If one is teaching a
course on the American novel, the loose narrative structure and somewhat inchoate characterization of *The Innocents Abroad* make it a
useful contrast to formal novels. Indeed, the book's original epistolary
format, its roots in newspaper reporting, and its affinity with platform
lecturing, all make it a good example for discussing the genesis and
heterogeneity of the form of the novel.

The Innocents Abroad is also a good text to teach in any course that focuses on culture. As Mark Twain, Sam Clemens spent a lifetime satirizing his own culture in particular and the human race in general. This essay will show how one can effectively teach *The Innocents Abroad* by employing its motif of examining cultural artifacts. On its most general level, this motif raises the question of how people are enculturated. More specifically, it invites comparisons among cultures. More specifically still, the motif indicates how the text can be read as an initial crystallization of Clemens's satire of American post-Civil War, white, Anglo-Saxon, Protestant culture. By approaching *The Innocents Abroad* as his first prolonged critique of American values, one can, first, establish links to the popular culture of the day—newspapers, travel books, the lyceum and lecture circuit; second, illustrate how the Twain character functions in the satire; and third, discuss cultural values in a way that not only highlights the 1860s but also opens up an important issue of the 1990s—multiculturalism. Finally, Twain's adventures and misadventures in *The Innocents Abroad* cause one to ask very basic questions about what it means to be civilized and cultured. Before I elaborate these generalities with specifics from the book, some background on the popular culture from which *The Innocents Abroad* emerged should be helpful.[1]

In the 1840s and 1850s, the rising middle class in America had turned to popular magazines and etiquette books to learn about domestic manners. About to embark in 1867 on a tour of Europe and Palestine, the *Quaker City* tourists studiously read guidebooks by Murray and Baedeker to learn what one should visit abroad. In a sense, then, the five-month cruise of the *Quaker City*, from 8 June to 19 November 1867, was symbolic of the still relatively unformed manners and tastes of the American middle class. Indeed, as Twain would insinuate in *The Innocents Abroad*, the middle classes, when they did travel in foreign lands, revealed their innocence by turning to a myriad of travel volumes, even some that told them how they should *feel* as they gazed upon places that the guidebooks claimed were worth visiting. As we shall see, Twain would both embody this innocence and satirize it.

Travel books, whether by amateurs or professional explorers, had been popular in Europe since the "discovery" of the Americas. As the United States spread across the middle latitudes of North America, books by explorers and tourists formed a staple of the publishing industry. And the lyceum—started in the 1820s as a way to disseminate practical and scientific knowledge, and matured in the 1850s as a formal lecture circuit to disseminate social and philosophical ideas to the villages and towns of the United States—also fed the public's appetite for information, poetical description, and pseudo-analyses of exotic places and people, whether in North America or not.

In addition, newspapers big and small had long since formed the habit of printing letters from travelers, often from current or former members of a town or village. These letters might describe the big cities of the eastern seaboard, or detail life in the new territories of Oregon or in the gold and silver fields of California and Nevada. The first extant letter of Sam Clemens—published in brother Orion's newspaper, the *Hannibal Journal*—is dated 24 August 1853 from New York City. Sam had left Missouri to see the world's fair some weeks before. Orion would later publish a number of Sam's letters in another newspaper that Orion owned and edited, the *Muscatine* (Iowa) *Journal*, while Sam was in St. Louis, Washington, D.C., and Philadelphia.

These strands of popular culture meant that Sam Clemens, who was on the East Coast early in 1867, writing as "special traveling correspondent" for the San Francisco *Alta California*, did not have to work hard to convince the editors of the *Alta* to put up the $1,250 fee for the *Quaker City* cruise itself, plus $500 in gold for expenses. Those editors had already given Clemens a wide latitude for his weekly letter to them, originally expecting that he would travel leisurely around the world and back to San Francisco. Having already had ample proof of Mark Twain's appeal—due to letters from the Sandwich Islands (Hawaii) published in the *Sacramento Union* in 1866—the *Alta* editors expected that any letters would be a cut above the usual correspondence from travelers and would therefore delight their readers. Given the popularity on the West Coast of the Mark Twain persona, and given the continuing popularity of travel books and correspondence to newspapers from travelers, combining that persona with those genres must have seemed like a good investment to the *Alta California* editors. Even Horace Greeley apparently recognized a rising star, for Clemens also contracted with Greeley's *New York Tribune* as a correspondent after Clemens's success lecturing in New York City in May 1867.

In addition to helping place *The Innocents Abroad* in its historical moment, this background also helps students understand a basic attitude that guided Clemens as he wrote the original letters and then as he revised and expanded them into book form between February and June of 1868. Essentially, this attitude consisted of his maintaining an emotional distance not only from the particular events recounted but also from the conventions of the travel book genre itself, an emotional distance that is proper for a skeptic who is also a comic writer.

Equally helpful is a foregrounding of the goals of the travel book genre as they bear on the traveler's habit of sightseeing. One function of the usual guides and travel books of the nineteenth century was to provide a means by which the reader can move closer to the exotic, whether that proximity is literal (leading one to the actual sight that must be seen) or imaginative (leading one to an experience of the sight or attraction via representation). In addition, travel books provide information which may contextualize the specific attraction and so organize an individual's knowledge of what he or she is experiencing. Thus these books articulate a set of ready-made perceptions about an attraction that frames the individual's emotional response. As Clemens portrays them in *The Innocents Abroad*, these "frames" are more properly characterized as "screens," screens which provide a sense of comfort to tourists by preventing them from being at a loss for a properly cultured response once they are face to face with the specific attraction. If the basic function of the guide/travel book is to move the individual closer to the exotic, this screen effect prevents him or her from coming too close to it by actually having to look closely and formulate fresh judgments. The narration and description of these books thus mediates experience in two opposing directions, promising the thrill of the unknown that characterizes the exotic while creating a sense of safety.

This paradox, of course, parallels the fundamental emotion of travelers in a foreign country. Obviously, one travels abroad for pleasure, to experience foreign ways—food, customs, manners, etc.—but that encounter inevitably produces anxiety, not just about logistics, about getting lost or stranded, but also about being lost or stranded in an encounter with otherness that individuals in the foreign countries represent. Most tourists wish to meet "friendly natives" and experience their ways *without* becoming too involved with specific individuals. Hence, few people who travel actually linger long enough to "break into" another culture and experience it at a depth beyond the surface sampling of the tourist, a tendency exemplified by the *Quaker City* passengers.

After some biographical information about Clemens and some background on the popular culture that sustained his Mark Twain persona, I usually try to discuss the functions of travel books by bringing out the psychology of traveling just mentioned. This strategy illustrates for the students how the structures and conventions of travel writing entail a rhetoric meant to engage an individual both as reader and as traveler. If this link between rhetoric and experience can be made, the student will, ideally, appreciate the conventions of travel writing and therefore be well-positioned to understand how Clemens uses and abuses them. My gambits for engaging the students are questions designed to evoke their own emotions about traveling, even if those excursions have remained within the borders of the United States. What was different about where you went? Were the people friendly? Did you try local dishes? Did you like the food? Did you travel as part of a tour group? Did you spend any significant time with individuals from the local area? Did you participate in any festivities? Were you invited to visit or even eat dinner at someone's home? Coupling their own emotions with some sense of the conventions of travel writing and the historical moment in which Clemens wrote *The Innocents Abroad* primes the students for the comic distance that Mark Twain creates as he enacts and parodies both the role of the travel correspondent *and* the psychology of a tourist.

The first part of the text, then, to which I draw their attention, is the preface. In it, Twain warns the reader that he does not write in the "usual style of travel writing." If this is not wise of him, it is at least honest, he claims, implying that the usual style is essentially mendacious. How so? Because the usual style tells the reader "how he *ought* to look at objects of interest beyond the sea."[2] Rather than narrating and describing what is the party line of the ostensibly cultured, Twain's purpose in *The Innocents Abroad* is to suggest how the reader would see things "with his own eyes." The move here is sophisticated, for on the one hand merely going overseas implies a cultural importance to what is over there, yet on the other Twain will represent the independence of "the average American" by judging the specifics of what is over there for himself. Furthermore, Twain implies that culture as an icon, as something to worship (an idea promoted by nineteenth-century travel writing), is an idea that has more than a little phoniness and snobbery associated with it. In sum, Twain implies that his eyes are the average American's eyes, the eyes of someone who is plain-spoken and plain-living as well as free-thinking—the virtues of Jefferson's ideal yeomanry. The preface thus not only initiates the parodic distance from travel writing but establishes the implied audience.

The preface's attack on the conventions of travel writing sets up one of the running jokes in the text: the misleading nature of guidebook language. Either the descriptions bear little resemblance to the object described, or they are clichéd—in effect, pretenses of having an original thought (434). The thievery of ideas as well as poverty of thought implied in the repetitious and clichéd phrasing of guidebooks is openly ridiculed in chapter 10 when Mark Twain first produces a sentence in guidebook style and then follows it with a warning about its being copyrighted: "Toward nightfall the next evening, we steamed into the great artificial harbor of this noble city of Marseilles, and saw the dying sunlight gild its clustering spires and ramparts, and flood its leagues of environing verdure with a mellow radiance that touched with an added charm the white villas that flecked the landscape far and near. (Copyright secured according to law.)" (70).

This maneuver is typical of a basic parodic technique used by Clemens throughout *The Innocents Abroad*: reproduce a certain rhetorical style in such a way that the reader sees it as illegitimate, that is, as an object not to be taken seriously. The bracketed sentence makes it clear that the rhetoric is mimicked and thus comic. Without that bracketed sentence, however, the sense of mimicry is lost, a point easily made if one compares the description of a Pisan tear jug that comes later in the narrative (180). Such a comparison illustrates the protean quality of Mark Twain as a character in *The Innocents Abroad*, for he will not hesitate to (re)produce, in a manner to be taken seriously, the very same guidebook rhetoric he parodies. At other times in the text, Twain will mimic other rhetorics, for example, American newspapers (264) or theater reviews (202), but in general his parody remains targeted on the language of travel writing.

In a key passage late in the text (364–69), when he and his fellow tourists are in Palestine, Twain conducts an extended analysis of guidebook descriptions of the Sea of Galilee, quoting at length two examples after he has given the reader his own rather unflattering portrait of this "celebrated" body of water. For Twain, the Sea of Galilee has a "dreary" solitude about it and is "expressionless and unpoetical." The two quoted descriptions are of course very positive about the beauty of the place, but Twain will not let them stand unchallenged, correcting what he calls "misstatements" of details to make them conform to the unvarnished truth. Almost like a lawyer cross-examining a witness (the writers' descriptions are called "testimony" at one point), Twain probes the misleading nature of such descriptions: "Nearly every book concerning Galilee and its lake describes the scenery as beautiful. No—not always so straightforward as that. Sometimes the *impression* intentionally conveyed is that it is beautiful, at the same time that the author is careful not to *say* that it is in plain Saxon" (368).

Having exposed in some detail the false nature of such descriptive passages of famous sites, Twain goes on to suggest motives for such untruthfulness, whether one calls them "pleasant falsities" or hypocrisies "deliberately meant to deceive." Either the writers were fearful that writing the truth about places associated with the Bible would be unpopular, or the veneration they felt for such places "heated their fancies and biased their judgment." It amounts to the same thing either way: they were full of prejudices and had "their verdicts already prepared" and so could not write dispassionately. If prejudices are exactly what one seeks to shed by traveling, the rhetoric of travel writing instead creates its own set, substituting its own vision and thus screening tourists from forming their own perceptions. Twain finishes his analysis of descriptions of the Sea of Galilee by noting that the remarks of his fellow tourists on the sights they see have ceased to surprise and charm him because he has realized that they are constantly plagiarizing, thus exemplifying the problem: "authors write pictures and frame rhapsodies, and lesser men follow and see with the author's eyes instead of their own, and speak with his tongue" (369).

There is a complicating factor in this issue of how the rhetoric of travel writing actually prevents an honest look at whatever attraction such writing has brought one to see. Essentially, we have already noted this complication with the descriptions of Marseilles harbor and the Pisan tear jug: Mark Twain's willingness to propagate his own word pictures that reflect his own prejudices. The passage on the Sea of Galilee, for example, begins with a comparison to Lake Tahoe, the description of which is only a more elaborate version of the sentence that describes Marseilles and its environs and is then mocked:

> In the early morning one watches the silent battle of dawn and darkness upon the waters of Tahoe with a placid interest; but when the shadows sulk away and one by one the hidden beauties of the

shore unfold themselves in the full splendor of noon; when the still surface is belted like a rainbow with broad bars of blue and green and white, half the distance from circumference to center; when, in the lazy summer afternoon, he lies in a boat, far out to where the dead blue of the deep water begins, and smokes the pipe of peace and idly winks at the distant crags and patches of snow from under his cap brim; when the boat drifts shoreward to the white water, and he lolls over the gunwhale and gazes by the hour down through the crystal depths and notes the colors of the pebbles and reviews the finny armies gliding in procession a hundred feet below; when at night he sees moon and stars, mountain ridges feathered with pines, jutting white capes, bold promontories, grand sweeps of rugged scenery topped with bald, glimmering peaks, all magnificently pictured in the polished mirror of the lake in richest, softest detail, the tranquil interest that was born with the morning deepens and deepens, by sure degrees, till it culminates at last in resistless fascination! (365)

"Resistless fascination" is exactly what all travel writing seeks to create in its readers. It is what causes Mark Twain's fellow tourists to speak of what they see with words that are not their own. We may not hoist Mark Twain on his own petard because in a footnote he all but admits his prejudice about Lake Tahoe, but his description of that body of water is pure travel writing rhetoric, calculated to create an impression of beauty and languor and to stir a yearning for such idyllic moments. In short, Mark Twain's description is mimetic, not parodic of the effect Lake Tahoe had on him; it creates "resistless fascination." That rapture overwhelms any interest in presenting the unvarnished truth or even making a joke.

Inevitably, then, places in *The Innocents Abroad* exist where readers might feel as though Mark Twain is putting them on. He seems to create word pictures in the mendacious style of travel writing's rhetoric and leave out the clue—the bracketed sentence that follows the sentence about Marseilles—alerting the reader that this instance is parodic and not to be taken seriously. Because Mark Twain has done such a good job of alerting the reader to the virtual impossibility of any travel writing being original and genuine, it therefore becomes an open question as to how the reader should react to such examples as the descriptions of Lake Tahoe and the Pisan tear jug.

Clemens, it would seem, has some awareness of how his oscillations between parodic and serious travel writing undercut each other. At least, the confusion of such mutual undercutting seems to be represented as happening to Mark Twain when he tells the story of Abelard and Heloise, "stripped of its sentimentality." Mark Twain counts on the reader to be familiar with—indeed, already taken in by—other renditions that make much of the story as a romance. Foolishly believing in the romance of Abelard and Heloise was his fate, Mark Twain says, and he declares he will not in the future waste any sentiment until he is sure that his "attentions" are deserved. In short, Mark Twain should have read the romantic versions of the Abelard and Heloise story as parody. The specific target here, sentimentalized narrations of Abelard and Heloise, echoes the attack on misphrasings of travel language. In both, the signifier apparently has little or nothing to do with the signified. But if Mark Twain is fooled, then so can the reader be fooled, even by Mark Twain's own rhetoric, which can sincerely call forth sentiment, as we have seen with his set piece on Lake Tahoe. The list of "attentions" paid to the graves of Abelard and Heloise—tears, *immortelles*, and a bunch of radishes—complicates this question of Mark Twain's constancy, however, suggesting the foolishness of Mark Twain the character as well as the cleverness of Sam Clemens the parodist. The incongruity of the radish as a tribute to the lovers makes Mark Twain seem silly in his failure to understand the "truth" of Abelard and Heloise, but it also can function as the bracketed sentence does in the Marseilles example, alerting readers to Clemens the implied author who expects them to appreciate the multileveled nature of his satiric gibes. In effect, *The Innocents Abroad* offers a Chinese box of sentimental conventions for the reader to laugh at: Mark Twain's response to the sentimental tale is enclosed within a travel book narrative the conventions of which are themselves offered as comic targets because they too create a distorting prejudice about what they purport to tell. Nevertheless, Clemens wants his readers to be moved by his own highly colored rhetoric. At bottom, the reader of *The Innocents Abroad* must be constantly ready for both parodic and sincere versions.

This sometimes dizzying sequence of rhetoric and responses, then, leaves the reader wondering whether he or she should *ever* take Mark Twain seriously, which is precisely the comic effect that Clemens had achieved with hoaxes earlier in his career while in Nevada writing for the *Territorial Enterprise* in Virginia City. Moreover, it is said that

Clemens achieved the same paralyzing effect face-to-face. Justin Kaplan reports that Clemens had that effect on his fellow *Quaker City* passengers (41), and Paul Fatout (62) and Fred Lorch (47), in their books on Clemens's platform performances, report on one joke of Mark Twain used in early tours that often had the same effect on audiences. Also noted in these studies is how Mark Twain would suddenly shift tones (Lorch, 37) or make fun of his own seriously delivered descriptions (Fatout, 59–60).

Thus, it is important for an understanding of *The Innocents Abroad* to be aware of how adept Clemens is as a mimic and to ask if he is serious in offering a rhetorical set piece. Moreover, because Clemens was on the lecture platform before and after writing his letters and then during the rewriting of them as *The Innocents Abroad*, pointing out the similarity between written narrative and oral delivery helps students understand how Clemens created and shaped Mark Twain's character early in his career.

Analyzing one of the main targets for satire in *The Innocents Abroad*—the rhetoric of travel writing—has brought us to a consideration of "Mark Twain" as a comic device. I want now to contemplate briefly Mark Twain as a "character." On the comic level, Mark Twain as character is the shape-shifting trickster who inverts what is usual to create satiric laughter, a clown who carnivalizes the genre of travel writing. Considered as a character within a quasi-novelistic narrative, Mark Twain represents the quintessential American, brash yet naïve, pragmatic yet sentimental. Such contradictory impulses invoke Walt Whitman's self-description in section 51 of "Song of Myself": "Do I contradict myself? / Very well then I contradict myself / (I am large, I contain multitudes.)" Mark Twain contains, if not multitudes, at least five aspects: (1) the reporter of dry facts (e.g., 42, 129); (2) the innocent whose ignorance is charming (e.g., 55, 89, 98, 295–97); (3) the vandal or sinner whose ignorance is repellent (e.g., 56, 83, 185, 407); (4) the guidebook rhetorician who purveys the beauty, sentiment, and picturesqueness of the excursion (e.g., 58, 112, 156); (5) the honest skeptic (e.g., chap. 53; 367).

This amalgam of roles is related to the earliest days of Samuel Clemens as a writer for the *Virginia City* (Nevada) *Territorial Enterprise*. Part reportorial and part fiction, the writing practiced by Clemens (and others) in the early 1860s in Nevada and California (often called "Washoe Journalism") was a perfect way to learn how to become adept at the multiple roles and shifting rhetorics that characterize *The Innocents Abroad*. In a course on Mark Twain, the book can be usefully described as a climax of that Far West newspaper and magazine experience. The kaleidoscopic role-shifting within *The Innocents Abroad* creates many of the comic effects of the narrative, provides a brisk pace, and allows for the simultaneously parodic and serious use of what was usually expected from travel writing. All of these elements contributed to the popularity of *The Innocents Abroad* in its day, and they preserve its readability today.

The variety of roles that Mark Twain must play is an effect of what might be called the dramatic conflict of *The Innocents Abroad*, which is essentially a question of culture clash. As Mark Twain encounters and evaluates other cultures, he begins to ask questions about his own. It is this ability to recognize faults in his own culture, even if his criticisms of other cultures are virulent at times, that makes *The Innocents Abroad* a useful platform for discussion of cultural values. The clash of cultures actually begins intramurally, for Mark Twain represents the subordinate category in a two-tiered division of the *Quaker City* passengers. He is one of the Vandals or sinners, to be distinguished from the saints and true Pilgrims on the trip. This initial division foreshadows the broader clashes between cultures and helps define Mark Twain's critique of the white, Anglo-Saxon, Protestant culture that the pilgrims represent.

To get to that satirical center, we must first discuss three other components that serve as foci for the book's satire: (1) the American sense of inferiority vis-à-vis European culture that provokes a desire to become cultured; (2) the American sense of superiority about their way of life that provokes a fear of loss of identity through the process of becoming cultured; (3) that sense of superiority magnified into the chauvinism and orientalism which claims that the WASP culture of the United States *is* civilization.[3] Mark Twain, of course, will represent each aspect of these American tourists encountering otherness. Although *The Innocents Abroad* is not organized in a clear linear pattern, a useful way to present the book is to offer these three aspects as a sequence, which is then followed by a look at what I have called the satiric center of the narrative: the Pilgrims are actually Vandals, and American Christianity, which seems to have the clear moral edge on Catholic Europe and the Islamic Ottoman Empire, carries its own compromising faults. In what remains of this essay I will suggest exemplary pieces of the text to illustrate each aspect.

At different places in the text, Mark Twain declares that he "travels to learn," and it might be stated as a general proposition that the proper way to travel is to keep an open mind about everything so that one may learn. But for the Americans on the *Quaker City* cruise, this point has a barbed quality because for the entire life of the Republic, that is, up to 1867, many people felt that the United States had no "high" culture of its own. From this viewpoint, the fine arts in the United States are essentially imitations of the Europeans. Literature, for example, is usually said to be derivative of the English. It is one thing to appreciate the art treasures of another country and feel as though one's own country has something comparable; it is quite another to feel as though one's culture has nothing.

A good focal point for this sense of cultural inferiority comes in the chapters on Italy and Mark Twain's discussion of the Old Masters, essentially the artists of the Renaissance. In Venice, Mark Twain says he has "striven to learn," "humbly wished to learn" whatever he can about artworks because no chance exists in America to acquire a critical judgment. In the Vatican museums at Rome, the sheer number of paintings overwhelms the viewer, and only Raphael's *Transfiguration* makes a positive impression, a reaction that gives him some hope of learning to appreciate the Old Masters beyond the little he is able to do so far. The elaborate rituals for viewing these artworks—accounts of guides as well as those in guidebooks—reflect received opinion on the fine art of Europe: it is one of the pinnacles of culture. Not to like it is to admit one's lack of education. When Mark Twain says that he does not like the Old Masters—not much, anyway—he dismays his friends who had urged him not to reveal his own deficiency by admitting his dislike. He had promised to keep such "uncouth sentiments" to himself (171). In Yankee fashion, Mark Twain will later say that he can judge Italian commerce better (182), but he also will fight back on aesthetic grounds typically American, claiming as his aesthetic guide "that great Monarch of all the Old Masters, Nature" (172).

Mark Twain also fights back with another typical weapon—laughter—when he highlights the comic deadpan of the doctor, which made him look like "an inspired idiot" (209). The doctor—with his foolish questions about penmanship (when shown a manuscript written by

Columbus) or about the difference between a bust and pedestal (when shown a statue of Columbus)—manages to satirize not just the implied importance of European culture as represented by any number of artifacts, but also the implied demand for the tourists' admiration. The duty of the traveler—to learn—is the target for laughter in the climactic exchange between the doctor and his guide:

> "See genteelmen! Mummy! Mummy!"
> The [doctor's] eyeglass came up calmly, as deliberately as ever.
> "Ah—Ferguson—what did I understand you to say the gentleman's name was?"
> "Name? He got no name! Mummy! 'Gyptian mummy!"
> "Yes, yes. Born here?"
> "No! *Gyptian* mummy!"
> "Ah, just so. Frenchman, I presume?"
> "No! *Not* Frenchman, not Roman. Born in Egypta!"
> "Born in Egypta. Never heard of Egypta before. Foreign locality, likely. Mummy—mummy. How calm he is—how self-possessed. Is, ah—is he dead?"
> "Oh, *sacre bleu*, been dead three thousan' year!"
> The doctor turned on him savagely.
> "Here, now, what do you mean by such conduct as this! Playing us for Chinamen because we are strangers and trying to learn! Trying to impose your vile secondhand carcasses on *us*! Thunder and lightning, I've got a notion to—to—if you've got a nice *fresh* corpse, fetch him out! Or, by George, we'll brain you!" (212)

By feigning in this exaggerated way, Mark Twain and his fellow Vandals satirize the expectations on both sides—from snobbish Americans and Europeans alike.

This sort of scene shows Mark Twain's struggle to assert some independence, to maintain an identity, at the same time as he makes concerted efforts to absorb European culture. At the close of Henry James's *Daisy Miller*, the American expatriate Winterbourne, reflecting on his role in the social demise and subsequent death of Daisy, feels that perhaps he failed to understand her thoroughly American ways because he had " 'lived too long in foreign parts' "—had become a European, in effect. Mark Twain makes fun of such a possibility when he notes that some American travelers have been adding French phrases to their names when signing themselves into a register in an Italian hotel (e.g., Lloyd B. Williams, *et trois amis, ville de* Boston, *Amerique*), and when he tells of a man who acted as though he were French upon his return home. It may not be "pleasant to see an American thrusting his nationality forward *obtrusively* in a foreign land, but oh, it is pitiable to see him making of himself a thing that is neither male nor female, neither fish, flesh, nor fowl—a poor, miserable, hermaphrodite Frenchman!" (168). What complicates this critique of affectation and the blurring of cultural identities is its entanglement with the laudable goal of learning about other cultures. When one understands another culture, one is, to that extent, assimilated into it. Too much assimilation, however, results in a Winterbourne or the man who pretends to be French when he is among his countrymen. Thus, when Mark Twain says, "We wish to learn all the curious, outlandish ways of all the different countries, so that we can 'show off' and astonish people when we get home" (167), he is not simply attacking the obvious perversion of motive for learning other ways. He is also uncovering a negative side to the traveler's penchant for learning: too much learning of "outlandish ways" undermines an American sense of self.

Part of Mark Twain's counter against such loss of American identity consists of examples of American pride about specific aspects of their homeland. To begin with, there are the comments on democratic values that throughout the nineteenth century have been the bulwark of that pride in their young society. Thus, the miles of paintings in the Louvre are beautiful aesthetically, but politically they are signs of a nauseating "adulation of princely patrons" (100), and Italy, the chief exhibit for the aesthetics of the Renaissance, builds and maintains such beauty by grinding the people to death with taxes (184). Similarly, Odessa is praised because it resembles an American city, with streets that are broad and straight, stores that have a "stirring business look," and people who are "fast walkers" (278). All these details imply the order and industriousness of the United States. Critiques of foreign ways also imply the superiority of the United States in technology, education, and hygiene. Coupled with the assertion that European sites of natural beauty such as Lake Como are inferior to American instances of natural beauty (e.g., Lake Tahoe), Mark Twain's implicit defense of the United States sums up the American viewpoint that had been and was continuing to be built in the nineteenth century: Europe may have beautiful art and quaint traditions, but no European country can match the American landscape, American system of government, or American industry.

Once Mark Twain's argument has been laid out in these terms, it is probably a good time to invite students to decide how much has changed since the 1860s. What artistic achievements can the United States claim? Do we still boast about our landscape, system of government, and industry? The discussion here often produces not just a good look at what young Americans today see as the best and most distinctive elements of their culture, but also a clearer sense for them of the roots of such claims. Students begin to sense a connection with Mark Twain's America.

I have tried to suggest how the narrative of *The Innocents Abroad* reveals two sides to the American tourists' attraction to the otherness of Europe. On the one hand, they feel culturally inferior and wish to overcome that lack by learning, in some depth, about foreign ways; on the other hand, they feel culturally superior to Europe and fear the potential loss of identity that is implicit in a thorough understanding of foreign ways. The brilliance of Clemens is that he uses Mark Twain's quirky, shifting personality to represent both sides. The next stage is the orientalizing that virtually equates WASP culture with civilization. Having shown the students how Mark Twain represents a brief for American virtues, I next try to show how in his encounter with the peoples of the Middle East he represents the exaggerated, chauvinistic form of that brief.

This thematic sequence is suggested, to an extent, by the movement of the narrative as it chronicles the itinerary of the *Quaker City*. If Western Europe elicited the initial engagement and recoil from foreign cultures (see 187, where Mark Twain says that the true religion is Protestant), the countries of what we now call the Middle East and what the American Pilgrims think of as the Holy Land, deepen the conflict between keeping an open mind about one's own culture and accepting the values of other cultures. The Catholicism of Europe is nothing as an obstacle to acceptance compared to the Islamic Ottoman Empire, which controlled the Middle East in 1867.

Encountering the Islamic cultures of the Middle East brings out in Mark Twain the most virulent strain of American chauvinism. In effect, his sense of separateness from Catholic Europe disappears, and, behind a united Western front, he characterizes negative attributes as intrinsic to the peoples of the Ottoman Empire, effectively orientalizing them in a derogatory fashion. Thus, Smyrna is "just like any other Oriental city" (292), which means that it is dirty, smelly, disorderly, etc. (see 263, 326, 335, 362), and the people in a village in Palestine are "beggars by nature, instinct, and education" (363). The attack is even stronger when the people are portrayed as essentially evil: the "natural instincts" of the "Muhammadans" prevent moral behavior (263); Greeks, Turks, and Armenians lie and cheat naturally (264–65). Such characterizations move toward racism when Mark Twain compares Arabs to American Indians (339–41; 384; 394); the same characterizations apparently rest in the smugness of theology when Mark Twain says (jokingly?) that the torments inflicted upon him by Arabs are turned into "sweet consolation [because he] knew that except these Muhammadans repented, they would go straight to perdition someday" (452). All of these comments represent the dark side of American and Western pride in self and culture. They easily lend themselves to discussion of the recent rise of intolerance of different peoples in the United States and other parts of the West (e.g., violent attacks against Turks in Germany; American skinheads who planned a race riot and were arrested in July 1993).

If orientalizing can be described as a discourse for maintaining a distinctive distance between self and an other perceived as too different to entertain any notion of underlying sameness, too different to fulfill the traveler's duty to learn about foreign ways, one can argue that another of Mark Twain's aspects—the guidebook rhetorician who creates and then peddles the beauty and sentiment of the excursion—functions in a similar way. In effect, when Mark Twain employs the rhetoric of travel writing to create word pictures, he uses the mediation of language to maintain enough of a distance from the other to sanitize it and to make it nonthreatening. We are back to the psychology of the tourist that I mentioned at the outset: the true traveler wishes to get close to the foreign culture he or she is visiting, but at the same time most people are fearful of getting too close. The modern answers are photographs, which frame out unpleasant features, and material souvenirs, which allow a tangible possession of a foreign culture. Photographs are especially helpful in maintaining a distance. They are like nostalgia itself, which selectively filters out the negative aspects of traveling and highlights the positive.

In *The Innocents Abroad*, such selectivity occurs when Mark Twain consciously creates set pieces of description, and they are taken seriously. The lecture circuit audience as well as the travel book audience expected such word pictures. Before Clemens left for Europe on the *Quaker City* cruise, he had dazzled lecture hall audiences on both coasts with descriptions of an eruption of Kilauea volcano he had witnessed while touring Hawaii in 1866. By all accounts, this description, which appears in its best-known form in *Roughing It*, was one of the more effective portions of his "Sandwich Islands" lecture. As I noted, *The Innocents Abroad* uses such descriptions seriously as well as parodying them. My point here is that at times these descriptions have as one of their functions a screening effect that sanitizes as it aestheticizes (anesthetizes?) experience. Moreover, this screening effect is linked to the distancing created by orientalizing.

Often these word pictures are referred to as "picturesque." Clemens in *The Innocents Abroad* seems to use "the picturesque" in a variety of ways, not all of which are relevant to the prior history of the term but which probably reflect what was commonly meant in 1867.[4] My focus is a narrow one: the "picturesque as screen" effect. This screening and distancing function bears a resemblance to an aesthetic favored by Hawthorne in his famous definition of "Romance" in the preface to *The House of the Seven Gables*. This similarity is clearly demonstrated in Mark Twain's description of Venice (156–58), wherein the city is a "beautiful picture" *only* by the light of the "charitable" moon. The "treacherous" sunlight reveals the true Venice—"decayed, forlorn, poverty-stricken, and commerceless." Such a contrast leads to another theme of *The Innocents Abroad*, the innocent Mark Twain disabused of his boyish pictures of such places as Venice (158–62), and it is obvious from this and other passages in the book that nostalgia's selective memory employs the imaginative distance implied by the "mellow" moonlight (see 381, 424, 433). Often, merely achieving a physical distance from a large object is enough to invoke the picturesque-as-screen. Such is the case with Naples. Up close, there are "disagreeable sights and smells," while from the slopes of Vesuvius the city is a "picture of wonderful beauty," and the "frame of the picture was [itself] charming" (227–28; see also 243, 257, 325). The metaphors of "picture" and "frame" are self-consciously employed, and the creation of an aesthetic is deliberate.

Such conscious efforts to make an aesthetic out of experience are literalized when Mark Twain climbs Mount Tabor in Syria and views the plains through the "picturesque framework of a ragged and ruined stone window arch" (375–77). As in the aestheticizing of Naples, even the frame is picturesquely charming, a redundancy that seems to emphasize the need to create such "pictures" at a time in the United States when photography for the masses had not yet arrived and landscapes were most often rendered in steel engravings. The pleasure of this view from Tabor is such that it jogs a memory of a villa near Genoa that Mark Twain had forgotten to mention when writing about Italy. In the midst of the gardens of this villa, the visitor may take in the prospect through a pane of yellow glass set up for the purpose. Far from deriding such artificiality, Mark Twain says that the device yields "the faintest, softest, richest picture that ever graced the dream of a dying saint" because it casts the view "into enchanted distance and shuts out from it all unattractive features." This describes exactly the "picturesque-as-screen" in *The Innocents Abroad*.

When one views a landscape, such screening and distancing seem merely part of the process of picture-making—of composing a landscape painting, steel engraving, or photograph. When the same process is applied to people, the link to orientalizing becomes apparent. To a certain extent, Mark Twain goes through this process with the Neapolitans in the passage cited earlier. But when Mark Twain says that Arabs around a well in Palestine are "picturesque," as a "Bible picture," as a "grand Oriental picture which I had worshiped a thousand times in soft, rich steel engravings" (393), he cannot sustain the aesthetic illusion because the desolation, dirt, fleas, smells, and other ugly features are too palpable. The picturesque aesthetic in *The Innocents Abroad* functions partly to screen out such unattractive features. Whether denying the humanity of Arabs by calling them "naturally" immoral or transmuting their humanity by blocking out disagreeable elements in order to compose a word picture for a souvenir, Mark Twain in these phases suggests both the subtleties and the obvious shrillness of his cultural chauvinism. (Given the large percentage of students at the University of Hawaii with Asian or Pacific Island heritages, this section of my presentation of *The Innocents Abroad* generally elicits many different reactions, all of them animated.)

This leads us to the final phase of evaluating Mark Twain's performance in *The Innocents Abroad*. Having allowed the students to absorb the fact that Mark Twain, in one of his many facets, represents the intolerance of WASP culture, I go on to show how other portions of the text illustrate a completely different attitude, thus constituting the most daring part of Clemens's satire, a critique of his own culture. Notable in this part of teaching the book is a passage on the "naturally good hearted and intelligent [Syrians who], with education and liberty would be a happy and contented race" (318). Here, Mark Twain contradicts his other assertions about the natural propensities of Arabs and Muslims, and he sounds like a liberal humanist of the Enlightenment who believes that all people can be educated and improved. Significantly, this comment comes in one of several discussions and condemnations of the Ottoman Empire (404, 423, 424). At such times, Sam Clemens uses his Mark Twain persona to move past tactics that make faults essential elements of Middle Eastern peoples and instead attributed these faults to political institutions. (That distinction itself is usually worth a great deal of discussion among students.) Even in the midst of his most intolerant statements about the Ottoman Empire and its Arab and/or Muslim inhabitants, Mark Twain realizes that if he wishes "to profit by this tour and come to a correct understanding of the matters of interest connected with it, [he] must studiously and faithfully unlearn a great many things . . ." (349). Further, Mark Twain must learn to acknowledge the faults of his own culture.

That culture symbolically manifests itself in the behavior of the *Quaker City* tourists, especially those who initially had been labeled Pilgrims—that is, those who were apparently the best of the group. What the reader discovers along with Mark Twain is that these so-called Pilgrims are Vandals too, no better than the Mark Twain who, at the beginning of the voyage, is reprimanded for using his penknife to carve up the ship's rail (29). Indeed, the Pilgrims exhibit more propensity for destruction than Mark Twain because they insist on taking home pieces of monuments as souvenirs. The vandalism gets so bad that not only the Ottoman officials, but the British government too, warns the *Quaker City* tourists about their behavior (308–9). Blucher is represented as the worst of the offenders, but they all do it (276), and a running joke of the author's during the Middle East phase of the trip is the way that the Americans blithely hammer off pieces of any monument that suits their fancy, including the Sphinx! (458; see also 328, 382, 392, 401, 404, 455).

Such behavior, however, is not the worst that the Pilgrims have to offer. Talking about the way the Christian Americans had assaulted a mosque, breaking pieces from the foundations while stepping with booted feet upon prayer rugs, Mark Twain says that these actions were the same as "breaking pieces from the hearts of [the onlooking] old Arabs" and "inflict[ing] pain upon men who had not offended us in any way." Then he goes even further. "Suppose a party of armed foreigners were to enter a village church in America and break ornaments from the altar railings for curiosities, and climb up and walk upon the Bible and the pulpit cushions?" (392). By not only portraying the wantonness of the Pilgrims, but also reversing the situation and seeing it through Muslim eyes, Mark Twain clearly indicates the extreme depth of cultural insensitivity exhibited by the Americans.

This specific instance of the Americans' lack of charity should be seen as part of Clemens's broad critique of the Pilgrims from the *Quaker City*. It is not just that their claim of being morally superior Christians seems to be overtaken by their growing reputation as souvenir-hunting Vandals who are willing to desecrate what is sacred to another culture. They are also complacent hypocrites, ready to abuse horses and mules in order to maintain a ban on Sabbath travel (322), and self-righteous dogmatists, ready to traffic in thickheaded interpretations of the Bible (294, 297, 360, 398). Mark Twain labeled the Pilgrims self-complacent and self-righteous as early as Marseilles (75), and even while crossing the Atlantic, when the Pilgrims wished to stop the boat in midstream for Sabbath or selfishly prayed for a wind to aid their one boat and thus hinder the many boats crossing the other way (36). If the *Quaker City* Pilgrims are truly representative of America's best, as they themselves would contend, then the portrait of them that Mark Twain draws implies a harsh critique of American society.

In fact, to the extent that the Pilgrims' souvenir-hunting vandalism turns the culture of others into commodities, their behavior is not far from Clemens's attack on the way that the Roman Catholic Church has commodified Christianity. This commercialism is most blatant, perhaps, in Naples, where the blood of Saint Januarius is said to liquefy every year, and the hair of an effigy of the Madonna used in a procession is said to grow (225). Rome (196), Milan (129), and Paris (96–97), however, all demonstrate a tendency to blur the line between exhibition of sacred objects to fortify the faithful and exhibition to fortify the church's bank account. In the Holy Land, exhibition for profit reaches new heights. Travelers are "expected to pay for seeing [relics]" (382). Not content with charging pilgrims to view supposedly authentic sacred objects (Mark Twain and company see numerous pieces of the true cross all over Europe and the Holy Land, for example), the church, claims Mark Twain, has in effect created sacred places in which to view them (381–82). In Jerusalem, such entrepreneurial spirit extends to the pillar to which Jesus was tied when whipped before his crucifixion (406), to his prison cell (408), and to his tomb (412).

The behavior of other Christian sects and the Protestant Pilgrims from the *Quaker City* is also linked by their quarrelsome natures. The Christian sects who maintain chapels in the Church of the Holy Sepulcher must be kept separate or they will fight (404, 411). Similarly, the Pilgrims are all too ready to quarrel among themselves (358). In both cases, Clemens satirizes Christians who fall far short of true Christian behavior. Instead of being spiritual pilgrims, representatives of what is fine and good in American culture, the *Quaker City* Vandals represent its barbarisms, its grasping materialism, and its misplaced pride.

This satiric inversion leads to another question that *The Innocents Abroad* provokes: what constitutes civilized behavior? Ancient Greece and China illustrate that it has long been customary for one culture to label another barbaric simply because the other is different. And at times Mark Twain makes the same judgment: dancing dervishes, for instance, constitute a "barbarous . . . exhibition" (261). His dismissal of the Old Masters marks him as uncivilized as surely as does his carving up of a rail of the *Quaker City*. But the Catholic church's Inquisition was barbaric (197), and savagery is found even in the Bible itself (395). Moreover, even though Mark Twain claims that the English version of civilization is superior to the Spanish and Italian (465), Muslim Egypt is presented as *the* symbol of civilization (460–61). These shifting perspectives are matched by the moods of Mark Twain, who can deliver meditative remarks occasioned by viewing the Sphinx (457) or claim to destroy and eat a beggar in order to calm himself (186). It is a useful exercise to ask students if these shifting perspectives and moods represent or prefigure the kind of cultural relativism espoused by the multiculturalism of the 1990s. At the least, they depict a mind that is open to experiences of the exotic and that explores the significance of those experiences. In a final analysis, the scope of Mark Twain's travels in *The Innocents Abroad* necessitates asking basic questions about culture itself; it also leads one to questions about human nature. What does it mean, for example, to say that "the nomadic instinct is a human instinct?" (426). Clemens at one point plays with the novelistic convention of addressing the audience as "gentle reader" by changing it to "savage reader" (288) because, he says, a change would be refreshing.

But much of *The Innocents Abroad* suggests the truth of that characterization: culture does not eradicate savagery so much as cover or modify it.

The Innocents Abroad was Sam Clemens's first prolonged look at American culture as it stacks up against other examples of civilization. Having completed that scrutiny at the end of the 1860s, Clemens would soon turn his complete satiric attention to the American experiment as it unfolded during the rest of the nineteeth century.

Notes

1   Arguably, the examination and critiquing of American values via a comparison with another culture started in Mark Twain's letters written on the Sandwich Islands (Hawaii) in 1866.

2   Mark Twain, *The Innocents Abroad*, Signet Classic Edition (New York: New American Library, 1966), 15. All further references will appear in the text.

3   My use of "orientalism" is based on Edward Said's book. For Said, "orientalism" names a discourse that enables a Western knowledge of the Orient that represents Westerners as intellectually dominant and morally superior, thus effectively assisting Western imperialism. For Clemens's account of his Middle East tour, the emphasis rests on cultural imperialism, but Said's thesis argues that cultural imperialism is always entangled with its political counterpart.

4   See Martin Price (Works Cited, below) on the standard uses for "picturesque."

Works Consulted

Bode, Carl. *The American Lyceum: Town Meeting of the Mind.* 1956. Reprint. London: Feffer and Simons, 1968.

Clemens, Samuel L. *Mark Twain's Letters, Volume 2—1867–68.* Ed. Harriet Elinor Smith and Richard Bucci. Berkeley: University of California Press, 1990.

———. *Mark Twain's Letters, Volume 3—1869.* Ed. Victor Fisher, Michael B. Frank, and Dahlia Armon. Berkeley: University of California Press, 1992.

Fatout, Paul. *Mark Twain on the Lecture Circuit.* Carbondale: Southern Illinois University Press, 1960.

———. *Mark Twain in Virginia City.* Bloomington: Indiana University Press, 1968.

Kaplan, Justin. *Mr. Clemens and Mark Twain.* New York: Simon and Schuster, 1966.

Lorch, Fred W. *The Trouble Begins at Eight: Mark Twain's Lecture Tours.* Ames: Iowa State University Press, 1968.

McKeithan, Daniel Morley, ed. *Traveling with "The Innocents Abroad": Mark Twain's Original Reports from Europe and the Holy Land.* Norman: University of Oklahoma Press, 1958.

Metwalli, Ahmed M. "Americans Abroad: The Popular Art of Travel Writing in the

Nineteenth-Century." *America: Exploration and Travel.* Ed. Steven E. Kagle. Bowling Green: Bowling Green State University Popular Press, 1979. 68–82.

Moritz, Albert. *America the Picturesque in Nineteenth-Century Engraving.* New York: New Trend, 1983.

Price, Martin. "The Picturesque Moment." In *From Sensibility to Romanticism.* Ed. Frederick W. Hilles and Harold Bloom. New York: Oxford University Press, 1965. 259–92.

Rogers, Franklin R. *Mark Twain's Burlesque Patterns as Seen in the Novels and Narratives, 1855–1885.* Dallas: Southern Methodist University Press, 1960.

Said, Edward W. *Orientalism.* New York: Random House, 1978.

Scott, Frank W. "Newspapers, 1775–1860." *The Cambridge History of American Literature,* Vol. 1. Ed. William P. Trent, John Eskine, Stuart P. Sherman, and Carl Van Doren. New York: G. P. Putnam's Sons, 1918. 176–95.

Steinbrink, Jeffrey. *Getting to Be Mark Twain.* Berkeley: University of California Press, 1991.

Appendix: A Schedule for Teaching *The Innocents Abroad*

Day 1: Background
1. Popular culture; biography of Clemens.
2. Function of travel books.
3. Comic distance of Mark Twain.
4. The psychology of being a tourist (some discussion).
5. The book's preface—parodic distance and implied audience.
6. Chapter 10 quotation sets up two topics for further reading: the running joke about the misleading nature of travel book language; the character of Mark Twain.

Day 2: Mark Twain's Character
1. Follow-up on travel book language.
2. Mark Twain's character: (a) Parodic or not? Abelard and Heloise example. (b) Link to platform techniques. (c) Five aspects to the character.

Day 3: Culture Clash
1. The Pilgrims vs. the Sinners.
2. Americans feel inferior to Europeans. (Discussion).
3. Americans feel superior to Europeans. (Discussion.)
4. American chauvinism and orientalism. (Discussion.)

Day 4: Aesthetics and Satire
1. The rhetoric of the picturesque.
2. The Pilgrims as Vandals.
3. Critiquing Christianity.
4. What is meant by "civilized"?

Connecticut Yankee: Twain's Other Masterpiece
Lawrence I. Berkove

Teaching *Connecticut Yankee* can be an exceptionally rewarding experience because the book is far better than is generally realized. Written at the height of Twain's powers, *Connecticut Yankee* approaches the skill, complexity, and tragic force of *Huckleberry Finn*, and it is definitely one of Twain's greatest works. Students react positively to it, for it illuminates the thought and art of Mark Twain in unique and surprising ways. Despite its ultimate pessimism, students appreciate it for its honesty in articulating moral and philosophical issues that they are confronting. Because teaching *Connecticut Yankee* is closely tied to interpretation, in this essay I will explain my interpretation of the novel simultaneously with my method of teaching it.

As with many great novels, there are some obstacles to a satisfactory reading of *Connecticut Yankee*, but they are on the surface and can be resolved at a deeper level. Teachers who prepare for them will be richly repaid by an unusual amount of student participation and a variety of insights and aesthetic enjoyment. They will be able to turn to good advantage what are thought to be difficulties but are better regarded as opportunities: the change in the novel from a humorous to a tragic tone, the fact that Twain's art and ideas are not yet thoroughly understood, the novel's seeming lack of structural and thematic unity, and the unexpected impact on it of Calvinistic thought.

The first problem—the shift in tone from humorous to tragic—is easily understood. It stems from the fact that virtually no one reads Mark Twain without some preconceptions, stemming from his popular reputation as a humorist, of what to expect. Readers who anticipate a book full of laughs will not be disappointed in the earlier chapters, but the later chapters will puzzle and upset them. The first lesson to be taught a class by way of preparation, therefore, is that although Mark Twain was a humorist, he was not *only* a humorist, nor was his humor, typically, an end in itself. Some background is necessary to understand what follows from this premise.

Mark Twain was a hoaxer. Perhaps no other writer in literature had so profound an appreciation and mastery of the hoax. It is Twain's primary literary technique and runs through his entire oeuvre, from "The Dandy Frightening the Squatter" (1852) to the late "What Is Man?" (1906) and the posthumously published *The Mysterious Stranger* (1916). *Connecticut Yankee* is intricately laced with hoaxes.

A hoax is a deception. In its familiar forms of tall tales and practical jokes, it is often humorous, especially when the butt of the humor is someone whose pompousness or overconfidence strikes an audience as ripe for a comeuppance. In its extended and specialized sense as a fraud or swindle, however, or to those who are the butts of cruel practical jokes, hoaxes may be quite painful or even tragic. Pascal Covici has noted that "the humor of Mark Twain often turns out to be no laughing matter."[1] Readers expect the target of the hoax to be one or more of the characters in a work of fiction; it always comes as a shock when they learn that *they* are the author's real target. In Twain's most important works, and certainly in *Connecticut Yankee*, clues to underlying main themes are often presented disarmingly, in humorous contexts or in seemingly offhand statements, and they are easily overlooked. Thus, readers often discover with shock at a book's ending that they have missed the point of what is happening in the same way that characters in the work have. Twain does not do this gratuitously, but as a way, first, to make the reader experience the force of the hoax and, then, to reflect on its nature. Thus, it is a mistake to dismiss as bad writing what may seem to be narrative problems or unsatisfactory conclusions; chances are that they are part of a subtly laid hoax.

The deepest pattern for Twain's hoaxes is to be found in his religion, which he interpreted heretically. Students may be surprised or upset to learn that Twain did not believe that God was benevolent, but anyone who reads *The Mysterious Stranger* fragments, or *What Is Man?* or *Letters from the Earth*, works composed after *Connecticut Yankee*, cannot reach any other conclusion, and evidence has long been established that Twain viewed God as a trickster and a tyrant. The origin of Twain's views is in the Calvinistic doctrines he learned as a youth, especially those which taught that God had predestined existence, had made human nature corrupt, and had assigned most human beings to hell. By creating Adam and Eve as fatally limited, Twain reasoned, God set them up from the first to make the wrong choice in the Garden of Eden. Subsequent generations of humans, now burdened with original sin, do even less well in the postlapsarian world of temptations and tribulations. Doubly damned by both predestination and a nature so corruptly sinful that even lives totally spent in apparently virtuous thought and action will not redeem them, humans cannot do otherwise than to merit hell. The fact that they have consciences only makes it worse, because they then castigate themselves for failing to do better, even when it is impossible for them to do so. As Twain viewed life and the "damned human race," therefore, humans were programmed to fail from the beginning of creation by a Catch-22 system. They are thus the butt of God's rather grim practical joke or hoax. Twain saw this predestined pattern repeated in nature, history, society, and individual human beings. He objected to its injustice and deception and devoted much of his literature to describing existence as he saw it in the forlorn hope that he could expose its cruelty. But until the 1890s, when his reputation was established, he dared not express these views outright since that would have alienated the readers of his time. One of Twain's greatest abilities was that of writing at two simultaneous levels: one a plot entertaining enough to be enjoyed, the other a serious but submerged counterplot that, if detected, would reveal to his readers that an instructive hoax had been played on them so that they might fully appreciate what it meant to be taken in. *Connecticut Yankee* perfectly exemplifies this approach.

This takes us to the second problem: that Twain has depths not yet adequately understood. He is a magnificent writer, much better even than some of his advocates realize. The same care that we are accustomed to take with every word and phrase in a Henry James novel may be profitably applied to *Connecticut Yankee;* Twain is no less accomplished an artist. Many scholars see in Twain flashes of brilliance, but not the consummate artistry that characterizes great literature. As a result, a good deal of scholarship engages in a sort of special pleading. Impressive ideas and flashes of literary skill are recognized in both *Huckleberry Finn* and *Connecticut Yankee;* but although we are asked to credit Twain with literary greatness, his novels are widely believed not to hold together. Expecting *Connecticut Yankee* to be funny, many commentators, recognizing that there is no way to find humor in the conclusion, have reasoned that Twain changed his mind mid-course, and that the novel consequently breaks in two. But if we do not expect the novel to be humorous, then it succeeds—powerfully—as a serious hoax.

Another objection to the novel's artistry is the appearance of elements of apparent autobiography. As resemblances between Twain and the protagonist Hank Morgan emerge, some critics feel this detracts from the integrity of the book as a work of fiction. This is a peculiar objection, for it is not at all uncommon for authors to create characters with resemblances to themselves, and for those characters not always to be admirable. Authors write best from what they know, and they ought to know themselves best. As long as Mark Twain is thought to be only a diamond in the rough, someone who can start a novel but not finish it, and who almost but not quite transcends the lack of formal education or some stabilizing feature of his personality or economic condition, there will be ingenious explanations of why *Connecticut Yankee* appears to fall short of formal excellence. Again, this approach is fatally flawed by an incomplete understanding of Twain's genius and neglects the fact that some of the world's outstanding writers succeeded despite the lack of a formal education or perfect personalities. Although Ben Jonson claimed that Shakespeare had "smalle Latin and lesse Greek," he still recognized Shakespeare's greatness. We know next to nothing of Homer and relatively little about Cervantes, yet today no one doubts their surpassing literary achievements. We are in the position of knowing a great deal about Mark Twain, but it would be a case of not seeing the forest for the trees to be so convinced for biographical reasons that Twain was artistically limited as to deny actual evidence of the success of *Connecticut Yankee*.

A third problem is the question of the novel's unity—that is, the harmonic relevance of all parts to its final effect. Most experienced novel readers prefer novels in which there are no loose ends and everything seems to flow together synergistically. We must admit that *Connecticut Yankee*'s unity is not immediately obvious. The first half appears to be funny; the conclusion is grim. There are seemingly digressive chapters in it, such as those in which Hank Morgan appears to serve, transparently, as a mouthpiece for Twain's personal biases. There are also important passages that a careful reader might find difficult if not impossible to accept. Nevertheless, each case where an objection might be raised is actually, paradoxically, evidence of the novel's unity. I will explain.

The best way I have found to proceed with *Connecticut Yankee* is to require that the class finish a first reading of the novel before a discussion of it takes place because it is necessary to move back and forth in the text. Having already informed my students of the previously stated objections to the novel's structural and thematic unity, and my belief that these objections can all be overcome and the novel seen as a work of extraordinary and surprising power and brilliance, I have piqued their curiosity and presented them with a challenge. This approach in itself is a refreshing change from the conventional way of dealing with classics of literature; now both the author and the teacher are out on a limb and something new may be discovered. Since I have required the novel to be read before discussion of it begins, they will already have comprehended the force of the objections to its unity and be interested in how I can prove the contrary.

I begin the proofs by asking my students to allow, for the time being, two basic assumptions. The first is that Hank Morgan is a fictional character, under Twain's control at all times, even (and maybe especially) when he seems to most resemble Twain. The second is that *Connecticut Yankee* should be judged as a unified novel; if its parts can be seen to be unified, then the novel is successful; if not, not. Students have usually been willing to grant these requests because they are seen to be reasonable and potentially beneficial. My students consistently have been eager to be engaged in fresh discovery. Once the assumptions are granted, we can proceed with solving the problems raised above.

The first of them is the question of how the novel is organized. It is constructed as a fiction in two senses of the word: that we are reading something that is not fact, and that even the fictional information we receive is not dependable. The plot is conveyed within several narrative frames. The outermost one, in the "A Word of Explanation" and "Final P.S. by M.T." chapters, is told to us by a narrator who refers to himself as "I" and signs himself "M.T." This narrator must be fictitious, although "M.T." would seem to signify Mark Twain; if not, we have to believe that Twain actually had the experience of meeting Morgan and reading his manuscript. The narrative was supposedly preserved by Clarence, who also contributes the penultimate chapter "A Postscript by Clarence." Unless we wish to believe that the events literally happened, then Clarence's part in the narrative is also fictitious. Inside these frames is Hank's account, supposedly written retrospectively as a record of his experiences in sixth-century England.

Apart from noting the obvious, that Hank must also be fictitious, we have to deal with his reliability as a narrator. This is a critical element of the novel, and the failure of readers to recognize him as unreliable has commonly misled them. Hank is not unreliable in that he deliberately lies to us or withholds information. On the contrary, he gains our confidence by his openness, his good nature and good sense, and his benevolent intentions toward his new situation. In addition, we can identify with him because he is like one of us: an average American, and not someone from a class above or below us with a lifestyle or values that we do not share. He also reminds us (frequently) that he is democratic, and we see that his enemies are the enemies of the common man: tyranny, ignorance, and superstition. Nevertheless, Mark Twain once described him as a "nincompoop," and the fact of the matter is that however much Hank professes to understand the events and personalities he encounters, he does not understand them enough, nor does he even understand himself. He almost never questions his own judgment, his true motives, or his actions, despite a growing inconsistency between what he professes and what he is and does. As a consequence, he is as much the victim of his own unreliability as we are.

He believes himself to be the "boss," in control even when his schemes begin to go awry or backfire and when surprises happen to him. Inasmuch as it is difficult to see Hank as unreliable from the outset, it is best to defer discussion of Hank's reliability until the class is well into the discussion of the novel and is scrutinizing the text more carefully. As the novel is reviewed, abundant evidence will be found to demonstrate that Hank's character has remained fixed throughout the novel, and that just as we have been hoaxed into trusting him, he has been hoaxed into believing himself in control of events.

A more subtle organizing element in the novel is its pervasive and critical use of dreams.[2] As early as the "A Word of Explanation" chapter, the narrator tells us how his adventure began with his reading of Thomas Malory's "enchanting" book, Morte d'Arthur, "a dream of the olden time." As he reads, he himself "dream[s] again." While in this mood, the stranger he met earlier comes to his room, begins his narrative, then becomes sleepy and gives "M.T." a palimpsest to read while he retires to his own room. Even in the second line of chapter 1, Hank describes the summer landscape: "as lovely as a dream and as lonesome as Sunday"—apparently contradictory impressions. A young girl appears with a hoop of red poppies in her hair—the allusion to opium supplying another suggestion of dream state—and walks "indolently along, with a mind at rest, its peace reflected in her innocent face." Mental indolence and innocence again appear to be contradictory.

Once Hank has been brought to Camelot, he "moved along as one in a dream." Every day he awakens expecting his dream to have vanished, but it persists. He continues to half believe that he is still dreaming until Clarence informs him that he is to be burned at the stake the next day. He compromises the difference between dream and reality when he realizes the imminent danger of the situation: "I knew by past experience of the life-like intensity of dreams, that to be burned to death, even in a dream, would be very far from being a jest, and was a thing to be avoided, by any means, fair or foul, that I could contrive" (chapter 5).

This is a good point at which to pause and discuss with the class if we can really know dream from reality, and whether there is ultimately any great difference between them when it is possible to die for real in a dream just as it is in "reality." The novel continues to make many references to dreams, including waking daydreams, such as King Arthur's dream of conquering Gaul (chapter 31) and Hank's dream of creating a republic (chapter 42). Again, the point to be emphasized is that much more of our lives may be spent in "dreams" than just those obvious times when we are sleeping, and that the line between dream and reality is not as sharp and provable as it appears to be. Inasmuch as Hank's dying words at the novel's end raise further questions about what is dream and what reality, the topic is one that has to have been deliberately built into the text. If students are asked to track all references to dreams in the novel, they will find distinct and compelling patterns that will lead to lively discussions.

Another, more subtle principle of organization inheres in the fact that the novel begins at the end. Everything has already happened to Hank Morgan in the sixth century when Clarence takes over. Everything has already happened to Clarence when a "reborn" Hank takes over again in his proper age, the nineteenth century. Almost everything has happened to the reborn Hank when the narrator, "M.T." takes over, and everything *has* happened by the time M.T. finishes with a P.S. The reader is therefore induced to get emotionally involved in what is essentially a history of past events that are beyond change. The point at issue here is Twain's main theme: *that everything has already happened and that the hope of change is a vain dream.* If this idea sounds hellish, it is no accident. Twain's frequent references to the "damned human race" literally reflected his conviction that life was part of hell and that any other belief was illusion. This is both a powerful and a deeply disturbing notion, and therefore I do not state it at the beginning of a study of *Connecticut Yankee* but let the idea take shape gradually, as the class comes to see that it, and only it, can account for the novel's events and effects.

After the discussion of how Twain's deeply held but heretical beliefs about religion appear to be at odds with his reputation as a humorist, I explain that it is not my purpose to deny that Twain is a master humorist; that would be patently insupportable. I resolve the apparent contradiction by pointing out, as Covici maintains and as I have noted, that Twain's humor "often turns out to be no laughing matter." Humor is often disarming, and I therefore urge students to look carefully for serious issues beneath the humor. Twain's humorous effects are often a sugar-coating over some bitter or pessimistic idea, or they are a strategy to set up the reader for a hoax. Additionally, once the seriousness of the counterplot is realized, humor serves, by its incongruity, to intensify the novel's tragic effect.

My discussion of the text begins with a demonstration of its formal unity. My first points relate to the frame structure; its presence at least suggests that Twain made an effort to impart shape to the novel. Next, I move on to show that everything in the novel, from the first chapter on, points inevitably to the final Battle of the Sand-Belt. This is a critical part of my argument. It is necessary to demonstrate it, if only to counter the claim that the novel "breaks" between a humorous beginning and a grim end. Indeed, everything I say about the novel furthers this point, because I use it to advance my interpretation that the novel is a work of tragedy rather than of comedy, and that its main theme is the denial of the possibility of human freedom. Some of the evidence that supports my position follows.

We know from biography that the first part of *Connecticut Yankee* which Twain worked out was the section dealing with the Battle of the Sand-Belt.[3] It is not surprising, therefore, that the first chapter of the novel, "A Word of Explanation," contains some quiet allusions to the violent end. When "M.T." is told by the stranger that he *saw* the bullet hole made in the armor of Sir Sagramour le Desirous, his reaction is "electric surprise." These words are the first foreshadowings of the uses of guns and electricity at the Battle of the Sand-Belt. Later in the chapter, the foreshadowing continues ironically as Hank recounts how he learned his real trade in the "great arms factory"—the Colt

Company—of Hartford; he learned to make "guns, revolvers, cannons, boilers, engines, all sorts of labor-saving machinery." It may be a bit unusual and more than a little grim to describe guns, revolvers, and cannons as "labor-saving machinery," but that is how Hank's guns and revolvers function in the Battle of the Sand-Belt.

Hank later in the book muses on the determining force of heredity and training and how humans early get into molds they cannot break out of. But in the first chapter we see the mold into which Hank has been cast: a maker of armaments and other "labor-saving machinery." He remains unaware of how this fact determines what he will do in sixth-century England, but once these considerations are mentioned to students, they quickly see how this beginning shapes his actions. A disturbing pattern emerges in the novel of his association with explosives and killing, and each incident contributes incrementally to the momentum leading to the final battle.

The first use of explosives occurs in chapter 7, when Hank destroys Merlin's Tower; the second is in chapter 23, where Hank restores a fountain with dynamite. The next reference to it occurs obliquely, in chapter 25, where Hank listens with great pleasure to a cadet from his military academy lay out "the science of war" and "wallow in details of battle and siege, of supply, transportation, mining and counter-mining . . . infantry, cavalry, artillery, and all about siege guns, field guns, gatling guns, rifled guns, smooth bores, musket practice, revolver practice. . . ." This passage is reminiscent of the scene in Book II of *Gulliver's Travels* where Gulliver enthusiastically tells the King of Brobdingnag of the wonders of gunpowder and is surprised when the King responds with horror at the "inhuman" invention. It is relevant to note here that the first modern educational institution Hank founds in Arthur's kingdom is a kind of West Point, and the cadet is a proud product of Hank's "civilization."

Another incident occurs in chapter 27, when Hank dispatches a couple of hostile knights with a dynamite bomb. "Yes, it was a neat thing, very neat and pretty to see. It resembled a steamboat explosion on the Mississippi; and during the next fifteen minutes we stood under a steady drizzle of microscopic fragments of knights and hardware and horse-flesh."[4] By this time, even those students who are sympathetic to Hank can see that he is deadly and that his humorous way of describing events conceals a personality insensitive to the horror of his actions.

Hank introduces revolvers in chapter 39, "The Yankee's Fight with the Knights." As Hank shoots knight after knight out of the saddle, the rest of the knights break and run. At this, Hank declares "The march of civilization was begun." Hank is not ironic, but Twain is.

When the knights again assemble to attack him after the Interdict, we discover in chapter 42 that Hank's "civilization" consists not only of factories but also of bombs hidden in each factory that can be detonated from a central location. With this discovery, the ominous association of Hank with deadly "labor-saving machinery," quietly begun in "A Word of Explanation," has ripened to the point where most students can see that the mass destruction of the Battle of the Sand-Belt is the logical conclusion of an unmistakable pattern that Hank himself does not recognize. The modern civilization that Hank wishes to bestow upon the sixth century is in reality deadlier by orders of magnitude than the crudely violent one of King Arthur's age. The point is made subtly in chapter 10, "The Beginning of Civilization," when Hank unconsciously associates nineteenth-century civilization with hell as he compliments himself with having surreptitiously introduced modernity into the sixth century. He crows about how nineteenth-century civilization is "booming" under the nose of the sixth century and how it is "fenced" away from general view. It is now an "unassailable" fact, like "any serene volcano, standing innocent with its smokeless summit in the blue sky and giving no sign of the rising hell in its bowels." He thinks of himself standing with his "finger on the button . . . ready to turn it on and flood the midnight world with light." All of the quoted words and passages clearly foreshadow the Battle of the Sand-Belt with Hank's unassailable strong point, the booming of the guns, the electric fences, the spotlights, and the flood. The association of this civilization with hell is explicit. Does Hank see it? No. Does Twain? With this unusually dense linkage of clues, can there be any doubt?

Another way in which everything leads to the Battle of the Sand-Belt is developed by the way that Hank attempts to further democracy. Hank talks a lot about democracy, but his words are contradicted by his actions. That Hank considers himself a "Yankee of the Yankees" associates him in most readers' eyes with democracy. Even his title of "Boss" seems mild and homey compared to titles like "king," "emperor," and "Caesar." But it quickly becomes apparent that he has tremendous power and is not hesitant to use it, and that he is feared like a mysterious stranger from another world—which he in fact is.[5] The more Hank reflects on despotism, the more attractive it becomes to him. Each time he seems to reject being a despot, he actually moves closer to that role. Furthermore, it is no accident that of all surnames Twain could have given to Hank, he chose one that links him with Morgan le Fay.[6] At first, the two will seem antithetically different, but when Hank is compared at the end with Morgan le Fay, similarities will appear. And at what point in the novel do we learn Hank's last name? Chapter 39! Why is it so delayed, if not to both establish and obscure the comparison?

The more power Hank acquires, the more he thinks of himself as inherently superior and the more his democratic professions are contradicted by his admitted ambitions. He looks down on—most undemocratically—the people he encounters, and he never treats any of them as his equals. On the contrary, he repeatedly confesses his resentment at not being a noble, and has hardly a good word to say about kings. Only Arthur repeatedly demonstrates kingly qualities that wring admiration from Hank, despite himself.

Hank claims to scoff at magicians like Merlin, but then brags about the magic he himself does. Ask your students to define magic. Most will say that it consists of tricks that are not understood. Hank's tricks are technological effects that no one in the sixth century could understand, but every reader of the novel does. Clearly, therefore, to us he is no magician. But, despite Hank's scorn of Merlin, Merlin *is* a real magician. In chapter 3, Hank ridicules Merlin's tiresomely windy repetition of how he directed Arthur to acquire the sword Excalibur from a mysterious hand in a lake. Hank calls it a lie, but if we give credence to the story of Arthur, Merlin's account is accurate, and Arthur, who is also in the hall, does not contradict Merlin. Merlin also casts a spell at the end of the novel that puts Hank into a thirteen-century sleep. Merlin has powers beyond understanding.

Hank also aspires to be a prophet, and in chapter 8 he ventures to prophesy future history. This passage is particularly interesting for several reasons. One is that Hank's "prophetic" powers are really a unique kind of hindsight. A second is that Hank (apparently inadvertently) compares himself in this passage to "adventurers," "wantons," and "drabs"—hardly a compliment. A third is that Hank here demonstrates a knowledge of history. In other words, he knows what "will" happen because from his vantage point as a nineteenth-century person, it already has. This is a highly significant point that we will return to shortly. A fourth, and final, significance of the passage is Hank's apparent unawareness of the fact that prophets do not make things happen, but merely predict what has been destined. Only God can predestine and make things happen.

Hank increasingly wishes to be "adored" and "revered." Heretofore, Hank compared himself with other humans, but this new aspiration implies divine status. This may be an unconscious goal from Hank's perspective, but that Hank is in competition with God is a facet of the novel which Twain must have deliberately constructed. As early as chapter 7, Hank resolves to emulate Robinson Crusoe in that he would have to "invent, contrive, create, reorganize things." The first verb is innocent, but "contrive" has a negative connotation, and "create" is reminiscent of Genesis 1:1. "Reorganize things" also sounds innocent until one reflects that for Hank to undertake to reorganize the sixth century into the nineteenth century means he will have to overwrite the history that has already occurred and been recorded and remake the world according to his pattern. In effect, Hank is about to challenge God on His creation. Later in the same chapter, Hank resents Merlin for spreading a report that Hank does not create miracles because he cannot. Of course, Merlin is correct, but Hank spends the rest of the chapter giving the illusion that he can make miracles happen.

In chapter 8, Hank compliments himself for having "done my entire public a kindness in sparing the sun." We know that Hank did not literally spare the sun but merely used his knowledge of past eclipses to predict that one which already had occurred was about to happen. This is a critical point, which I will soon develop further, but right now the issue is that Hank seems to have convinced himself that he is capable of creating miracles.

Chapter 26, "The First Newspaper," further develops Hank's tendency to think of himself as divine in its allusions to the birth of Christ as told in the gospels of Matthew and Luke. The original meaning of gospel is "good word" or "good news," and it is this sense that Twain uses when Hank says that "[o]ne greater than kings had arrived—the newsboy. But I was the only person in all that throng who knew the meaning of this mighty birth, and what this imperial magician had come into the world to do." The central passage is worth quoting. Hank shows the newspaper to some monks, who cross themselves and describe it as "a miracle, a wonder! Dark work of enchantment." When he finishes reading from it in a "low voice," he gives it to the monks to handle.

> So they took it, handling it as cautiously and devoutly as if it had been some holy thing come from some supernatural region. . . . These grouped bent heads, these charmed faces, these speaking eyes—how beautiful to me! For was not this my darling, and was not all this mute wonder and interest and homage a most eloquent tribute and unforced compliment to it? I knew, then, how a mother feels when women, whether strangers or friends, take her new baby, and close themselves about it with one eager impulse, and bend their heads over it in a tranced adoration that makes all the rest of the universe vanish out of their consciousness and be as if it were not, for that time. I knew how she feels, and that there is no other satisfied ambition, whether of king, conqueror or poet, that ever reaches half way to that serene far summit or yields half so divine a contentment.
>
> During all the rest of my séance . . . I sat motionless, steeped in satisfaction, drunk with enjoyment. Yes, this was heaven; I was tasting it once, if I might never taste it more.

The religious imagery in this passage is unmistakable, and so is its similarity to the account of Christ's birth in the manger. Notice, moreover, that Hank's perspective is that of a parent—and one who is in heaven. And what is this newspaper, the Camelot *Weekly Hosannah* (a Hebrew word meaning "please save us," used to praise God), about? This first issue that Hank reads from so dramatically is about the "miracle" of Hank's restoration of a well. In other words, Hank creates his own gospel to praise himself.[7]

Hank's power continues to grow. But when he seems close to the point where he can realize his "dream" of advancing England abruptly into the nineteenth century, the Interdict strikes. From one point of view, the Interdict is not only sudden, it is entirely unsuspected and seems like a flaw in the novel. But from God's point of view, Hank is aspiring to rival Him. It is therefore logical that God's church be the instrument that brings Hank down. The Roman Catholic Church is treated with some criticism by Hank, and because he is afraid of its power, he tries to neutralize it by encouraging the development of a host of Protestant denominations. But, at the end, it is the only institution that is still strong enough to oppose Hank, and if it is authoritarian, it is still better than Hank's authoritarianism, which, as we see in the Battle of the Sand-Belt, is a more hideous and deadly despotism than the "despotism of heaven." As much as Mark Twain himself hated the grip that the church had on men's minds and hearts, he recognized in this novel that its power might be all that stood between man and a worse and more fallible master—man himself.

Despite Hank's frequently repeated affirmations that he understands human nature, he does not. Nor does he reflect on what he has become. Instead, he brags a great deal about his power: "I was no shadow of a king; I was the substance; the king himself was the shadow" (chapter 8). He is condescending to the villagers of Abblasoure in chapters 31 to 34 and decides to confer on them the benefit of his supposedly superior understanding of the theory of political economy. When they realize, however, that he has tricked them into confessing some illegal acts, they fear for their lives, for he has the power of life and death over them. He admits only that he has "overdone" his trick a little, but it is obvious that he has fundamentally overestimated himself and underestimated them. When he is sold into slavery (or, it can be said, *back into* slavery, for he began in the sixth century as a slave), he has been given a lesson in political economy far more sophisticated than the one he thought to teach: in a *completely* free market, where titles and political "rights" are not recognized, a man is ultimately worth only what some buyer is willing to pay for him in the expectation of some capacity for utility. This is an elementary lesson in natural, practical economics. The villagers already understand it, but Hank does not.[8]

Hank claims at several points in the novel that he has destroyed the institution of knighthood, but, as we know, it outlasts him. To put it down each time, he has to use more and more force, which he does even when it should be clear to him—as it is clear to everyone else— that England is with the knights and not with him. This confrontation, of course, raises the question in a new way of how democratic Hank actually is. Can Hank be democratic in any meaningful sense of the term if he looks down on all of his constituents and is a frightening Boss to them, if he is never elected to any term of office, if he insists on opposing the majority of the population, and if he even will kill whoever opposes him—no matter how many—in order to create his "dream of a republic"? The novel remarkably anticipated the predicament in which the United States found itself in Vietnam, where, in the name of democracy, it waged war against the majority of the population. Twain's Hank, especially insofar as he may be thought of as a representative American—"a Yankee of the Yankees"—therefore raises interesting questions for a class: What is democracy? Is Hank democratic? If not, how did he get to be what he is? Is he really benefiting England? Is he better or worse than the leaders that the English already have? Can a democracy be wrong? If the majority is not always right, how is right determined? And so on.

Many ironies in the novel also can be linked to this theme. Take, for example, Hank's invention of "Man-Factories," in which he intends to transform groveling peasants into men suitable for democracy. But ask your students if men can be mass-produced in a factory. Then ask how successful Hank was at doing so. What became of all his "men" when the Interdict struck? At the end, he is left only with boys. Or take Hank's plan to start a patent office. That sounds fair, but with his thirteen-century start on the rest of England, who is going to benefit from that office? Does Hank, in fact, invent anything himself? Does he not simply remember how to build what he knew in his own century? If a rough parallel can be established between, on the one hand, a nineteenth-century Hank and sixth-century England, and, on the other, developed countries and undeveloped countries in our time, what can be inferred about Mark Twain's views of democracy and of progress?

These themes and others will be found readily enough by students who are encouraged to think of Hank's character as consistent and to look for other evidence of unity. The hardest part of teaching the novel, however, consists of the case for its denial of the possibility of freedom. The evidence for this denial is more subtle than the previous patterns, but it is abundant.

We go back to the beginning of the book for this theme and ask some hard questions. Virtually every student today is familiar with movies or literature about time travel, and with the possibility of changing the future if someone could get to the past and cause some things to be different. Now it is time to ask if it is not more likely that it is impossible to change the past. Given a perfect and omnipotent God, His plan for the world would also be perfect (i.e., complete, incapable of improvement, and immutable). Therefore, even if an individual from one age were by some miracle permitted to visit another age, that miracle would also be part of God's plan and the time traveler would not be free to alter the course of the other age's history, which God had predestined at Creation. Insofar as students are at all familiar with their religions or with the Bible, it is productive to point out that both the Old Testament and the New Testament describe a God who is omnipotent and omniscient, who defines the future, causes things to happen, and will not be frustrated.

It is not necessary for students to be religious believers to interpret this novel, but they must be open-minded enough to appreciate that Twain had some relevant views on God and on freedom vs. predestination and that those views show up in ways that cause things to turn out as they do. It may be enough to ask: if there is a God who is omnipotent and omniscient, then, logically, how can we be free? One way I define freedom is: the ability to surprise God. If this definition is used, it should be apparent that either God cannot be surprised, or He is not omniscient and omnipotent. For most religions, predestination is easily understandable, but freedom is the great mystery. For Twain—at least as I understand him—there was no mystery. He believed that freedom could not and did not exist; it was an illusion.[9]

The evidence for predestination in *Connecticut Yankee* is substantial. The most dramatic evidence is Hank's ability to predict eclipses. Of course, he does not really predict them; he knows about them because they have already occurred, but new ones are predictable. This is important because the very ability to predict them implies a fixed and immutable order in which any eclipse is, from a cosmic perspective, already an accomplished fact. Hank never reflects on this fact, nor does he grasp a corollary: that because no change is possible in an immutable system, neither he nor anyone else is free. *Connecticut Yankee* also implies that time replays itself in endless, simultaneous recycling. That Ecclesiastes may intend this continuous cycle when it says that "there is no new thing under the sun" may be an unconventional and also disturbing view of biblical revelation. Nevertheless, have your students look at the first chapter of Ecclesiastes and ask them to consider how much of the novel is explained by it. You may wish to assign themes based on individual verses.

Hank not only knows about eclipses, but he also knows a good deal of history: personalities, events, and dates. He knows these things because they have already happened and are fixed. Changing the time of an eclipse is a revision of God's plan that is beyond him, but so also is history unchangeable. It was not *meant* for him to have any lasting effect on the sixth century, and that is the way it works out. In other words, all the plans he lays and everything he does are only evanescent. They are not going to last; everything is an illusion. He is taken in by it, and so is every reader who thinks or hopes that Hank is going to be successful, all the while suppressing the real-world knowledge that nothing "modern" happened in the sixth century and that the nineteenth century did not occur until the nineteenth century.

Hank is optimistic and energetic, but everything that he thinks he accomplishes just sets him up for a harder fall at the end. He thinks a lot but never reflects, and so he misses some clues, including a major one that almost all readers also miss. It occurs in chapter 2 just after Clarence tells Hank that it is 19 June 528, and Hank wonders how this can be verified. If there is any troublesome passage in the novel, this is it: "But all of a sudden I stumbled on the very thing, just by luck. I knew that the only total eclipse of the sun in the first half of the sixth century occurred on the 21st day of June, A.D. 528, O.S., and began at 3 minutes after 12 noon." The chance that anyone would just casually happen to know this detail is almost nil. Students always snicker when we start to discuss it because it is something they are sure is forced on Twain's part. If a coincidence, it is mind-boggling. Hank calls it "luck," but what is luck? Ask the class to define the word. Where does it come from? If there is an omnipotent and omniscient deity, where can luck fit in? All through the novel there are similar, though not so dramatic, examples of luck, or coincidence, or chance, or Providence. Again, define "chance" and "coincidence." If we grant an omnipotent and omniscient deity, there can be no luck, no coincidence, no chance. Nothing happens by accident in a predestined world, i.e., one ruled by Providence.

It never occurs to Hank (not to mention most readers) that he was *meant* to know this strange bit of information, just as he was meant to know history, and just as he was meant to know the trades he learned in the Colt factory at Hartford, so that the Battle of the Sand-Belt would occur, and yet all his efforts would turn out to be vanity. This is the message that Twain would communicate through the efforts and failure of the Yankee Hank Morgan: that only what is meant to happen, happens.

Chance, accident, luck, coincidence—euphemistic cloaks for Providence, itself a euphemistic term for God's control—are what truly drive the events in this novel. In chapter 2, Hank says that "being a practical

Connecticut man, I now shoved this whole problem out of my mind till its appointed day and hour should come." *Appointed?* Hank speaks more truly than he realizes. All events in the story fall into their appointed times and places.

Take, for instance, the tournament in chapter 9. Sir Gareth and Sir Dinadan are about to joust with each other when, "by malice of *fate*," Sir Dinadan sits by Hank and tells him the one joke that Hank hates most. When he finishes, Sir Dinadan laughs at his own joke "like a *demon*" and goes off to the contest. When Hank opens his eyes he sees Gareth strike Dinadan very hard "and I *unconsciously* out with the prayer, 'I hope to gracious he's killed.' But by *ill-luck*" Gareth crashes into Sir Sagramor, who catches Hank's remark and thinks it meant for him. I have italicized the three words here that are thematically linked to each other. An ominous fate or ill-luck rules this event, and Hank participates, even though unconsciously. So what? Where does it lead? It leads directly to a challenge to Hank from Sir Sagramor four or five years in the future. That in turn leads directly to chapter 39, "The Yankee's Fight with the Knights." In that fight, Hank makes a lasso and its "snaky spirals" yank Sagramor out of his saddle. Other challengers arise, and Hank "snakes" five more to the ground. Sir Lancelot comes forward and the "fateful coils" do their work again. Hank has earlier described this contest as a "duel of the gods," and now that he appears to have won, he basks in the applause, "drunk with glory," and thinks, "The victory is perfect—no other will venture against me—knight-errantry is dead." Hank is full of hubris, and his comeuppance is about to happen. He has been overconfident, as usual, and Sagramor challenges him again after Merlin steals the lasso. Hank meets Sagramor with a secret weapon, never before used, a revolver, and kills him. Other knights charge Hank, and he shoots them out of their saddles. When the rest break and flee, Hank thinks to himself, "Knight-errantry was a doomed institution. The march of civilization was begun."

We have already discussed the irony of this passage. Hank is hubristically overconfident again; knight-errantry is not doomed, and "civilization" is not what Hank thinks it to be. He sees none of this, but the reader can—and the reader also can understand that everything has led up to this point, and this point leads to the Interdict, and the Interdict leads to the Battle of the Sand-Belt. This novel is not disjointed at all, but, on the contrary, tightly organized. The real control in Hank's life is invisible, but the reader can detect Providence's shadowy presence obliquely through Hank's references to such clues as "dreams," "chance," "luck," "accident," "fate," "demon," and "snakes." These words reappear in chapter 42 when Arthur and Mordred's armies face each other to parley for peace. Neither side trusts the other. A ghost warns Arthur in a dream, but the battle is precipitated by "accident": a snake bites a knight's heel, the knight forgets the order not to lift his sword and takes it out to slash at the snake, and the battle takes place— as recorded in the story of Arthur, and as was therefore immutably fated.

Two main points remain to be discussed. The first is the Battle of the Sand-Belt itself. Hank is abandoned by all of his civilization except for Clarence and fifty-two boys. Why boys? Because, being young, they were the only ones he succeeded in indoctrinating. Now, why fifty-two? There are fifty-two weeks in a year, so perhaps this is an allusion to the passing of time. (Another reference to time might be in the name of Hank's wife, Alisande—i.e., all is sand). There are also fifty-two cards in a deck. This allusion therefore may be to chance, luck, fate—or to deception, if the deck is considered stacked.

Hank and his supporters are located in a cave surrounded by thirteen electric fences set in sand. Why thirteen? There are thirteen cards in a suit. Sand reinforces the pattern of time, and cards the design of fate. But an additional, more powerful answer might be supplied by considering the circular fences as an allusion to Dante's hell. Draw thirteen concentric circles, each one representing the circling electric fences. Inside the inmost circle draw another circle. That represent's Hank's cave. Call the space inside that circle the nineteenth century. Then the next spaces moving outward are the eighteenth, seventeenth, sixteenth centuries, etc., until you come to the space inside the outermost circle. That will be the sixth century. If my surmise is correct, what Twain is implying is that all of existence is within hell, and progress is a damned delusion, for, as in the *Inferno*, the closer one gets to the center, the deeper and more awful is the damnation.

The innocent little girl Hank first sees in Camelot, therefore, with her mind at rest, is damned, born into a cruel age and destined for a hard life. But her damnation is ameliorated by her inactive—dreaming—mind. The married couple Hank takes out of Morgan le Fay's hellish dungeon have achieved some peace of mind by escaping their lot through dreams. If Hank were successful in awakening them, and they saw what toll the years in the dungeon had taken on each other, how damnably cruel it would be! In Twain's circles, the more the mind is exercised, the more it conceives of hell; the more conscious it is of its situation, the more hell it suffers. Hence, Hank's final dreaming wish to be reunited with his wife, Sandy, is more than an expression of natural affection, it is also a pathetic request to return to a simpler existence in one of the outer circles where the dreams are not so "real" and "hideous."

One of Dan Beard's original illustrations of chapter 18 depicts a barred slit window with an inscription over it: "All hope abandon ye who enter here." The quotation from Dante is not in the novel's text, but Twain had read Dante and he approved the illustration. There is, however, an important difference between Dante's hell and Twain's in *Connecticut Yankee*. Dante's hell is separate from the rest of the world and is complete; *Connecticut Yankee*'s hell merges with the world and is as endless as time.

The last point to be considered is how Hank reached the sixth century. He tells us he got into a crowbar fight with a man called Hercules and was laid out "with a crusher alongside the head that made everything crack," and he then woke up in sixth-century England. Ask your students what would normally happen to someone hit a crusher to the head with a crowbar wielded by a Hercules. Realistically, he would be killed. We must at least, therefore, entertain the possibility that Hank died in that fight and that he is able to move between time periods because he is not a creature of one life, but that he has a sort of life-in-death existence, doomed—or damned—to wander forever with haunting memories of other lives. This is suggested to us by Hank's brief, tragic, but unpursued glimpse of his essential individuality in chapter 18 as a "microscopic atom . . . in this plodding sad pilgrimage, this pathetic drift between the eternities. . . ." This is a chilling as well as powerful insight into the depth of Twain's double despair at the "damned human race" and the cruelty of its existential delusion.

The purpose of this interpretation, of course, is not to convince anyone of its literal truth—I do not recommend using literature as a medium of divine inspiration, and do not myself believe in the novel's paradigm of hell any more than I do in Dante's—but it is meant to help readers understand Twain and to appreciate him as a great artist. *Connecticut Yankee*, like *Huckleberry Finn* before it, is a denial of the possibility of human freedom.[10] This is a remarkable book to come out of the American nineteenth century, which we think of as so dedicated to the affirmation of freedom, but the truth is that Twain, like many of his fellow nineteenth-century authors, e.g., Melville, Dickinson, Crane, and Bierce, among others, had serious doubts about the nature and extent of human freedom. What ultimately keeps Twain from being a depressing author as well as a tragic one is, paradoxically, his American hatred of slavery, cruelty, and injustice, even if the tyrant is a malevolent deity. Twain may even be described as a literary Prometheus who, regardless of great personal cost, devoted himself to bringing the light of truth to man. Both in Twain's literature and in his heart was a deep and sincere yearning to be free. That may be why Hank at times resembles Mark Twain, because as an actor in the drama of life, Twain, like Hank, sought freedom; but as an author-observer he did not believe man was worthy of freedom or that freedom was even possible.

As the underlying structure of *Connecticut Yankee*'s themes is uncovered and students discover its astonishing unity and artistic sophistication, they will take away a fresh respect for Twain and for literature. They will not begrudge its not having been consistently humorous when they recognize that it has caused them to be more thoughtful about human destiny and that it has made a difference in their lives.

Notes

1   Pascal Covici, Jr., "Humor," *Mark Twain Encyclopedia* (New York: Garland, 1993), 380. Covici's section on "Hoax" in the encyclopedia is also worth reading, but a fuller discussion of both these topics is in his *Mark Twain's Humor: The Image of a World* (Dallas: Southern Methodist University Press, 1960).

2   I discuss the centrality of the dream motif to the novel in "The Reality of the Dream: Structural and Thematic Unity in *A Connecticut Yankee*," *Mark Twain Journal* 22 (Spring 1984): 8–14. Information from that article is abstracted in this essay, but the full explication contains many additional details that should be helpful in the classroom.

3   See Howard G. Baetzhold's entry on *Connecticut Yankee* in the *Mark Twain Encyclopedia,* 174–78. He recapitulates an earlier essay (listed in the entry's bibliography) on the course of the novel's composition and notes that as early as 1886 Twain had revealed to an audience his plan to have Hank, from behind electrified barbed wire fences, machine-gun Arthur's enemies. Baetzhold takes cognizance of the facts that Twain's views about the novel began shifting soon afterward and that Hank ultimately fought the chivalry of England instead of Arthur's enemies. Baetzhold, understandably, places interpretive emphasis on Twain's remarks about the novel that he was writing, whereas I place greater emphasis on

the text itself and on the Calvinistic beliefs that constituted Twain's deepest convictions and that were meshed with his creative impulses.

4 Considering that Mississippi River steamboat explosions were normally regarded as horrible disasters, that Twain's brother was mortally injured in one, and that Twain never forgot the anguish of watching his brother and others die, Hank's description of the explosion as "very neat and pretty to see" must have been loaded by Twain to be bitterly ironic.

5 The motif of a sinister, mysterious stranger first appears in Twain's works in "The Celebrated Jumping Frog of Calaveras County" (1865), and it recurs over the rest of his career. Usually, however, the mysterious stranger is seen from the standpoint of characters with whom readers can identify; he is an outsider, an "other." In causing time, the world, and everything that is in it to be viewed in *Connecticut Yankee* from the perspective of a mysterious stranger, Twain powerfully inverts the motif and subtly implies that no matter how potent a mysterious stranger may seem to humans, even he is controlled by an omnipotence beyond him.

6 The name "Morgan" also has relevant negative associations with the famous pirate, Henry Morgan, and the powerful financier, John Pierpont Morgan.

7 A more complete interpretation of the relevance of chapter 26 to the rest of the novel can be found in my article, "The Gospel According to Hank Morgan's Newspaper," *Essays in Arts and Sciences* 20 (October 1991): 32–42.

8 Hank's pratings about market value reflect theoretical discussions in nineteenth-century America about the value of labor. Twain, on the other hand, had been personally familiar before the Civil War with the institution of slavery, and afterward he knew first-hand that "wage slave" could be more than a figure of speech. Theory, therefore, becomes in the novel another sort of dream that blinds one to hellish reality. For an extended discussion of the significance of political economy to the novel, see my article, "*A Connecticut Yankee*: A Serious Hoax," *Essays in Arts and Sciences* 19 (May 1990): 28–44.

9 Twain's religious background can be readily learned by reading the section on Calvinism in any reputable encyclopedia or handbook of Christian theology. I have dealt more specifically with the degree to which Twain adhered to the Calvinistic teachings of his youth and how he applied them to his major writings, in "Mark Twain's Mind and the Illusion of Freedom," *Journal of Humanities* [Kobe, Japan], special issue (March 1992): 1–24. Because it is presently difficult to get access to this publication, I will send an offprint to anyone who sends me a request and a self-addressed envelope with adequate postage.

10 My interpretation of *Huckleberry Finn* is developed in "The 'Poor Players' of *Huckleberry Finn*," *Papers of the Michigan Academy of Sciences, Arts, and Letters* 53 (1968): 291–310.

A Connecticut Yankee in the Postmodern Classroom
James S. Leonard

Mark Twain's *A Connecticut Yankee in King Arthur's Court* is a novel marked by bizarre inconsistencies. Much of the book is satire of the best Twainian sort, although even here a considerable confusion arises at times as to just who is being satirized and what constitutes the "normal" perspective from which the situations' absurdities are seen. The novel's tone overall is that of a children's book, and it has most frequently been read and taught as one. (I recall book reports on it when I was in junior high school.) But the tone of jovial fantasy is violated by some rather gruesome turns in the narrative, about which the narrator—himself the perpetrator of some of that gruesomeness—seems mostly indifferent. Thus, we are left with three major interpretive possibilities: (1) ignore the violence and read the book as light satire; (2) overpower the seeming contradictions with a reading that marshals textual clues to construct a seamless web of textual unity; (3) emphasize the inconsistencies *as inconsistencies* to see what the text's contradictory nature will yield. In teaching *A Connecticut Yankee*, if we have to resort to the first of these three possibilities (as, for example, movie and television versions of the story have typically done), we falsify the material to such an extent that we would probably be better advised to choose another novel (and perhaps another author). The second possibility represents the classic formalist approach, which works well in most classroom situations. (Lawrence I. Berkove's essay in this volume gives an excellent discussion of how to do it.) But I'll choose door no. 3. This is a somewhat unsettling approach, for the teacher as well as the students, because it calls the integrity of the work and authorial control by its creator into question. However, it can pay big dividends because it opens up the text to student engagement in a way that the formalist's drive to closure may not. (My terminology probably makes it evident that I teach literary criticism as well as

American literature. But one really does not have to be a critical theory wonk to make this approach work.)

I like to start my discussion of *A Connecticut Yankee* in an unlikely place—the poetry of Marianne Moore, who wrote, in her poem titled "Poetry," that poems properly assume the qualities of "imaginary gardens with real toads in them." I ask my students to analogize a bit, as Moore herself was doing here, and see that Mark Twain brandishes a comparable formula in his title: the Connecticut Yankee, a real toad, is transported in Twain's story into Arthurian Britain, an imaginary garden. (The main point of the "Connecticut Yankee" designation, after all, is that the protagonist is an ordinary, practical guy.) Or we could say, following the fuller contours of the thematic situation, that Sam Clemens's own nineteenth-century New England (again the ordinary and practical) becomes the real toad that has left its ecological niche for the mythical garden of Arthurian Romance. This is a bit of a mind-wrenching thought, but with some prodding (perhaps akin to Jim Smiley prodding his jumping frog), most students can follow it. I then complicate the matter further by suggesting that, as Moore knew very well, real toads do not *really* inhabit imaginary gardens. Such gardens are peopled by imaginary toads that are *pretenders* to the real; the real vs. imaginary dichotomy is not so straightforward as it at first appears. What sets *A Connecticut Yankee* apart in this horticultural economy is the way that Twain, anticipating Moore's characteristically modernist aesthetic principle, converts it into a thematic one. What we want to see as irreducible difference in kind between Hank Morgan's solid, "realistic," commonsensical New Englander temperament (or values) and the mythical context in which he finds himself is, naturally, a humorous narrative impetus for Twain. But the more we look at the image of this supposedly real toad (that is, Hank seen through his manuscript's rendition) as figuration against the ground of its adopted habitat, the more we can see it as a matter of one imaginary *garden* transported into another, more distant one, as if in search of that elusively ultimate, archetypal Garden that must mythically predate them both.

In this somewhat indirect beginning to our examination of Twain's novel, we have established intertextual connections at both ends: Genesis and *Paradise Lost* (i.e., the "archetypal Garden") as predecessor texts, Marianne Moore's poem, with its modernist assumptions, as successor text. Thus, *A Connecticut Yankee*, rather than existing as a freestanding, internally complete structure, can be seen as one statement, or series (or jumble) of statements, in a continuing conversation. I point out to my students that Morgan's "manuscript" is a standard nineteenth-century fictional device for creating verisimilitude—a modern descendant of Plato's reliance on the dialogical Socrates, Chaucer's faithful copying of the tales told by the Canterbury pilgrims, Milton's rehearsal of the text provided by his muse. Within the mainstream of American fiction, it is preceded by Hawthorne's discovery of Surveyor Jonathan Pue's manuscript concerning the life of Hester Prynne and succeeded by Henry James's third-hand receipt and presentation of the governess's manuscript in *The Turn of the Screw.*

At the same time, however (problematization being never far away), I try to help the students see how Twain's verisimilar moment (again, like the real toad) undercuts itself, signaled by the manuscript's identification as a "palimpsest," inscribed across "traces of a penmanship which was older and dimmer still—Latin words and sentences: fragments from old monkish legends, evidently" (10). Such a palimpsest, I concede, is perfectly possible in a mechanical sense and, given a recorder other than Twain's "Yankee historian" (10), might reasonably have been expected. But to think that the Boss, virtual ruler of Britain, revolutionizer (at least) of sixth-century industry and economy, and, most notably, publisher of the world's first newspaper, could find no more suitable writing material than this previously worked-over parchment is to think, as Lemuel Gulliver would say, "the thing that is not." How to explain this anomaly is a good topic for discussion. But "explaining" is not the main point; in this discussion we are more interested in the interpretive operations that Twain encourages us to perform in order to *make* the matter explicable.

Students are intrigued by the degree to which the palimpsest is not a "realistic" explanation so much as a clear signpost warning of thematic significance ahead. As such, it thwarts the drive toward realistic expectation, itself becoming one term of a broadly conceived textual palimpsest, overlaying the narrative with a kind of visible thematic aspect. Hank Morgan's narrative is (somewhat) straightforwardly presented as the text of nineteenth-century Connecticut written over that of sixth-century Arthurian Britain.[1] I ask the students to see the difference between the two as the primary thematic space of the story. Hank Morgan is, in fact, the name of that difference—paralleling and extending "Mark Twain" as the name by which Sam Clemens designates the difference between himself and his public/authorial persona. The persuasive force of "Twain's" narrative charm is evident in the ease with which his palimpsest ruse serves its verisimilar purpose, seducing (over)eager readers to accept uncritically the superimposition of Morgan's no-nonsense "Yankee historian" commentary across the Latin fragments from antiquity.

And we can turn the analogy yet another way. Morgan's manuscript is a material compression of the book's title: the text of modern realism overlaying the predecessor text of medieval romance and, beyond that, the still hazier reaches of monkish legend—with the spaces between plainly calculated to be filled with meaning. But we can see that the mark of thematizing intention also inserts some doubt regarding Yankee matter-of-factness. The more Hank Morgan comes forward as thematizing author, the less reliable he becomes as purveyor of history. Having a thematic ax to grind, he proliferates interpretation in a way that supersedes interest in unvarnished fact. These supplementary functions (to apply Derridian language to the narrative situation of *A Connecticut Yankee*) coexist within a narrative relationship that is at once both the basis for verisimilitude in the novel and the condition of its impossibility. Assessed from the point of view of thematic significance, the palimpsest difference which creates thematic space also brings that thematization into question—underscoring (by overwriting/overriding) the inaccessibility of one of the terms (Arthurian Britain) of the comparison. (Twain's phrase "monkish legends" is a less indirect admission of that inaccessibility, identifying what has been overwritten as more mythic than historical.)

What all of this amounts to is a sort of vortex of authorial strategies and meaning possibilities that I want the students to explore. If they find it a bit dizzying, so much the better; there is strong indication that Twain did, too. What I do not want them to do is simply "read through" the textual details without pondering their formal and thematic significance. With respect to authorial strategy, I propose that Twain's evident desire to distance himself from his narrative by the layered authorlessness of a palimpsest text makes simple sense. After all, his stand-in, Hank Morgan, faces some considerable narratological problems, and feels a corresponding authorial anxiety.[2] With the narrative responsibility that Twain has foisted onto Hank, it is no wonder that the time-traveling Yankee, appearing to Mark Twain the tourist, seems "unspeakably old and faded and dry and musty and ancient" (5) while telling his story. As authorial mastering mind, Hank attempts purportedly new readings—of texts and contexts—that claim to perfect any previous ones; but as the chaotic data he encounters routinely resist/overthrow interpretattions, he becomes representative of the (inevitably) frustrated need for a definitive interpretation.

We can easily see that the interpretive impulse is stimulated by differentiations of the type that Twain's novel sets out: United States/ Britain, sixth century/nineteenth century, monarchy/democracy, practicality/pageantry, justice/injustice. But as we read, these (and other) seemingly solid differences tend to slip into confusion or sameness. Monarchy is vilified, but Arthur at crucial moments is admirable; knightly romance is discredited, but Sir Launcelot and his fellows emerge at times as genuinely virtuous; the peasants' situation warrants sympathy, but they keep proving themselves personally undeserving; superstition is the enemy, but Hank frequently invokes it; violence is to be eliminated, but Hank commits it on an unprecedented scale. This recurrent interruption and overthrow of universal propositions by specific counterexamples opens the thematic door to a horrifically vertiginous universality of sameness/repetition that smacks of (among other things) determinism. The broad indication, in terms of "Arthurian plot," seems to be that (after all) the sixth century looks a lot like the nineteenth. In terms of authorial plotting, the problematic is a revision of the palimpsest; that is: is this new inscription (or any new inscription) importantly different from its predecessor(s)? Even with reference to Twain's own work, when, for example, Hank Morgan occasionally slides into Huck Finnisms ("Hank" re-forming "Huck"?), as with "[it] was too many for me" (13), or shows a reflexive reliance on Mississippi River region analogies, such as the mention of Guenever's "furtive glances at Sir Launcelot that would have got him shot in Arkansas, to a dead certainty" (21), students familiar with Twain may perceive a briefly discomposing lapse of style—that is, of the differentiation that allegedly constitutes Hank Morgan—and an intrusion of Twain/Clemens into the narrative.[3]

What we have established here is an interpretive scenario in which we find Mark Twain grappling with problems of textual logic, narrative technique, and both desired and undesired thematization. We see Hank Morgan not just as a character in his own story but as an image of Mark Twain himself, solving writing problems in parallel with Hank's ingenious political solutions. In inscribing the palimpsest text across its monkish predecessor, Morgan/Twain/Clemens (or Hank/Huck/

Mark) discovers the difficulty of suppressing not only monkish legends but a whole array of other forerunners to the present narrative (including Twain's own previous products), leaving poor Hank with an unavoidable depression over the inevitability of plagiarizing earlier writings. The joke about the humorous lecturer that propels the plot is, along with the palimpsest text itself, a prime emblem of this anxiety. The connections that this joke raises to the humorous lecturer-writer Mark Twain, and to his own problems of originality and connection to his audience, make it one of my favorite moments in working with *A Connecticut Yankee.*

The joke is inescapable, having been retold for centuries, accumulating a genealogy that now overshadows the joke itself. And though Hank both laments the universal repetition and complains that the anecdote "never saw the day that it was worth the telling" (48), one cannot help enjoying the incongruity that against this background Twain and Hank have made certain that the joke does not escape yet another retelling. The logical necessities of the narrative require Hank himself to recite the joke to the reader:

> While Sir Dinadan was waiting for his turn to enter the lists, he came in there and sat down and began to talk; for he was always making up to me, because I was a stranger and he liked to have a fresh market for his jokes, the most of them having reached that stage of wear where the teller has to do the laughing himself while the other person looks sick. I had always responded to his efforts as well as I could, and felt a very deep and real kindness for him, too, for the reason that if by malice of fate he knew the one particular anecdote which I had heard oftenest and had most hated and most loathed all my life, he had at least spared it me. It was one which I had heard attributed to every humorous person who had ever stood on American soil, from Columbus down to Artemus Ward. It was about a humorous lecturer who flooded an ignorant audience with the killingest jokes for an hour and never got a laugh; and then when he was leaving, some gray simpletons wrung him gratefully by the hand and said it had been the funniest thing they had ever heard, and "it was all they could do to keep from laughin' right out in meetin'." (48)

The self-conscious reflexiveness of this joke and the circumstances of its (re)telling in *A Connecticut Yankee* provide a wonderful opportunity for meditation on "Who is Mark Twain?"—one of the undercurrents we have been attending to in our look at the novel's devices. In the way that it cross-sections the narrative's relation to Twain's own situation and concerns, it also takes us some distance toward the "What is literature?" destination—which to me is the primary consideration in any examination of a particular literary text.

The logic of recurrence that the joke encapsulates multiply recurs in Twain's novel: the nineteenth century is a retelling of the sixth across the numerically unholy gap of thirteen centuries; the United States may be a retelling of its mother country, Great Britain; and more generally, one violent, repressive, insensitive society after another shows itself to be a dismal reiteration of predecessors. In fact, the text as a whole begins to view itself as a reflection of a kind of universal repetition compulsion. Repeatedly, the desire for difference asserts itself; repeatedly, it collapses into depressing sameness. The text of Human Nature seems insistently to resist revision; and as Freud tells us, death presents itself as the only effective weapon against this sort of compulsion. It asserts itself as such with a vengeance in *A Connecticut Yankee* when Hank Morgan decides that the only practicable way to kill off the evils of chivalric tradition is to kill *all* the knights: another bone-chilling occurrence of the logic of the supplement in which the theoretical good of social change substitutes itself for human feeling and, it seems, for any recollection that human beings are involved. This instance of transcendent principle obliterating (or at least hiding) the bare face of human presence exemplifies Hank's flawed understanding of his palimpsest situation, from its simple but violent beginning to its cataclysmic end—to be remedied only by his own death. In the tragic economy of narratological succession, the birth of the thematized text requires the death of its subject(s). The author murders not to dissect but to contain against unwanted, and therefore nonthematic, variations, or worse still, against the undesired thematization of hopelessly plagiarized repetitions. The students notice how in this approach to Twain's novel we have joined both the author and his protagonist in a reflection on the primacy of interpretation as central to the search for valid understanding. The text has become, in Roland Barthes's phrase, a "playing field"—with palimpsest-like layers of interpretive possibility.

By this point—and out of this maze of considerations—students begin to develop a feel for Twain's use of the palimpsest formula in *A Connecticut Yankee* as a makeshift solution—for authoring and plotting and setting—that exposes its thorny problematic, and as a bonus, the inaccessible ideal solution. Returning for a moment to Marianne Moore's garden/toad analogy, we might say that Mark Twain is an imaginary garden inhabited by the real toad Samuel Langhorne Clemens, and that Twain in turn becomes the real toad inhabiting the imaginary Hank Morgan, the (again relatively) real inhabitant of the fabrication known as the Boss. Moving back in the other direction, we might ask: for what real toad is Sam Clemens the imaginary garden context?

This question, in some sense, takes the imaginary garden out of the literary text and locates it in someone's real backyard. The summary point here is that in *A Connecticut Yankee* the real vs. imaginary/mythical, whether for author or setting (and at some point[s] these are the same), keeps shifting as the perspective changes. Against the background of Arthurian Romance, nineteenth-century New England advances a comparatively convincing reality claim. Likewise, Arthurian Britain (in its fictional guises rendered not only by Hank Morgan but by, among others, Twain's predecessors Malory and Tennyson) seems real if juxtaposed against more distant "monkish legends"; and in the farthest reaches lies the ever-hazier path to the singular *original Garden*—the hypothetical stopping point for the interpreting/mythologizing impulse.

The impact of that original Garden for *A Connecticut Yankee* can be showcased for students by a look at Hank's description of the setting in which he awakes after being kayoed by a crowbar-wielding workman named Hercules (speaking of the mythological) in the (seemingly) too-real setting of nineteenth-century New England: "When I came to again, I was sitting under an oak tree, on the grass, with a whole beautiful and broad country landscape all to myself—nearly. Not entirely; for there was a fellow on a horse, looking down at me—a fellow fresh out of a picture book" (8–9). Here the "beautiful and broad country landscape" bears, for an instant, the look of the mythical destination of pure origin, but immediately we see that Hank's journey has fallen short (he is not alone; neither he nor his "book" is original). Hank has arrived too late. He finds that the "Garden" has long since departed (its demise represented most specifically and consistently in the novel by the Church as socialization, and therefore perversion, of the aspiration to metaphysical perfection). This is the first of many wish-fantasy escapes for Hank that later (or sooner) degenerate into nightmare. Particularly notable is the phrase, "with a whole beautiful and broad country landscape all to myself," exposing his search for originality as a yen to escape not just from one society but from human society altogether. His misanthropy seems motivated by the authorial sense that society is inexorably marred by thematic/mythic ambiguities and the violences they generate. This necessary insufficiency is thematically visible only within the ironic space between Hank Morgan (the roundly socialized nineteenth-century Yankee) and Mark Twain (the skeptical authorial persona whose cool comprehension exceeds the boundaries of Hank's sometimes feverish earnestness)—Hank having been too much infected by the mythologies of his own society to easily throw off their influence. From the novel's new vantage in its real/mythological sixth-century setting, the mythological aspects of Hank's former garden in the nineteenth-century landscape become increasingly prominent—for the reader if not for Hank himself.

On the biographical front (which always seems of interest to students), Clemens's own attraction to mythical romance (noting his private expressions of a fondness for Malory and a reverence for certain of Malory's characters, as well as his authorial romanticizing of noble savage figures like Huck Finn and Jim) wages war in *A Connecticut Yankee* with his stylistic commitment to realism and his thematic/ philosophical commitment to demythologizing. Here again it is the substitution of one romance for another. In *Adventures of Huckleberry Finn* the seemingly incorrigible romanticism of Tom Sawyer (which may actually mask the roots of a predominantly conventional relation to society) is supplanted by the ostensibly realistic but actually incurably idealistic views of Huck Finn; in *A Connecticut Yankee* what really galls in the sixth-century context is the ordinariness of the characters once we get close to them, and the mythology that looms more and more monstrous as the novel proceeds is the nineteenth-century myth of progress, culminating in Hank's incredible inhumanity offered up to that progress at the last battle. And that final battle in turn yields up its own mythological aspect. Its supposed finality dissolves into another repetition of misdirected brutality by which the relatively powerful overcome the relatively powerless in a (fortunately) futile and shifting quest for ultimacy. The novel is in this sense unstable (or contradictory) to the end.

Hank's subscription (and ours?) to the myth of progress takes the form of political (democratic), social (egalitarian), and economic (capitalist) theories in whose name he tries to do battle, both metaphorically and literally, with the Arthurian codes of honor and natural virtue—codes that seem atheoretical to the sixth century just as the nineteenth century's values seem natural to Hank, but which, like Hank's, bear the marks of violent and destructive ideological assumption best visible to the "uninitiated" outsider. Here Twain's *Yankee* gives students a handle on what is, for obvious reasons, a tough question to grasp: does some mythological covering inevitably blind one to one's own ideological (and narratological) prejudices? The demythologizing effort plays out for Hank as only—to borrow a phrase from a Wallace Stevens poem—"inescapable romance, . . . disillusion as the last illusion" (468). This means that the "reality" of Moore's "real toad" depends on seeing the otherwise questionable amphibian (a kind of biological palimpsest) from its own perspective(s). This is, in a sense, the trick of first-person or fully sympathetic third-person narrative: to bring the reader inside the fabric of mythological/ideological assumption and thereby blind the reader to its mythological/ideological nature. The trick of Twain's perversion of such techniques is to repeatedly strike the hollow note (as in Hank Morgan's casual justification of thoughtless violence)—a stratagem that seems to leapfrog beyond modernism toward the disruptive effect of the postmodern. The trick of our interpretive strategy, in turn, is to similarly cross and recross narrative boundaries so that students see the text from both inside and outside. Their efforts to pin down the relation between the two should lead them through an exploration of interactions among text, intertext, and authorial intention.

It is easy for students to be carried along by the amusing surface of *A Connecticut Yankee in King Arthur's Court*. And closer attention to the texture of the text seems, at first, to punish (with confusions) rather than reward. The task of the approach recommended here is to turn the tables on the palimpsest by turning those punishments into rewards. This is a novel that plays well in the 1990s precisely because it is troublesome. The *Yankee*'s "unraveling" profoundly exposes the palimpsest nature of the text (all texts?), the self, and the self-serving ideological intention at each layer—but only if we aggressively confront its difficulties. If we persuade our students (and in the process ourselves) to squarely face the novel's problematic nature, this imaginary toad can lead a meaningful life in the real garden of their (and our) own experience.

Notes

1 Hank's work-over of the palimpsest's underlying text joins interestingly with Roland Barthes's observation that "mythical speech is made of a material which has *already* been worked on so as to make it suitable for communication" (110; Barthes's emphasis).

2 Hank is, of course, not the only stand-in; Clarence takes a brief turn at narration in his "Postscript," and the frame narrator (Mark Twain the tourist) is certainly not identical with the usual persona of Mark Twain.

3 Whether or not this actually is a "lapse" (i.e., unintended or unrecognized) on Twain's part is still another issue—one that, fortunately, need not be resolved here.

Works Cited

Barthes, Roland. *Mythologies.* Trans. Annette Lavers. New York: Hill and Wang, 1972.

Clemens, Samuel. *A Connecticut Yankee in King Arthur's Court.* Norton Critical Edition. Edited by Allison R. Ensor. New York: Norton, 1982.

Stevens, Wallace. *The Collected Poems of Wallace Stevens.* New York: Knopf, 1954.

120   James S. Leonard

Opportunity Keeps Knocking:

Mark Twain Scholarship for the Classroom

Louis J. Budd

By the time of his death in 1910, Mark Twain had functioned as hero of
the American public for at least fifteen years. Therefore, his writings
could have been used to narrow the gap that was growing between the
literary standards preached by the middle class and those of the mass
culture catered to by the first stage of big-business journalism and publishing. Sensitive to that gap, Twain was willing to serve as a bridge,
and he could have made a difference. Contrary to the impression common today, he enjoyed more respect then than now among the cliques
that in every society appoint themselves as the palace guard of the
highest or most sophisticated (by their own terms) level of culture.

However, in 1910, departments of English were striving to establish
their specialized claim to curatorship of high literary culture. They
played safe by denying almost all of the living writers, especially Americans, any right to deserve their attention. As for Twain, he was especially suspect because of his popularity—a handicap that nobody could
shake off until Robert Frost, who knew how to conduct academic politics with a masterly air of the required naïveté. Furthermore, Twain
could sometimes get downright coarse as well as bawdy. A few passages in *Letters from the Earth* offend even the undergraduates of today
who flaunt graffiti on the T-shirts they wear to receptions with the
faculty. The faculty of 1910 felt much surer about their standards,
social or literary, and they abandoned Twain to readers with no grounding in philology and to the nonacademic critics, many of whom would
desert him after Van Wyck Brooks's searing indictment in 1920, which
in the cause of liberating the American consciousness tried to exorcize
one of its freest spirits.

Meanwhile, Twain's mostly silent constituency had kept the faith, as
they proved in 1935, when the centenary of his birth brought an astonishing spread of recognition, both in this country and abroad. The de-

tails can be sampled in Thomas A. Tenney's monumental *Mark Twain: A Reference Guide* (1977). I will single out only the fact that Nicholas Murray Butler, the president of Columbia University, organized an exhibit and a program of speeches. Throughout Twain's life he had won unlikely friends such as the now elderly and ever more conservative Butler, than whom nobody was more respectable. But no Twain boomlet developed in college curricula. After 1945 came the initially healthy rigors of the latest New Criticism, which took ten years to find aesthetic virtue in Twain and then only in *Adventures of Huckleberry Finn*. Although he has gained more ground in the curriculum since then, my sense is that the majority of the faculty, especially in a department of English oriented toward publication, still do not rate him as an important literary figure and would not let him any further up the status ladder than courses for nonmajors or for the secondary schools. Such faculty ought to read William M. Gibson's concise *The Art of Mark Twain* (1976), which states a persuasive case for his multifaceted craftsmanship, or Everett Emerson's *The Authentic Mark Twain: A Literary Biography* (1984).

However, as we all know, enrollments in optional English courses have been dropping steadily. The time may be near when those colleagues who have declared that they would rather starve than teach science fiction or film—or Mark Twain—will be called on to honor, or else eat, their words. Diehards may find that the name has two literal meanings. Perhaps they will find consolation in deconstructionism, which rediscovered that every term or sign can be attacked as imprecise. As the disarray among the guardians of high culture becomes more glaring and their kind of belles lettres dissolves further into avant-garde faddishness, they may also find that they have been standing guard over nothing, like Jay Gatsby at the end of chapter 7 in Fitzgerald's novel. But the state of enrollment, or rather nonenrollment, by career-oriented students seems precise and real to me.

Fortunately, as an opening for regaining some lost ground, Twain's popularity continues to hold up with the public. At airports, when natty businessmen finish groaning over their prime rate and go to the book displays, they can find and do often buy a couple of his books. Hal Holbrook is still going strong, and television ads can use a Twain figure without bothering to call his name. Young Americans have already acquired a good feeling about him and some knowledge of his writings, almost as often *Letters from the Earth* as *Huckleberry Finn.* They flock into courses devoted entirely to his work.

Therefore, my main point is that Twain still offers a shining opportunity for a department of English to establish better rapport with students by teaching a worthwhile writer in whom they are already interested. Of course, defensible differences of opinion swirl around Twain. But the lingering notion that he poses no philosophical or aesthetic complexities will fail the test of fact. So, to restate my point more specifically, Mark Twain scholarship is vitally useful for the teacher and then the students. I assume that we would not expect students to dig deeper than we do, that Sinclair Lewis was clowning when he invented an instructor who discourages classroom questions with, "Go to the library and make a report to the class on that." The shrewd student, by the way, may simply go to the annual chapter on Mark Twain in *American Literary Scholarship.*

By scholarship, I do not primarily mean anthologies of critical essays. Teachers overestimate, I think, how much students care about the tense battles among critics. Furthermore, the belief that disagreements among the initiated will strike sparks among beginners does not confront the possibility that subtle disputation can prove intimidating instead. The pressing need of students is to read widely in the original works, to range beyond the shopworn texts and acquire an individualized sense of Twain (or any other writer), to find fresh items they enjoy, and maybe even to come to feel like a prospector who has located pay dirt. Therefore, the teacher needs to become and stay familiar with the two Twain editions in progress so that, having revivified his insights at the source, he can guide students toward finding their personal Mark Twain. As the ad man likes to put it these days, they deserve it.

Above all, the teacher of literature needs to know the Iowa/California Edition of the Works of Mark Twain (simply the California Edition by 1993), which has produced nine volumes and is picking up speed toward its goal of republishing in definitive texts all of his writings. John Gerber is the founding father of this project (and also the editor of its *Tom Sawyer* volume), which typically contains an authoritative study of the origins and revisions of each of its texts. The California Edition will include not only the full-length books but also the many hundreds of shorter pieces that help add up to the millions of words that Twain wrote when he was not joking to interviewers about his laziness or devoting his energy to his many-geared business deals.

Also important is the Mark Twain Papers edition, now through his notebooks up into 1891 and five volumes of his letters from 1853 through 1873. The admirable goal is to publish everything of interest among the materials held at the University of California at Berkeley, evidently the finest single collection for any author. This edition will continue to present unknown sketches and essays and will include the complete autobiography. Still, the personal letters, fully annotated, may prove its richest part for nonspecialists. Has there ever lived another person as crotchety and erratic and yet as spontaneously humorous as Twain? Every teacher of literature is obligated to his or her students to see whether Twainians like me are demented in claiming that, in spite of dismaying lapses of touch, Twain's best wit can flare up even when he is perpetrating one of his most dismal stories, indeed, whenever he goes to his post—a pun meaning that even his hurried letters can soar into memorable comedy.

Because his comedy could achieve flights too stunning, even stunting, to be sustained for long, he can often be taught most effectively through his shorter pieces. A kind of market-research proof of this proposition lies in the sales of Charles Neider's several anthologies, which are still available in paperback. Among collections of short pieces, Walter Blair's Riverside Edition has had the best balance, but there are four interesting anthologies along cultural-political lines. Tom Quirk's edition in 1994 for the Penguin American Library even improved on Blair. Our calling more attention to shorter pieces—such minor classics as "The Recent Carnival of Crime in Connecticut" or "The Private History of a Campaign That Failed"—will both reinforce *Huckleberry Finn* and spread the inhuman load of reverence it is asked to bear. Incidentally, the Iowa/California Edition, which covers the novel's contemporary reception, brings us back closer to what Twain and his contemporaries saw in *Huckleberry Finn*. The edition identifies, for instance, the review that pleased him for understanding his novel best. As Harold Kolb showed in his brilliant article in the *Virginia Quarterly Review* (1979), too many readings today press one case among clearly parallel possibilities. The Iowa/California Edition, furthermore, reproduces the original illustrations. Recent scholarship has argued convincingly that Twain paid so much care to the illustrations for all his books that they carry an integral part of his intended effect.

In talking first about *Huckleberry Finn* I do not mean to pass over *The Adventures of Tom Sawyer* or, backing up further, to pass over *Roughing It* or *The Innocents Abroad*. I *would* pretty much let undergraduates ignore *The Gilded Age* unless they are politically minded, ignore *A Tramp Abroad* unless they are following some special interest such as the construction of Twain's travel books, and just ignore *The Prince and the Pauper* altogether if they want to. But *The Innocents Abroad* lasted as his best-known book during his lifetime, and for anyone wanting to use Twain as a focus for social or intellectual history or for popular taste, this is the place to start, with much strong scholarship available and with even better soon to come. *Roughing It* (magisterially reedited in 1993 by the Mark Twain Project) is a fine place to pick up the ongoing discussion of his persona—in other words, of how Twain projected what was somehow taken to be his own personality behind the tall tales and other antics. The narrative voice in the "Old Times" section of *Life on the Mississippi* has been analyzed so expertly that it offers a classic point of entry into the workings of Twain's humor as well as into how his persona worked its strategies of survival, both within the books or fictions and in the world of his book-buying audience. The Mark Twain Library (hardcover or paperbound) edition of *Tom Sawyer*, with the original illustrations, helps us understand why so many tributes from outside the academy greeted its centennial year, which coincided with the country's bicentennial. Above all, the scholarly and critical writing on *Tom Sawyer* can help us perceive that it carries lasting substance and that the sophisticated reader can admire it on its own terms.

A Connecticut Yankee in King Arthur's Court, handsomely reissued as part of the Iowa/California project, can also be had, if need be, in a first-class Norton Critical Edition. It shows especially well the clash between the author's intentions, stated with unusual precision for him, and the criticism confined to the implied logic of the plot. As for Twain's attitude toward *Pudd'nhead Wilson*, it was far more casual than most of the current criticism, which finds dark profundities not visible in the novel's initial reception. More generally, the materials, most of them still interesting, that show Twain's reception during his lifetime make a baseline for measuring the readings of succeeding generations, a worthwhile enterprise unless we believe that our collective I.Q. has risen right along with the national debt.

For *Following the Equator*, I will rest on the old saw—it is a good enough book for people who think that it is. But *The Mysterious*

Stranger presents both a specific opportunity and a challenge. Students keep trying to tell us that, even in the version that scholarship has exposed as having been cobbled together by Twain's literary executor, *The Mysterious Stranger* still works, that its mixture of amusing fantasy and grimness keeps nagging at their interest, that it fits sociologist Robert N. Wilson's category of novels that "ask radical questions about the nature of man and about his role in the social and physical universe he inhabits." The currently liveliest and most intriguing Twain scholarship analyzes his mind and art through the last fifteen years of his life, while the practical challenge of *The Mysterious Stranger* lies in whether any editor can offer a rounded text that we are collectively willing to teach without boring students about the technicalities of textual editing. I can cheerfully ring in the word "boring" since, having dabbled in textual problems, I appreciate the labor that some have dedicated toward laying out the career of a Twain manuscript so minutely that anybody with enough patience can, in the privacy of his/her own home—as certain mail-order advertisers used to say—reconstruct the process of its inspiration. On that last problem the relevant chapters in Walter Blair's and Hamlin Hill's history of American humor (1978) will at least help substantially.

Ready-made student interests lead back finally to *Letters from the Earth* and those drugstore or airport sales, which tap a different audience or maybe just a different side than the soft-porn paperbacks in the next row. When parents of students—fathers more than mothers, I find—learn that *Letters from the Earth* has been assigned, they want to hear what the academic verdict is. They unflinchingly accept the darker side of Twain. They also accept his speculations about literalist Christianity, letting him question it sardonically while they abhor mild expressions of doubt from somebody else. I suspect that this tolerance operates within a broader sense of Twain, or Samuel L. Clemens, as a personality.

In the much-plowed area of Mark Twain biography, Justin Kaplan (1966), Hamlin Hill (1973), and Guy Cardwell (1991) have now filled in the worst case that can be urged against him. Nobody has repeated the charge in 1906 that he was a paid agent of the British Foreign Office or the charge in 1978 that he cavorted incognito and begot an illegitimate daughter in Hannibal during the 1880s. So many researchers have sifted the Mark Twain Papers that no major scandals can still be hidden there. So, as Hill put it, the issues between the Heretics and the Idolaters are clear. They are vibrantly human issues that students take to heart rather than to their ghostwriter for term papers.

Of course, Twain was also an engaging personality, and it is always hard to resist the temptation to weave in one-liners. But his career epitomizes central problems in American culture, which is also simply another culture—that is, another version of human society. Those problems involve the virtue of spontaneity versus social discipline, the price of success, and the possibility that high culture has no firmer referents of position than the Sunday school heaven that he mocked; with poignancy he exemplifies the nineteenth-century crisis of faith, the ways rationalism can slide toward a self-devouring determinism or even a solipsism, which is ironical for such a master of presenting himself to an adoring public.

In case I have not made it clear, I conclude by declaring that Twain scholarship is an exciting, open field, though the fine-grind explication of *Huckleberry Finn* during the last twenty years may be like the gas-guzzler, ready for the museum where Henry Ford wanted to put Twain's childhood home. There is much left to learn and to speculate about. Perhaps the most valuable scholarly article of 1979, for instance, followed up the surprisingly few leads about the six months that Twain spent as a typesetter in Cincinnati in 1856–57. If one has students who get rapport from knowing that Mark Twain slept here or there, they can do sleuthing in a surprising number of cities and can unearth new perceptions of Twain and, indeed, perceptions by Twain since he was interviewed so widely. My own fate has proved to be a pursuit of Twain through the columns of newspapers, and after thirty years I can report—like the detectives he made fun of in "The Stolen White Elephant"—that the trail is still fanning out. The teaching of Twain can arouse interest leading to student involvement that will repay all parties at better than the current prime rate, wherever that stands. It is a golden opportunity—Mark Twain would have called it a sure thing—to reinforce our departments of English.

II   Rediscovering *Huckleberry Finn*

"Huckleberry Fun"
Everett Carter

The first thing to say about *Huckleberry Finn* is that it is a funny and pleasurable book. A true professional, Mark Twain wanted his writing to earn its and his way, and he knew that the best way to find readers was to mine the vein of humor whose first product was the pure gold of "The Jumping Frog of Calaveras County." He subscribed easily, comfortably, instinctively to the oldest traditions of his craft—that it should delight and instruct, and in that order. First, to give delight, to give pleasure, and *Huckleberry Finn* constantly gives the deepest, the primary kind of pleasure—that of the child in all of us. He also wanted to instruct, and the instruction in *Huckleberry Finn* is the important undertone. The overtone is the delight, the triumph of pleasure over pain, of hope over fear, of life over death; the undertone is the flow of satiric criticism. First the pleasure, then the instruction.

The novel's delight is immediate: "You don't know about me, without you have read a book by the name of 'The Adventures of Tom Sawyer,' but that ain't no matter. That book was made by Mr. Mark Twain, and he told the truth, mainly." That "mainly" sets the tone; the story will be playful, will imitate life but at the distance of pretense, will be like life, but at a safe remove. The book will have the perspective of youthful deflation of the adult world; it will establish the identity of the true author, who will control both the overtone of comedy and the undertone of satire.

The next sentences in chapter 1 contemplate the important pleasure of the happy ending. Huck reminds us of the triumph of the first installment of his small saga—the winning of $6,000, "all gold," that was his part of the reward for the downfall of Injun Joe. With this emphasis, the reader is pointed in the direction of true comedy; the $6,000, "all gold," will be there at the conclusion to symbolize, in hard cash, the happy ending.

The language of the opening sentences furthers the comic tone. Part of our delight in it is our admiration of its wit—our appreciation of the expert manipulation of language to imitate the speech of a partially educated boy of a specific region. Another joy is the more selfish pleasure of superiority; we laugh at those who know the rules less well than we, and who inhabit an area where an "inferior" dialect is spoken. A further invitation to smile is in the manipulation of the sentence's rhythm: the "mainly," coming after the pause of the comma, and after the speaker has apparently finished his thought. We hear, and see, the comic lecturer as he pauses, looks innocently about him, and adds the deflating "mainly."

The next sentences establish the important element of hedonistically happy childhood, the return to infantile messiness. "[I]t was rough living in the house all the time, considering how dismal regular and decent the widow was in all her ways; and so when I couldn't stand it no longer, I lit out. I got into my old rags, and my sugar-hogshead again, and was free and satisfied." The comic tone of this passage is signaled by the words "regular and decent," reminding readers of *Tom Sawyer* that it was the Widow Douglas who had "snaked" Huck out of the "wet" and had given him the first of many homes he would long for. Huck's rebellion is the cheerful, lighthearted protest of the child against the acknowledged moral superiority of the parent. The Widow's attitudes are the moral touchstones of the book; her position is emphasized by the immediate introduction of the ugly Miss Watson, who will be the truly repressive figure, the one from whose tyranny both Huck and Jim will escape. Huck's wallowing in the mud is comic when it occurs in the context of the good and beneficent parent who will be there to clean him up; it becomes serious rebellion in the context of an evil "parent," Miss Watson, and the soon-to-be-introduced real parent, the awful Pap Finn. Huck accepts the moral authority of Widow Douglas, avowing himself a believer in the Widow's "Providence," a beneficent one in which "a poor chap would stand considerable show," and a heretic in Miss Watson's repressive religion under which "there warn't no help for [a poor chap] any more."

After introducing himself, after alluding to the author of his story, after telling of the Widow and Miss Watson, Huck describes his meetings with Tom and with "Miss Watson's big nigger, named Jim." Both characters are shown first in their roles in the pure comedy. Jim will play the buffoon, yielding the easiest and most primitive stimulus to laughter—our feeling of superiority to someone beneath us. Tom will be shown as he constantly converts reality into make-believe. (Both will also perform important roles in the didactic elements of the novel, Tom as an exemplar of sentimental absurdity, Jim as the medium of the novel's satiric attack on Southern attitudes toward race).

With the coming of winter, Huck is dismayed by signs of the reappearance of his vicious father. He immediately transfers titular ownership of his fortune to Judge Thatcher, who has been caring for it, giving Huck the reasonable 5 percent interest it has been earning. By the transfer, Huck places the money out of his predatory father's reach. Judge Thatcher, along with Widow Douglas, is a good "parent," and with her he provides a stable moral center, located in a "decent and regular" society, a center that is necessary to establish the comic aspect of the satiric undertone. Pap Finn will be the contrast to this society, a contrast that will enable the reader to see the moral thrust of the satire. For the time being, however, I will concentrate on the pure humor of this first part of the plot, the delight in Huck's ability to triumph over obstacles and reach a "happy ending."

Kidnapped by his terrible father, Huck finds his life in danger. He resourcefully saws out a portion of a bottom log of his cabin prison and escapes in a canoe that has conveniently floated into his care. He meets Jim, who has escaped from his oppressor, Miss Watson, and together they live a short island idyll of childlike primitivism. Together they investigate a ruined house that has floated down the Mississippi, a "house of death"; in one corner lies a dead man. This brief episode focuses the comic tone. From the house of death they emerge joyfully with the small things of life, "an old tin lantern, and a butcher knife without any handle, and a bran-new Barlow knife worth two bits in any store. . . ." The list goes on, and ends with a wooden leg: "the straps was broke off of it, but, barring that, it was a good enough leg, though it was too long for me and not long enough for Jim." The conversion of possible pain and crippling to the joy of bacchanalian absurdity ends with Huck telling us, "We got home all safe."

Huck finds out that Jim has a price on his head. The two pile onto a raft and start their voyage down the Mississippi River. Never mind that freedom lay more certainly to the north; the tip of Illinois, a free state, lies south of St. Petersburg, and anyway the current flows south, and Mark Twain goes with the flow, even after the runaways miss the Illinois landfall in a fog. Before they do, they meet another life-threatening adventure and emerge from it unscathed. This time another derelict structure is involved, a wrecked steamboat named the *Walter Scott* (the symbolism will play a part in the satiric undertone, but in terms of the pure comedy the episode is another example of comic triumph). Trapped aboard the wreck with a gang of murderous thieves, Huck and Jim steal their boat, leaving the gang to drown. (Huck will try to save them by one of his wonderfully shrewd ruses, but the murderous gang will get their just deserts.)

At this point, Huck plays the same kind of thoughtless joke on Jim that he and Tom played in the first pages of the novel, showing the same childlike heedlessness. Huck's remorse, when Jim shows his pain, is the important first step in developing the major element of the novel's satiric purpose. (For the moment I will simply mark it and return to the comic overtone.) A steamboat smashes the fugitives' raft, and Huck alone starts on an important new adventure in the "House Beautiful" of the Grangerfords. The episode is largely satirical, with both the gentle satire on sentimental art, and the bitter satire on the Southern code of false honor. But it also provides another in the series of the novel's "happy endings." Escaping from the horror of the senseless, murderous family feud, Harney Shepherdson and Sophia Grangerford, with Huck's help, elope: "they'd got across the river and was safe." Jim, too, has escaped death, and Huck rejoins him on the raft and in the river.

When two Mississippi confidence men, the self-styled Duke of Bridgewater and Dauphin of France take over the raft (Huck, typically, has helped them escape from some of their angry victims), these "low-down humbugs and frauds" are the occasion for a variety of satires on nobility (these examples of royalty, says Jim, "do smell so") and on human gullibility (the poster for their public performance reads "Ladies and Children Not Admitted"; "If that don't fetch them," says the Duke, "I don't know Arkansaw"). The Duke and the Dauphin also provide us with the pure comedy of wit as they deliciously garble Shakespearean passages: "To be, or not to be; that is the bare bodkin / That makes calamity of so long life. . . . But soft you, the fair Ophelia: / Ope not thy ponderous and marble jaws. . . ." The rascals take their parts as well in the series of fortunate escapes and happy endings that continue to give readers the joy of deflected pain and averted danger. The most important of these episodes is the attempted swindling of Mary Jane Wilks and her sisters, a scheme that Huck characteristically thwarts with courage and craft. His success invokes the classical satisfaction of witnessing the dupers duped. The con men lose not only their stolen fortune, but all their earlier ill-gotten gains as well when Huck arranges for the restitution of the orphans' inheritance. Further gratification is provided by the eventual fate of the two swindlers. The reader does not, for the most part, share in Huck's sweetness of character that permits him to sympathize with the two frauds as they are tarred and feathered. Instead, we feel the comic satisfaction of witnessing poetic justice.

The last of the con men's villanies has been the selling of Jim for a share in the announced reward for his capture. The buyer, Silas Phelps, coincidentally, is Tom Sawyer's uncle, a happy coincidence since it creates the possibility of the eventual revelation of Jim's having already been freed. The last chapters, descending into the burlesque that often attracted Mark Twain's wayward genius, are devoted to the important objects of his satiric ridicule—the warping of Southern mentality by the falsehoods of meretricious literature, and the immorality of the Southern attitudes toward race. However, they are also the climax of the reassuring succession of affirmative endings. After Tom Sawyer has succeeded in getting himself shot (in the leg, of course—a curable wound), his rescue is effected by Jim, of whom the doctor says he had never seen "a better nuss or faithfuller, and yet he was risking his freedom to do it. . . ." The final scene comprises the classic comic finale: the revelation of an extraneous, gratuitous Providence, a "god from the machine," that turns the chaos into order and instantly transforms potential tragedy into comedy. Jim is in chains, and Huck is poor because "pap's been back before now, and got it all away from Judge Thatcher. . . ." No, says Tom, Jim is already "as free as any cretur that walks this earth! . . . Miss Watson died two months ago, and . . . set him free in her will." As for Old Man Finn, Jim reveals that it was his corpse that was huddled in "the house of death"; Huck's fortune is "all there yet—six thousand dollars and more. . . ."

It has taken ten chapters of satiric overkill to reach this happy conclusion. Convinced that false romanticism had been the cause of the moral downfall of the American South, Mark Twain put Huck and Jim through an ordeal by Tom's mad devotion to sentimental literature. In its first pages, the novel sounds the note of the first great comic novels in the Western tradition. Like Don Quixote, Tom substitutes the falsity of romance for the truth of reality. A Sunday school picnic is transformed into "a whole parcel of Spanish merchants and rich A-rabs." An old tin lamp becomes the means of summoning "a lot of genies." Unre-constructed by his early errors of fantasy, he drops into the Phelps plantation with the same warped vision: reality distorted by books of heroes: "Baron Trenck," "Casanova," "Benvenuto Cheleeny," "Henry IV." True comic satire, holding up vice and error to ridicule, must have a norm against which to measure the error, and Huck provides such a norm with his hardheaded empiricism. He looks at reality with his own eyes (like Mark Twain, he is after all "from Missouri"): "there warn't no Spaniards and A-rabs, and there warn't no camels nor no elephants. It warn't anything but a Sunday-school picnic. . . ." Then Mark Twain made sure to have him add the typically Twainian anticlimactic absurdity: "and only a primer class at that." Considering Tom's claim for the magical properties of an oil lamp, Huck does not reject it out of hand. Like the good empiricist he is, he "reckoned" he would "see if there was anything in it." He got a lamp, performed the experiment, rubbed away; nothing happened, and so he "judged that all that stuff was only just one of Tom Sawyer's lies." Faced at the end with the problem of freeing Jim from his captivity in one of the Phelps's slave cabins, Huck proposes his commonsensical solution: lift the bed leg up and remove the chain, take the key from the outside wall, and open the door. When Tom objects, proposing his ridiculous alternatives, Huck's response is: "I see in a minute it was worth fifteen of mine, for style, and would make Jim just as free a man as mine would, and maybe get us all killed besides."

The continuing satire directed against false romanticism is overshadowed by the deeper satire directed against the inhumanity of slavery and the ugliness of racial prejudice. The device of irony becomes the principal weapon of the satirist, using the small ironies that are effective devices of comic satire, not the large irony that is the hallmark of the tragic mode. Small ironies—reversals of meaning—are used to show us the disease of wrong human action when measured against a norm of health agreed upon by author and reader. A moral accord, the satiric covenant, is always present between author and reader, giving both the pleasure of the hope of reform, the comic possibility of a return to health. Large irony, universal irony, is fatal and unalterable, implying the malevolence of a seemingly rational but really absurd universe. The ironies of *Huckleberry Finn* are of the first kind, the comic ironies that imply the possibility of a return of a diseased society to health. Ironically, it is Pap Finn, the most evil of the Southern spokesmen for white prejudice, who inadvertently but surely establishes the norm of social health against which we measure his, and the unre-constructed South's, aberrations as he rails against the "govment" of the free Northern states. Pap, who "had been drunk over in town, and laid in the gutter all night," goes to "ripping again. . . . Whenever his liquor begun to work, he most always went for the govment. . . ." "Oh, yes," he whines, "this is a wonderful govment, wonderful. Why, looky here. There was a free nigger there, from Ohio. . . . And what do you think? they said he was a p'fessor in a college. . . . And that ain't the wust. They said he could *vote.* . . . Thinks I, what is the country a-com-ing to? . . . They call that a govment that can't sell a free nigger till he's been in the State six months. . . ." Pap Finn, very early in the novel, ironically establishes the moral norm against which Southern social inadequacies are to be measured, and from this point on the reader is secure in his alliance with the author when he creates his small, stable ironies. Whatever Pap Finn is for, the reader is conditioned to be against; whatever he is against, the reader is for. The social structure of the Northern free states becomes the standard of health from which Southern society deviates and to which, hopefully, it can be helped to return by the small ironies of comic satire. These ironies are bound up with the realistic vision that sees the boy as necessarily a product of the mores and attitudes of his society, and the characterization of Huck Finn will adhere to this reality. He will, in the course of his adventures, learn that Jim is not a thing, but a human being, and one of the best he has known. And yet, being a creature of his society, he cannot translate this knowledge from the individual to the class: blacks in the abstract will remain things for him, and his "conscience" will always chide him for violating societies injunction against stealing another (white) per-son's "things."

Twain has made sure to make this point by placing Huck's first crisis of "conscience" immediately after his discovery of Jim's warm human-ity. Huck has played another joke on him, this time letting Jim believe he was dead. Jim's sorrow and his dignified rebuke ("trash is what people is dat puts dirt on de head er dey fren's en makes 'em ashamed") plunges Huck into an agony of remorse in which Jim, who has been up to then a commodity, becomes a warm, dignified, loyal human being. But just a page later, when Jim says he is "all over trembly and feverish to be so close to freedom," Huck's reaction shows that his discovery of Jim's humanity has not been translated into a general truth about slaves and slavery. Huck feels "trembly" too; Jim, he tells himself, is almost free "and who was to blame for it? Why, *me*. I couldn't get that out of my conscience. . . . Conscience says to me, 'What had poor Miss Watson done to you, that you could see her nigger go off right under your eyes and never say one single word?' . . ." Jim goes on to say that "the first thing he would do when he got to a free State he would go to saving up money and never spend a single cent, and when he got enough he would buy his wife . . . and then they would both work to buy the two children, and if their master wouldn't sell them, they'd get an Ab'litionist to go and steal them."

Secure in the knowledge of his reader's assured complicity in the irony, Twain describes Huck's reaction: "It most froze me to hear such talk. . . . Here was this nigger which [note the "which"] I had as good as helped to run away, coming right out flat-footed and saying he would steal his children—children that belonged to a man I didn't even know; a man that hadn't ever done me no harm." He writes a letter to Miss Watson, betraying Jim, feels "good and all washed clean of sin," and then remembers Jim's love and loyalty. His "sound heart" triumphs over his false social "conscience." He tears the letter up. "All right, then, I'll *go* to hell." The complicity between author and reader is seamless: the ironies of Huck's inverted morality, his conviction that he is bad when he has done good, compels the reader to detest the society that has so warped the boy's sense of good and evil, and to cheer the "sound heart" that instinctively allies itself with the humanistic society that Pap Finn has earlier, unwittingly, established as the norm of moral health.

An appreciation of the overtone of pure humor and the undertone of satire should not ignore the depths of sadness and pathos that are there in the novel, as they are in most great comic inventions: the loneliness of Huck, the awful killings between the feuding Southern families, the pathetic drunkard murdered mercilessly by a Southern "aristocrat"; above all, the horror of a system that reduces people to commodities and trains its children to be unthinking accomplices in the crime. Anybody killed in the steamship explosion? asks Aunt Sally. "No'm. Killed a nigger." "Well, it's lucky; because sometimes people do get hurt." The numbing horror of this exchange between good-natured Aunt Sally and good-hearted Huck almost cancels out the fun and pleasure we feel in reading *Huckleberry Finn* and has convinced many modern readers and critics that the work is a tragedy. But this evidence of the power of social prejudice is a statement about a particular society, one that Mark Twain hoped could be reformed, and not a tragic statement about an inevitable human condition. We have learned about a norm of healthy social behavior through the ironic drunken rant of Old Man Finn. We know that Aunt Sally's moral blindness is not inevitable. Pap Finn's ravings have shown us that there are societies where humans can be treated as humans; the possibilities of social health are there in the depiction of the racial callousness of otherwise dear, sweet, humane Sally and otherwise warm, loyal, and loving Huck Finn, making this most painful of the satiric thrusts a part of an ultimately comic vision. The dominant mood of *Adventures of Huckleberry Finn* is an affirmation in which the undertones of healing satire merge with the overtone of pure humor to make it America's comic masterpiece.

Huck's Helplessness: A Reader's
Response to Stupefied Humanity
David E. E. Sloane

Adventures of Huckleberry Finn as a work of comic realism offers wonderful challenges to literary historians employing reader-response criticism as part of their critical methodology. The challenge lies in identifying how a great world classic, which *Huck Finn* unquestionably is, can be accused of so many faults, including a failed ending. As a "funny" book, marked by its sales through subscription agents rather than in bookstores, and identified by its comic illustrations, the novel received only scattered critical notices. Not only was it thrown out of the Concord, Massachusetts, Public Library, but even the leading humor magazine of its day, *Life*, attacked it. Modern critics, no longer concerned about the vulgar tone of the novel, have often taken the high ground of literary structure to attack it, claiming that the last fifth, which one of Ernest Hemingway's characters dismisses as only cheating, is such a falling off that it is an embarrassing failure in form and conception. Critics somehow construe this ending not as a planned closure, but as evidence of the basic fictional incompetence of a world-famous author whose collected and uncollected works will nevertheless stretch to seventy or more volumes when finally brought together by the University of California Mark Twain Project. Certain African American critics further complain of the last fifth of the novel that it completes Jim's degradation to the level of minstrel show darkie, which they sense has been most of his part throughout the novel, anyway. Finally, the complaint is made that the book lowers itself and falls away from the idyllic vision of the great raft passages in the middle, thus diminishing the luster of Twain's, and our literary culture's, greatest creation.

My position for purposes of classroom analysis is that such negative assessment is recklessly perverse, contradicted by the popularity of the book through time and by the author's capabilities demonstrated both elsewhere and in the book itself. The critic's first challenge is not to rewrite the book in an undemonstrable and possibly false exercise, but rather to make sense of the work as it exists, explaining how its parts correspond and develop in a symphonic creation of feeling and meaning that stands as a record of the author's visionary artistry. The primary questions are (1) what does the novel make a typical reader feel, (2) why does it make the reader feel that way, and (3) what do those feelings suggest about the author's ideology, about that of his culture, and about our responses to our world? The book is the artifact; our responses are some of the material for analysis; a fuller sense of varied social projections linked to our own expectations—all derived from the imagination and humor of Mark Twain—is the target. There must lurk in the text an essential "rightness" that makes it continue to be held so highly in our regard. Using a later commentary by Twain on slavery in Hannibal, in which he identifies stupefied humanity as the greatest evil of slavery, I argue in my classes that *Huck Finn* is an expression of pessimism, ameliorated by its last line and our hopes, and that the concluding portion of the book is appropriate to Twain's intention.

In getting at each of these points, I use my modest understanding of reader-response criticism as outlined by Kenneth Burke in a simply written and accessible eighteen-page essay, "Psychology and Form," in his book *Counter-statement*. Burke's idea in "Psychology and Form" is simply that fictional ideas, images, experiences, and various minor stylistic forms repeat themselves in symphonic progressions in great works of art, including music and literature, and that understanding how a motif is introduced in other than strictly informational forms can benefit us in understanding why some great ideas in a work of art bring us to a heightened emotional experience beyond the norm. *Huck Finn* is, of course, a chief candidate to be so discussed. Burke cautions us against the tyranny of the informational, as he calls it, emphasizing our awareness of the importance of both minor (literary devices) and major (the novel genre, in this case) forms in the artistic construction of the work of art—in this case the novel.

Huck's sensitivity and human sympathy lie at the core of the book. It is probably for this reason that so much controversy is aroused by the suggestion that his voice may be influenced by a black model, as proposed in Shelley Fisher Fishkin's *Was Huck Black?*, which received major coverage in the summer of 1992 from the *New York Times*, the *International Herald Tribune*, and *Newsweek*. It is the work of the plot and the various episodes of the novel to enhance our response to the hero's sensitivity, our urgent desire for the novel's success in the world, and our demand that there be a heroic outcome that satisfies our need for a dramatic climax through the creation of a reformed world and a reformed life experience for the major characters. These expectations are both informational—what the author tells us happens—and psychological—what the form of the novel tells, affirms, and seems to bring out in the crescendo of motifs, images, and word values at the end of the story to give the reader both release and satisfaction. The issue of Huck's sensitivity or humanity and its outcome is best approached by considering the three points of controversy identified above: first, the hostile critical reception of the novel; second, the position of Huck as an actor in the novel; and third, the overall message about the changeability of the people described in the book, and of people in their own culture generally. Bringing in some historical background materials and combining them with a reader's own responses to the novel seems to provide a picture of Twain the comic realist reinforcing through structure a message that he expressed elsewhere than in *Huck Finn*— that people could be unconscious of wrongs without being evil. Although true hearts could sometimes overcome social artifice, humanity generally was morally insensitive, selfish, and unlikely to reform. Humor and realism are central in this approach, so I am treating Twain as he was understood in his own time rather than as a disembodied "great writer," somehow totally free from time and place.

First, of course, we have with *Huck Finn* the arresting phenomenon of a world masterpiece that is frequently attacked on a variety of grounds by both conservative and progressive readers. The original review of *Huck Finn* by the comic magazine *Life*, generally attributed to critic Robert Bridges (not the British poet), is a case in point (reprinted in Sloane, *Mark Twain's Humor: Critical Essays*, among other sources). Bridges found the language unelevating and the experiences degraded; by the standards of literature usually approved for children in the 1880s, this is unquestionably the case. Even the dime novels of the period steered away from the sordidness in which the book wallows—crime, drunkenness, thievery—with the thievery often reenacted by Huck and Jim, although at a lower level of tension than by actors in major incidents such as the thieves on the *Walter Scott* or the Duke and Dauphin. Bridges particularly singled out for censure Huck's killing of the hog in chapter 7 to create the appearance of his own murder—a passage that is very important in the novel and in the reader's final estimation of the action of the novel—although today it is seldom pointed out as structurally or thematically crucial since it does not bear directly on racism, with which modern criticism is now preoccupied. In fact, the whole notice in *Life*'s review cites only six points in the novel, the demur about plot and morals (used as a jumping-off place for the commentary on five other points), Pap's delirium tremens, the hog killing, the family feud with its "six to eight choice corpses," the "Giascutus" story, and the funeral with its "sick melodeum" and "long-legged undertaker." Bridges lists the pig passage in sequence as second among his five items for attack: "An elevating and laughable description of how Huck killed a pig, smeared its blood on an axe and mixed in a little of his own hair, and then ran off, setting up a job on the old man and the community, and leading them to believe him murdered. This little joke can be repeated by any smart boy for the amusement of his fond parents" (Sloane, 214). From my point of view, Bridges's fascinated disgust with the incident is notable. He recounts it in loving detail, satisfactory proof for me that the episode is a striking and marked component of the text to a reader in the 1880s. As an analyst, however, I note that the message of the episode is underscored by Bridges's notice, and I see a likelihood that later readers will get the hidden message without noticing it. Up to this point, Huck has consistently taken a pragmatic line, seeing no point in Miss Watson's doctrine of gifts, for which he is labeled a fool, or in Tom's impractical Quixotism, for which he is labeled a "numskull." Arabs and elephants to Huck have all the marks of a Sunday school; none are valid, as tested by his two or three days of "sweat[ing] like an Injun" to conjure up genii, after experimenting, with similar pragmatism, by praying for a fishing line in response to Miss Watson's ideology.

Yet, with these tendencies established, we as readers have not experienced the translation of feelings into action. Chapter 7 achieves this translation while beginning a major motif that carries us forward to the last fifth of the novel. Chapter 6 featured our second view of "sivilization," as Pap succeeded Miss Watson's religiosity with the spread-eagle "call this a govment" speech and then degenerated into delirium tremens. Chapter 7 now offers Huck an opportunity to escape when he is left alone in the isolated cabin. The chapters are linked by Pap's references back to a stranger whom Huck claimed to be defending himself against with his gun at the end of chapter 6. As Huck develops his plan, he goes through a series of details that show him to be tremendously competent, creative, and effective. He secures the original canoe and loads it with detailed provisions, including coffee, sugar, cups, blankets, and other basic survival gear. He then surveys his entrances and exits and happens to see a wild pig: "hogs soon went wild in them bottoms after they had got away from the prairie farms. I shot this fellow and took him into camp" (Twain, 40). Pap, by the way, for those who like subconscious echoic connections of images, has previously had the hand of a hog and lain with the pigs in the tanyard, of course—a minor echo perhaps, but pigs and fathers are closely linked in a murderous context. The most important point is that Huck in several lengthy paragraphs of the gory passage cited by Bridges creates his own death scene. The detail is extended and convincing, and it must be, for this is Huck's first real demonstration to us of the tremendous power he has as a backwoodsman to overcome the minds of the prairie folk while using their own artifacts. Without telling us that Huck is extremely competent, Twain has demonstrated it, and, furthermore, he has demonstrated it in a way that links this competence to the experiences of the "sivilization" he is about to flee. Huck inserts an important statement as well: "I did wish Tom Sawyer was there; I knowed he would take an interest in this kind of business, and throw in the fancy touches. Nobody could spread himself like Tom Sawyer in such a thing as that" (Twain, 41). With this proviso, directly preceding the climax of Huck's invention with the bloody axe, Twain establishes the crucial motif that anticipates the entire action of the book's ending, and he will replay these lines during the raft trip, increasingly undercutting their appropriateness in application. Bridges noted the passages because he was reading the book in relation to his "idealist" expectations, according to Durant Da Ponte in "*Life* Reviews *Huckleberry Finn*" (Sloane, 213–15), and so the passage stands out for him as so repellent that he misses it as a major demonstration of the central figure's capability. This is Twain's success as a great and subtle plot builder. The compromise of that capability in Huck is heavily foreshadowed, too.

African American critics are also mixed, as a group, in their response to *Huck Finn*, as suggested by Leslie Fiedler in "*Huckleberry Finn*: The Book We Love to Hate" (reprinted in Sloane, *Mark Twain's Humor*, 217–34). Some of the dissatisfaction is on the basis that the ending makes Jim into a minstrel show darkie. Others are concerned with the image of blacks generally for its callousness—the word "nigger" is used more than 200 times in the mouth of the white Huck Finn; and when whites rather than blacks use "nigger," African Americans find this act uncomfortable, as well they might. Furthermore, Jim is seen as more or less childlike and overly contented in many sequences—again, particularly early and late in the novel, radically at variance with the militancy that finds its expression in modern African American novels, such as William Melvin Kelley's *A Different Drummer* (1959), or in an earlier generation in books like Arna Bontemps's *Black Thunder* (1936), or even earlier in J. T. Trowbridge's *Cudjo's Cave* (1864), a white author's antislavery novel unknown to most modern critics. But other sources, like B. A. Botkin's collection of narratives by former slaves, *Lay My Burden Down*, leave room for depictions of nonmilitant black Americans, which seems to square with Twain's own reminiscences. Fitting black Americans into the context of the novel, I am guided by remarks on the subject embedded in Twain's reminiscence of his mother, Jane Lampton Clemens, reprinted in Walter Blair's *Mark Twain's Hannibal, Huck and Tom.* Of his mother, he writes, including a passing observation on slaves in Hannibal, "Yet, kind hearted and compassionate as she was, I think she was not conscious that slavery was a bald, grotesque and unwarrantable usurpation. She had never heard it assailed in any pulpit, but had heard it defended and sanctified in a thousand. . . . Manifestly, training and association can accomplish strange miracles. As a rule our slaves were convinced and content" (48–49). We gain more insight when he writes of his father's plan to sell the slave Charley as described in a letter home: "[He] goes right on, then, about some indifferent matter, poor Charley's approaching eternal exile from his home, and his mother, and his friends, and all things and creatures that make life dear and the heart to sing for joy [Twain has previously described the singing of the boy-slave Sandy, sold away from his mother and at least not grieving when he is singing], affecting him no more than if this humble comrade of his long pilgrimage had been an ox—and somebody else's ox. It makes a body homesick for Charley, even after fifty years" (51).

In terms of the novel, then, the quiescence of Negro slaves does not indicate the author's acceptance of their status as normal. Rather, he is depicting a society in which *quiescence is normal.* Should we be surprised that he does this with some assertiveness? I don't think so. I think it is part of the situation that envelops Huck's conscience, and by extension the conscience of every reader immersed in the insensitivities of his or her own time and place—Twain's universal message.

Interpreters who cannot fathom this point are doomed to a hopeless misunderstanding of Twain's realism and the purposes to which he applies humor. Jim's rejection of Huck on the raft—as "trash"!—for lying to him is powerful enough to identify Jim's humanity in a world where he is already a fugitive by virtue of his runaway slave status. We read elsewhere of Jim's standing watches for Huck and of his sensitivity to his daughter and grief over mistreating her: we know all we need to know about Jim's humanity. Jim is thoroughly humanized, but his role in a slave state in 1845 will never be fully human. Yet, as Harry Wonham pointed out in a recent paper, when in chapter 8 Jim talks of not wanting stock because stock—livestock, a cow that later died—is too risky, he is also talking about himself: "I owns mysef, en I's wuth eight hund'd dollars. I wisht I had de money, I wouldn' want no mo' " (57); rejecting himself as a risk in favor of the money he is worth as a commodity is the ultimate dehumanization, but it is portrayed here by Twain as a burlesque. When Huck, arriving at the Phelps Farm at the end of the novel, responds to Aunt Sally's "Good gracious! anybody hurt?" with "No'm. Killed a nigger" (279), Twain completes the grotesquerie.

So we come to the problem of discovering how Twain's social insights and the demonstrated competence of Huck Finn our hero can account for the degeneration of the last fifth of the novel in terms of the heroic action and resolution we crave. Part of the logic of the ending for me has just been suggested in my brief remarks on Jim. I have always contended that readers are *supposed to be frustrated* by the last fifth of the novel, and I teach with that end in view. The last fifth of the action is *not* how we *wanted* the book to end. We—the readers, sentimentalists that we are—want the book to end with Huck and Jim emerging into a new consciousness of each other and maturing, but Twain's actual ending returns to the earliest childishness of the book, returns to St. Petersburg, returns to Tom's dominance of Huck, even though we know on the basis of chapter 7 that Huck can do as well or better than Tom. Why would Twain frustrate us so?

The question brings us to Twain's sense of his world as described elsewhere in his writings about St. Petersburg. Henry Nash Smith has condensed that sense into the useful chapter provided by Twain's own phrase defining Huck Finn as having "a sound heart but a deformed conscience" for his discussion of *Huck Finn* in *Mark Twain: The Development of a Writer* (also reprinted in Sloane, *Mark Twain's Humor*).

No realistic view of society could pretend that Huck and Jim would suddenly emerge into an enlightened society in 1845, or in 1885. Twain *the comic realist* is here a true realist who describes social experience without alternate demurs or interpretations by an omniscient but intrusive author. (Critics like Fishkin have suggested in many places that the racial climate in 1885 was growing increasingly gloomy, as repression and lynching mounted and the legal recourses of the post-Civil War period were successfully undermined by sophisticated white Southern opposition and Northern confusion and indifference—if not Northern racism, as well.)

The key to the last fifth of the book lies in Twain's thinking about the effect of "aristocracy" on democracy—an effect with which his entire canon is preoccupied through the 1890s. *Mark Twain's Hannibal, Huck & Tom,* gives one of the most telling insights into Twain's thinking in this respect in a lengthy but important passage on attitudes toward slavery in Hannibal. Twain had previously commented about Hannibal, "It was a little democracy which was full of Liberty, Equality and Fourth of July; and sincerely so, too, yet you perceive that the aristocratic taint was there. It was there, and nobody found fault with the fact, or even stopped to reflect that its presence was an inconsistency" (46). Twain continues on to suggest the more pervasive and awful effects of slavery when added to this other taint:

> It is commonly believed that an infallible effect of slavery was to make such as lived in its midst hard-hearted. I think that it had no such effect—speaking in general terms. I think it stupefied everybody's humanity, as regarded the slave, but stopped there. There were no hard-hearted people in our town—I mean there were no more than would be found in any other town of the same size in any other country; and in experience hard-hearted people are very rare everywhere. Yet I remember that once when a white man killed a negro man for a trifling little offence everybody seemed indifferent about it—as regarded the slave—though considerable sympathy was felt for the slave's owner, who had been bereft of valuable property by a worthless person who was not able to pay for it. (50)

Twain thus identifies the citizens of the Mississippi River town not as villains—as we the readers see them in the river town episodes during the raft journey itself, or as we see the duke and dauphin. They are representatives of a situation that *stupefied everybody's humanity.* The farmers are mean enough to Jim once he is recaptured after Tom Sawyer's wounding, and the outcome is less appealing than the sort of fictive experience that the raft episodes might have led us to expect, but could we really have expected any better of their stupefied humanity? Not only is the answer "no," but Twain underlines the answer by having the Doctor intercede for Jim as the farmers cuff him and having them respond according to their stupefied capability. If we as readers do not like this state of affairs, it seems inescapable to me that we never were supposed to like it. It is a matter of not seeing ourselves emotionally idealized, and at this point we are so commingled emotionally with the development of the novel's action that we are sullied and frustrated as Twain refuses to pamper us with a happy social resolution, even though he will concede us a happy outcome in the last couple of pages. Dickens's resolution of the plot of *Great Expectations* should warn us that comic novelists do not necessarily favor happy outcomes as much as their audiences do.

Nor can we expect of Huck a radical assertion of independence once he rejoins society. Comedy requires acceptance, not tragic rejection, and realism requires believability within the documented social context. If anything, to me as a critic this leads to an even greater tragic recognition of human dependency on the world, and I would contend that this message is consistent with Twain's later pessimism, and that it provides good evidence, furthermore, that that pessimism was part of his makeup from his earliest writing onward. If Huck's return to the shore world is conscious, it is Twain's trap for us. If it is unconscious, whether the ending is "bad" or "good" writing depends heavily on one's perspective. In noting the expression of sympathy for a murdered slave's owner, in the passage cited above, we have a paradigm for the Doctor's suggestion after Tom Sawyer is rescued that a "nigger like that is worth a thousand dollars" (Twain, 352) because of his helping the Doctor, sympathy expressed not in terms of Jim but rather in terms of Jim's value as a slave commodity—the value that Jim himself ironically expressed earlier in the novel. A study of chapter 42 in the California text, in fact, shows that Twain hammers home the point of Jim's ownership by repeated references to his owner and value ("he ain't our nigger, and his owner would turn up and make us pay for him," being a good example). Huck is back inside society at this point; protest is impossible.

The slapstick burlesque that led Huck to this point is Twain's chief use of comedy to demonstrate how stupefied humanity can become. Thus, the more egregious the comedy, the more obvious it should be to a reader that a radical falling off is taking place from the high point of the action at the end of the Mary Jane Wilks sequence and Huck's decision to go to hell for his friend. When we come to the end of the novel, we are frustrated that Huck is so completely subordinated to Tom Sawyer. Yet it is partly Huck who accounts for our frustration, consistently complaining about his own subordination to Tom: "Picks is the thing, moral or no moral; and as for me, I don't care shucks for the morality of it, nohow. When I start in to steal a nigger, or a watermelon, or a Sunday school book, I ain't no ways particular how it's done, so it's done" (307). The value of this passage, which reduces Jim by comic juxtaposition to the level of a watermelon is to again remind us of Hannibal—Sunday school and the intense emphasis on principle and morality on the cited page—while also reminding us of Huck's capability in using other tools—a saw and axe—to create his scenario in chapter 7. So, while echoing earlier experience, we now have the boy and the black man, who were elevated on the raft, again degraded by childish fantasy. Other comments by Huck include the statement, "there ain't *no* necessity for it" (300); "Confound it, it's foolish, Tom" (304); his rejection of one of Tom's ideas as "one of the most jackass ideas I ever struck" (309); and "Jim he couldn't see no sense in the most of it, but he allowed we was white folks and knowed better than him" (309). (The irony of this last statement seems to resolve for me the question of whether or not Twain was fully conscious of the irony of the racial situation he was writing about.) These are only a few of the demurs, comic and serious, that mark the entire run of the text, with the alternative being regulations, rights, and morals as construed by society. In fact, this section of the book leads up to its own crises as Tom introduces bugs, spiders, and snakes into Jim's prison cabin, making it even crawlier than the cabin of Huck's Pap's delirium tremens, causing Jim to rebel. Jim's two key statements are that he never knew it was so much trouble to be a prisoner (325), which may be read as an ironic gloss on the docility of slavery and its mildness in the Hannibal version recalled by Twain, and his decision to "keep de animals satisfied, en not have no trouble in de house" (327), which is a burlesque echo of one of the greatest moments of the book preceding Huck's "go to Hell" speech, that moment when he announces the raft ethic: "what you want, above all things, on a raft, is for everybody to be satisfied, and feel right and kind towards the others" (165).

Thus, at the end of the book, we find Tom Sawyer working extensively with the artifacts of his world; the fixation of the boys for spoons and sheets and the details of the household of Aunt Sally, for their prison escape parodies the usefulness of such detailed items in Huck's original "evasion" in chapter 7. Even the excuse given the Doctor for Tom's wound, "He had a dream and it shot him," seems to carry out the imaginary action of Huck taking the rifle at the end of chapter 6. None of these traces and echoes are informational facts of significance; rather they are restatements of motifs which, like minor themes in a musical composition, re-echo and carry forward feelings. The role of the yokel farmers who discuss the evasion's details would have a much stronger effect of symmetry with the raftsmen passage in place in the "restored" text of the California edition of *Huck Finn*. Having shown early in the book a range of rough, low characters, it seems reasonable that another local area should be populated by them. As with the raftsmen, they are rough and ignorant, but not cruel. Their appearance, however, is part of an overall sense of return and recapture, which is the dominant feeling of the last fifth of the book—that somehow we have not progressed. And so critics often speak of Twain's regressing to his low calling as a comedian rather than realizing the full import of his vision. Without the raftsmen passage, the yokels are an outré inclusion that is barely foreshadowed by such as the Bricksville loafers.

Tom's creation of the coat of arms is a burlesque restatement of the problem of Jim's status. Reference is made to slavery embattled. The depiction of Jim and Huck and Tom is grotesque: "runaway nigger, *sable*, . . . a couple of gules for supporters . . ." (Twain, 322). This lowering is followed by the aforementioned echo of the raft ethic, in the same chapter, when Jim declares he wants peace in the house among his insects and vermin, heaped on him by his insensitive friends rather than by his enemies (Twain, 325–27). This business supplies the reader-frustration that is to be released when Tom makes his great proclamation, that Jim is "as free as any cretur that walks this earth" (Twain, 356). The irony here is not localized, as a cynic would read the ending, and racist cynics consistently do; it is a cosmic irony derived from Tom's delusion as a member of his society—his stupefied humanity reflecting the stupefaction of all those about him. Jim's "freedom" once established, the Phelpses and everyone else go out of their way to treat

Jim well. The society is basically kind, as Twain contended of Hannibal. Slavery bred from aristocracy is the horror, and the last fifth of the book is the demonstration of its *effects*, which are as comic as the bizarre escutcheon fabricated by Tom, effects that are played out in a variety of guises throughout the whole conclusion of the novel. Why else drag in the coat of arms at all but to reemphasize this point to us the readers?

The truth is that Twain did not think that the level of sensitivity of typical Southerners was likely to be elevated. Huck's response to Jim is a personal response. It speaks to the assertion of his heart over his social training, but it does not cause that social training, or the society it represents, to disappear. In fact, I think that the source of the true power of the last lines Huck speaks derives from this fact. The last fifth of the book has successfully reasserted society's domination. The book was not really over with the climax and catharsis that we imagined to have concluded it at the end of the Wilks episode, even though Huck's elevation was. In true Twainian fashion, Twain gives us one more topper to top off the comic sequences leading to the conclusions. When Huck says, "I got to light out for the Territory [capital T—the realist's location, not a fantasy location] ahead of the rest, because aunt Sally she's going to adopt me and sivilize me and I can't stand it. I been there before" (Twain, 362), his "s" misspelling of "civilize" echoes the chapter 1 and 6 misspellings associated with Pap and Miss Watson and brings us back emotionally, by literary device, not by overt commentary, to our remembrance of both the evils that Huck fled and Pap's inhumanity and lack of sympathy toward Negroes, but also to his first emphatic display of competence in this tawdry and compromised environment. Now, with Jim's dignity compromised for $40 by Tom Sawyer's "reward," and with both Jim and Huck made silly by the action, insensitivity in sivilization has been reasserted. Thus, Huck's line is our great reaffirmation of the real truths underlying the novel—the importance of heart recognition and love between individuals. I suggest that it is even more powerful by virtue of the "failings" of the last fifth of the book, where Huck seems to have returned to his sivilization without any growth in humanity and wisdom. Twain was never, in a forty-year career, to come up with a political program to contradict this view, and it is because, I think, this is his root pessimism, upon which he overlaid his idealism as a visionary author.

Henry Nash Smith sees the last fifth of the book as Mark Twain in retreat as he "beats his way back from incipient tragedy to the comic resolution" (114), but I disagree that this is going back in a strategic sense. It is indeed going back in an emotional sense, but that is Twain's point: humans do not change and society does not progress. Huck was competent from early on, but he could not maintain his independence, even in the face of his sound-hearted knowledge. The working out of the ending in comedy is fortuitous in corresponding to a good outcome, but its real purpose is to show a truth of humanity that is far sadder than the comic overlay suggests. Getting locked into belletristic literary analysis of a writer like Twain obscures that message. The fact that the novel coalesces so many points at the very last moment of the book is not coincidental but rather the true greatness of a great work of art, formed along the lines of emotional response to echo and imply truths embedded in the action through a variety of symphonic rehearsals, misdirections, burlesques, caricatures, exaggerations, and, ultimately, triumphant gatherings of form and theme.

Works Cited

Blair, Walter, ed. *Mark Twain's Hannibal: Huck and Tom.* Berkeley: University of California Press, 1969.

Botkin, B. A. *Lay My Burden Down: A Folk History of Slavery.* Chicago: University of Chicago Press, 1945.

Burke, Kenneth. "Psychology and Form," in *Counter-statement* [1931]. Berkeley: University of California Press, 1968.

Fishkin, Shelley Fisher. "False Starts, Fragments and Fumbles: Mark Twain's Unpublished Writing on Race." *Essays in Arts and Sciences* 20 (October 1991): 1–26.

———. "Race and Culture at the Century's End: A Social Context for *Pudd'nhead Wilson.*" *Essays in Arts and Sciences* 19 (May 1990): 1–27. Reprinted in Sloane, *Mark Twain's Humor.*

———. *Was Huck Black? Mark Twain and African-American Voices.* New York: Oxford University Press, 1993.

Sloane, David E. E. *Adventures of Huckleberry Finn: American Comic Vision.* Boston: G. K. Hall-Twayne, 1988.

———. *Mark Twain's Humor: Critical Essays.* New York: Garland, 1993. (Includes the essays on *Huck Finn* referenced for Durant Da Ponte, Leslie Fiedler, and Henry Nash Smith.)

Smith, Henry Nash. *Mark Twain: The Development of a Writer.* Cambridge, Mass.: Harvard University Press, 1962.

Twain, Mark. *Adventures of Huckleberry Finn.* Ed. Walter Blair and Victor Fischer. Berkeley: University of California Press, 1985.

Teaching *Huckleberry Finn*:
The Uses of the Last Twelve Chapters
Pascal Covici Jr.

On the basis of a totally unscientific survey, I conclude that those of us lucky enough to have read *Huckleberry Finn* as children—to have read it, as we used to say, "just for fun," not because some teacher assigned it—found the book, including the ending, most satisfying. We didn't worry about the raising of issues—we were unaware that such things as "issues" lurked behind the text. But now we teach the book to young adults, some of whom had our sort of unforced early feeding, most of whom did not. We teach it as serious literature. The seriousness, however, comes from the humor, as I tried to suggest thirty-five years ago in *Mark Twain's Humor: The Image of a World*.

That, however, is my view, one that I'm happy to profess at the drop of a piece of chalk but that my sense of my role as educator leads me to withhold from precise articulation. I'm talking about a classroom, obviously, and not a lecture hall. When I lecture on Mark Twain's novel—or on anything else—I try to tell what I believe, giving the evidence, providing counterevidence, and doing my best to show why I think what I think, and why I think that what I think matters. But mostly I do my teaching, professing, and educating with groups of from twenty to thirty students at a time, and this is the context I intend to address here.

The problem that concerns me most is how to free up a class to discover independently rather than simply to ingest my views. Most of my students do not concentrate in English, although about half are majoring in one of the liberal arts rather than in business or engineering. As with any text, and especially with any very "rich" text, I am interested in getting them to read for themselves, something that we all hope they'll be doing for the rest of their lives. For the penultimate session on the book, we usually work over Huck's decision (in chapter 31) to "go to hell." I ask them to write out before that meeting a brief (no more than two-page) response to the following: " 'By the end of his book, Huck Finn has learned that slavery is wrong, and opposes it.' Do you agree or disagree with this statement? Why?" Because I try as hard as I can not to take sides in the argument that invariably ensues, they seem to feel OK about disagreeing with each other. I remind both "sides" of bits of text useful to their positions, and when someone asks—someone always does—what my own opinion actually is, I promise to say later on. Mostly, I haven't had to because somewhere in the course of discussion, a strong case for distinguishing between Twain and Huck emerges, and then for distinguishing between Huck's perception and the precepts of society that Huck thinks he honors. Most telling of all seems to be the uneven conflict between Huck's weak internalization of corrupt society (Huck's "conscience," as he calls it) and Huck's direct experiencing of Jim's large-spirited humanity.

Then, a few minutes before the end of class, I ask for summary statements—to which I contribute as necessary—and then shift gears by asking if they have any strong views about the last quarter of the book. A few of them repeat what they heard in high school; some have their own reactions; usually, the most I get is a sense that "It's good fun," along with the objection that there's too much of it. Nothing very profound, anyway. So I hand out the assignment for the next meeting: "Many readers find the last twelve chapters of *Huckleberry Finn* tedious or in various other ways uncomfortable to read: the treatment of Jim, Huck's subordination to Tom, and so on. Before entering into the discussion on what these chapters actually accomplish—if anything—consider how Twain ties them to the rest of the book. That is, find as many echoes from earlier in the book as you can and list them by page and chapter on a sheet of paper."

When the class next meets, I begin (their responses now in front of me) by looking at Tom's " 'What! Why, Jim is . . .' " (chapter 33). This I see as the keystone of Twain's entrapment of the reader, but—so far—no undergraduate has noticed that it echoes both Huck's self-interrupted response to Judith Loftus's mention that the townspeople suspect Jim of having killed Huck (" 'Why *he*—" [chapter 11]) and the Duke's similarly self-interrupted response to Huck's request to know to whom the king has sold Jim (" 'A farmer by the name of Silas Ph——' " [chapter 31]). In the two earlier cases, the checking of a spontaneous impulse to reveal the truth is followed by either silence or a lie. Only in Tom's case is this not immediately clear to a reader. I ask if anyone can remember his or her sense of what Tom might have been going to say: "Jim is dead," or "Jim is gone," or "Jim is wanted for your murder," but certainly not "Jim is free," they invariably concur. Then I reveal the two "originals" of this particular echo that they have missed, and they do indeed see that Twain-as-author is making interesting things happen.[1]

But if the "interesting things" that an author makes happen turn out to be so subtle, so rarefied, that only a professor can see them, then hasn't the author failed? This takes us back to their intuitive feeling that somehow, although for reasons seemingly inarticulable, most of them initially found the ending not only inoffensive but satisfying. So we go on to look at what the class's collected echoes accomplish. What latent chains of association might the text be forming in their minds?

On the one hand, there is the position most recently developed by Forrest Robinson but going back—by implication—to Ernest Hemingway's sense of the ending as "cheating."[2] By tacking on the unlikely propositions that Jim's freedom (a) has come about through the guilt of the social conscience as represented by Miss Watson and (b) is something that readers can see (maybe even are encouraged to see) as a happy ending for Jim and for his family, Twain allows us to pretend to ourselves that behavior that we know runs counter to social ideals of democracry and justice need not be viewed so harshly. Slavery isn't serious. Jim is now free; he'll be fine; his abuse by Tom was a cruel joke, to be sure, but we don't need to think about that as the book concludes; we can glory in Huck's distance from Jim, in Huck's compassion for Jim, and ignore the extent to which "human beings *can* be awful cruel to one another" (33:232).[3] The ending, that is, may "feel" right because it allows us to ignore the true nature of the world that Huck has been exploring, of the people whom he has been encountering.

On the other hand, the more one notices how those last chapters echo earlier motifs, issues, elements, the more difficult such ignoring becomes. Tom's dependence on "the books" attracts the attention of almost every reader. At the start of Twain's book, Tom's efforts to bring some drama into his friends' lives smacks of childhood's happy hours. That the other boys resign from the gang because they "hadn't robbed nobody, hadn't killed any people, but only just pretended" (3:12) suggests a failure of imagination as much as any maturing commitment to reality. To be sure, a reader can chuckle over Tom's insistence that captives be "ransomed" as the books demand, even though no one knows what the word means, but most of the chuckling seems to be sympathetic, nostalgic rather than condemnatory.

But by the end of the novel, Tom has lost favor with almost everyone. Huck (and we readers) want Jim freed. We're with Huck all the way when he encourages Tom to "let on" that picks are case knives. He says, " 'When I start in to steal a nigger, or a watermelon, or a Sunday-school book, . . . what I want is my Sunday-school book; . . . and I don't give a dead rat what the authorities thinks about it nuther' " (36:247). Back at the start of the book, when the "Spanish merchants and rich A-rabs" turn out to be a Sunday school picnic, and the robbers find themselves forced to give up even "a hymn-book and a tract" (3:12,13), the laugh is on the boys for interpreting literally Tom's deceptive (but still delight-filled) signifiers. The effect of Tom's escape plot is a bit more complex: so long as Tom seems merely to be bringing romance to bear upon reality—that is, rescuing Jim from slavery by the aid of various bookish devices—some readers can enjoy the phony excitement. Other readers feel impatience at Tom's foolishness, and, if not too distracted by the humor in the incongruities involved in applying the trappings of royalty and chivalry to the doings of raggedy boys and a slave, also feel some compassion for Jim and even wish that poor old Huck could get a little assertive over what Tom is doing to Huck's friend. But readers, as well as Huck himself, never doubt—despite all the commonsense disqualifiers—that Tom Sawyer, respectable member of St. Petersburg civilization though he be, is actually trying to free a slave.

Once the truth is out, all the pieces fit together with a crunch, and Tom as representative of respectable society gets most brutally crunched. "Religgion," as Tom calls it in his long "nonnamous letter" (39:270), has reared its head all through the book, and not merely as a matter of pretense or hypocrisy. But as a pretend cutthroat "from over in the Indian Territory," whose conversion to "religgion" is therefore indeed another pretense, Tom in his note echoes (most immediately) the king's performance as a pirate at the "Parkville" (the king miscalls it "Pokeville") camp meeting (20:131–32). And once a class starts thinking about theatrical performance, even the least imaginative students start making connections. (One undergraduate, who said in response to the assignment that he had absolutely no idea what I meant by "echoes," experienced an epiphany on this realization. He didn't give up his business major and become a dedicated student of literature, but he did end up enjoying what had begun for him as mere fulfillment of a distribution requirement.)

The crucial connection arises from the way in which Twain has the king comment on the success of his spurious conversion. After returning to the raft, he discovers that he has raked in "eighty-seven dollars and seventy-five cents. And . . . a three-gallon jug of whisky, too. . . . The king said, take it all around, it laid over any day he'd ever put in in the missionarying line. He said it warn't no use talking, heathens don't amount to shucks alongside of pirates, to work a camp-meeting with" (20:133). Why don't heathens work as well as pirates? Because the sight of a minister, however legitimate, bound for darkest Africa to convert the traditional "heathens" cannot hope to have the immediately sensational effect of a bona fide pirate. Pirates promise excitement, adventure of a theatricality perhaps to be equaled only by a converted cutthroat "from over in the Indian Territory." To the citizens of Parkville, enmeshed in dull lives, the presence of a mayhem-wreaking pirate is every bit as stimulating as is the anticipation of equally nonexistent cutthroats to the fifteen farmers with guns who crowd into the Phelpses' parlor and then let fly at two boys and a freed slave. The dishonesty of the king has its match in the dishonesty of Tom Sawyer. False religion, contrived excitement, theatrical effects: links aplenty join the king and Tom. Most students by this point are ready to volunteer the duke's brilliant last line on the poster advertising *The Royal Nonesuch* and his comment thereto: "LADIES AND CHILDREN NOT ADMITTED. / 'There,' says he, 'if that line don't fetch them, I don't know Arkansaw!' " (22:150). Of course he does, and of course it does.

These connections come at "great random" (to invoke Hank Morgan, another theatrical gent of Twain's invention), differing from class to class in their particularity as well as in their sequence. The important thing is that they do come. By now, everyone is going far beyond the generally stingy list of "echoes" handed in at the start of the class. I scribble their contributions onto the blackboard as fast as I can, but I also try to group the associations in anticipation of the summary I will try to articulate in the last ten minutes of the period.

The variety of possible directions generated by even my less-promising classes has always far exceeded what were my initial expectations. I myself have been led to see more specifically, therefore more usefully, into the interconnectedness and suggestiveness of Twain's novel than ever before. I find that I have been doing two different sorts of things in class these last few years. On the one hand, I have been helping my students respect their own associations; I have pushed them (as they have pushed me) to put into words why particular echoes might be significant. On the other hand, I have been using our collective success at such exercises in articulation to illuminate a principle dear to us professional readers but often unclear to the young victims of high school oversimplification: no single response does justice to what the text reveals. It is certainly "correct" to say that the reference to "religion" strengthens one's sense that good old Tom—who gives "Jim forty dollars for being prisoner for us so patient, and doing it up so good" (43:292)—is just as cruel a charlatan as the king, who sells Jim for 'forty dirty dollars'" (31:212). But it's equally "correct" to think that both Tom and the king can be seen as no worse—or, from yet another perspective—no better than the two perfectly decent representatives of society who, while hunting for escaped slaves, encounter Huck in his canoe near the raft on which Jim is hiding. Here, too, forty dollars—in the form of two twenty-dollar gold pieces (16:91)—illuminates the gap between active human compassion and the assumption that people are things to be paid for, or to be paid off.

And it is also "correct" to think about the extent to which Tom represents the society from which he pretends to be freeing Jim, representing it both as victimizer, through his penchant for concocting dramatic excitements and entertainments, and as victim of that same lust for the theatrical that he himself unleashes. Tom, to be sure, recovers from his gunshot wound, but apparently—at least in the doctor's view—only because of Jim's help (42:285). His own phony adventures almost do him in. Recipient of hot lead from representatives of his society, he is both a crooked instigator of theatrical delight, like the king, and a victim of that delight, like Buck Grangerford, like Boggs. How could we take seriously his apparently antisocial agreement to help free a slave?

But some members of the class, with equal validity, pay attention to the literary echoes, the titles Tom invokes during his planning of the "evasion" and the titles he refers to as the leader of his gang at the start of the book. This leads to Huck's evocation of Tom both before landing on the wrecked *Walter Scott*—" 'He'd call it an adventure. . . . And wouldn't he throw style into it?'" (12:67)—and during the exploration of that interestingly named ship—" 'Tom Sawyer wouldn't back out now, and so I won't either'" (12.67). And if no one else does, I recall that this emulation of Tom leads to Huck's efforts to use the books he finds on the steamboat to explain "to Jim about dukes and kings" (14:76), and then to the problem of King Solomon, his harem, and his apparent disregard for the value of a child. Jim, Huck will eventually conclude, "cared just as much for his people as white folks does for their'n" (23: 155), even though "[i]t don't seem natural" that this should be the case. And back we go to the end of the book, to the fact of Pap's death and recollections of how much this particular "white"—this "white to make a body sick, . . . to make a body's flesh crawl" (5:19)—"cared" for his son. And the death of Pap emerges in the context of the safety of Huck's $6,000 (43:293), the same amount that Huck returns to the Wilks orphans by placing it in the coffin containing their father's corpse.

I am sure that in Victor Doyno's classes, the literary references would lead to a fruitful exploration of sensational literature, of cheap foreign reprints, of Twain's sly thrust at Judge William Henry Blodgett's refusal to honor Twain's ownership of his own pseudonym.[4] (The king acquires the information for his appearance as the Reverend Harvey Wilks by first becoming " 'Elexander Blodgett—Reverend Elexander Blodgett' " [24:158–59].) And all of this, too, takes one back to the mainstream quality of Tom's plans for the evasion. Even the music to be used by Jim to soothe the rats with which Tom and Huck will infest the place of his captivity has its origin in the Grangerfords' parlor, where "nothing was ever so lovely as to hear the young ladies sing 'The Last Link is Broken' " (17:104), the very tune that Tom urges Jim to play on his jew's-harp as " 'the thing that'll scoop a rat quicker 'n anything else' " (38:263).

Just where the reverberations of a given echo end differs with each listener, thereby making this a fine book with which to bolster the self-confidence of students who feel that they cannot "do" English. For example: Huck finds the blade of an old saw (6:24), cuts his way out of Pap's cabin (Huck's prison), and makes sure that he has hidden all signs of the cut he has made, both before (6:25) and after (7:32) his escape. Tom plans to saw through the leg of Jim's bed (35:240) and to hide the sawdust by eating it. But after they hide it via ingestion, "it give us a most amazing stomach-ache. We reckoned we was all going to die" (39:267). Huck's adventures are real; Tom's are gratuitous. Huck respects Tom and wishes for his presence as one who would add "fancy touches" (7:33) and "style" (12:67); but by the time that he anticipates the possible effects of the "style" of Tom's way of freeing Jim, he can "see in a minute it . . . would maybe get us all killed" (34:234). Despite

Huck's respect for respectability and for the respectable, the respect that informs him that he is hell-bound because he is freeing a slave, he comes, finally, to express reservations even about Tom Sawyer. And all this from following up a saw blade. And as with the discoveries triggered by any particular set of perceived echoes, or associations, other readers can easily test this one against the general drift of the narrative. Does it fit? If so, why? If not, where did we lose the trail?

How does one read the low-keyed observation, in the book's last paragraph, about Tom's glory-seeking? Tom has "his bullet around his neck on a watch-guard for a watch, and is always seeing what time it is." Is Huck respectful, scornful, or simply reportorial? Jim, at the start of chapter 2, puts around his neck a nickel, Tom Sawyer's reimbursement for some adventure-facilitating candles. He "said it was a charm the devil give to him . . . ," and a very useful charm it turns out to be: the other slaves would "give Jim anything they had, just for a sight of" it, and "Jim was most ruined, for a servant." Jim's intelligent deception, disguised as merely the superstition of an ignorant slave, leads to monetary gain and release from labor. Tom's deception feeds a desire for glory. Which one has the better excuse for his chicanery? How much of a "devil" does Tom show himself to be? What does Huck think?

Huck acts on perception, as has by now become a useful commonplace. His conscience may make him feel bad—it is as corrupt as the society from which it comes—but his actions finally stem from his own experience. That experience turns out to be considerably deeper and broader than Tom's, but Huck remains the inarticulate observer. He can describe, but he does not analyze. Tom brings the whole book swirling into a reader's mind with the surprising observation that Jim is " 'as free as any cretur that walks this earth!' " (42:289). Huck reports the statement but says nothing about it. Pap's diatribe about the " 'free nigger' " from Ohio, actually " 'a p'fessor in a college' " (6:27), provides a useful perspective: how free is either the professor or his critic? How free are the "creturs" whom Huck has encountered? It takes very little to start a class going on the feuding families, on the victims of the king and the duke, and—perhaps most tellingly—on Tom himself.

The cross-dressing instigated by Tom in the evasion (39:268–69; 42: 284), as it resonates with Huck's disguise when he visits Judith Loftus (10:54; 11:55 ff.), has just recently begun to appear on students' lists, perhaps as feminist concerns enter the classroom. Laura Skandera-Trombley ("In Defense of Mark Twain's Judith Loftus," delivered at the

ALA meeting in 1992) has already had much to say about the drowned woman dressed as a man whose corpse leads "people" to assume that Pap is dead (3:11). Because this initial cross-dressing seems to pass by the attention of my particular readers, I point it out after we have discussed the possible significances of Tom's ludicrous insistence that Huck disguise himself as a " 'servant-girl,' " even though it is only for fifteen minutes in the middle of the night, to deliver the "nonnamous letter." And there is more. Tom himself, in a gown of Aunt Sally's that he will "hook," will be Jim's mother for a few minutes. Finally, at the moment of the actual evasion, while Tom stuffs Jim's clothes full of straw and leaves them on Jim's bed " 'to represent his mother in disguise,' " Jim will then " 'take the nigger woman's gown off me [Tom] and wear it, and we'll all evade together.' "

No one can keep all these details from chapter 39 straight. Tom Sawyer himself could not: is Jim really to " 'take the nigger woman's gown off of' " Tom? If so, how will Tom come to be wearing it, if he is to use a gown of Aunt Sally's? Well, on with the grand evasion! In chapter 42, when Aunt Sally sees Tom returning on a mattress with the doctor, she also sees "Jim, in *her* calico dress, with his hands tied behind him. . . ." Not "a" dress, which would be surprising enough, but "*her*" dress, a kind of lèse majesté that Twain gives Huck no time to follow up but that, however briefly, contrasts Jim's sterling behavior with the late-nineteenth-century clichés concerning black men and white women.

Tom's cross-dressing, ending in a bullet wound for Tom himself and unjust and prolonged captivity for Jim, emphasize the consequences of the playacting that means so much to Tom and to his society at large. It also has interesting ironic overtones in that the plight of Jim as a freed slave and the plight of women in Twain's view have immense cross-referential bearing on each other. Political, economic, and social helplessness—for any class interested in looking into such matters—will repay scrutiny. Huck's cross-dressing for the sake of finding out the lay of the land from Judith Loftus makes a clear contrast with the gratuitous pretense of Tom's phony escape plot. As a result of Huck's investiture in female garb, Huck learns of a plan to capture Jim, rushes back to Jackson's Island, and, in one of the more vivid episodes of reidentification of self in the book, calls out, " 'Git up and hump yourself, Jim! There ain't a minute to lose. They're after us!' " (11:62). No one, of course, is after Huck; but Huck has already, without fully knowing it, cast in his lot with Jim. Also, as Skandera-Trombley has so clearly reminded readers, Huck has found out what it means to be female: a girl is someone who cannot come within six feet of hitting a rat with a piece of lead, cannot catch, and even threads a needle differently from the way a man does. No wonder Huck says "us" to Jim; trying to play the part of a girl has taught him a little bit more (than have even Pap and the Widow Douglas) about what it means to be powerless.

Many of these points and questions emerge only in some classes. If a particular set of students is tired of beating the dying feminist horse— as by now it has become on some campuses, I gather, though not on my own—then so be it. But that initial, never-explained bit of crossdressing remains part of the book. What might it be good for? Does it have anything to do with Tom's almost equally grim disguises at the end? The woman dressed as a man, after all, was dead in the river. Whatever the reason for her disguising herself, for her—as for Jim and Tom and Huck—no evasion was possible, except for the final one of death. Skandera-Trombley suggests that Twain may have designed the nameless woman, and even Judith Loftus herself, to suggest involvement in the cause of abolition. Whether or not one finds this persuasive—the argument is complex, the statements "interesting, but tough" (17:100)—the position adds to one's sense that, beyond Huck's limited perspective, the mind of Twain works on and on.

For me, one fruitful sequence has been from the last cross-dressing in the book to the first, and then to speculations on possibilities. That is, Tom's observation that Jim " 'is as free as any cretur that walks this earth' " leads first to "creturs" encountered throughout the book who seem enslaved to the values and approvals of their neighbors. Then it raises questions about what Jim's "freedom" will really amount to. Further, it leads one to think of Tom, imprisoned as representative of his society, and of Huck, as having nowhere to turn. Neither the last nor the first cross-dressing has led to any "freedom." But Huck's—the second example—has led directly to the fabulous raft journey down the Mississippi. Where has Huck known love and (even if only at times) the feeling of freedom? On the river, with Jim. But now Jim's plans are to free his family. Where can Huck go? On and on down the river, to the gulf, and death? To the Injun Territory, ahead of the others, so as to avoid Aunt Sally's and other efforts to civilize him? "As free as any cretur that walks this earth" becomes Tom's final rattling of the chains that Tom does not even recognize. Twain does, however; and this is the grim note on which I like to end each class's encounter with *Adventures of Huckleberry Finn.*

I have tried to be suggestive without being simply vague, while making at least somewhat clear why it is that I find the ending of *Adventures of Huckleberry Finn* endlessly fascinating and extremely useful in the classroom. Whether in courses on American literature generally or in the particular "Mark Twain and the Tradition of American Humor" course that I often teach, the immediately accessible surface of this novel seems to give most students the confidence to look for more than they see at first. Although some of them (especially those who have read *The Adventures of Tom Sawyer*) have a hard time giving up their early adulation of Tom, they do seem to think about what Twain may have been getting at when he had Huck refer to the "stretchers" (1.1) in that earlier work. And once students begin to think, we have begun to do our job.

Notes

1 These two anticipations of Tom's prevarication came to my attention through the kindness of David W. Hiscoe, whose "The 'Abbreviated Ejaculation' in *Huckleberry Finn*" appeared in *Studies in American Humor* 1, n.s. (1983): 191–97.

2 Forrest G. Robinson, *In Bad Faith: The Dynamics of Deception in Mark Twain's America* (Cambridge, Mass.: Harvard University Press, 1986).

3 All references by chapter and page will be to the Holt, Rinehart and Winston edition of *Huckleberry Finn* (New York, 1948), with an introduction by Lionel Trilling.

4 Victor A. Doyno, *Writing "Huck Finn": Mark Twain's Creative Process* (Philadelphia: University of Pennsylvania Press, 1991), 189.

"Blame de pint! I reck'n I knows what I knows."
Ebonics, Jim, and New Approaches to
Understanding *Adventures of Huckleberry Finn*
Jocelyn Chadwick-Joshua

Is reading *Adventures of Huckleberry Finn* really hazardous to the health of students? What miraculous transformation do high school and college students experience when they hear racial slurs in films such as *Pulp Fiction, Natural Born Killers,* or the gangsta rap lyrics from Snoop Doggy Dogg or Tupac Shakur that makes them resilient to hearing this use of language and yet extremely sensitive to Jim's and Huck's use of their versions of Standard English in the slaveholding South? What fears do concerned parents feel about their children's reading *Huck Finn* that they do not feel about these films and raps? How can we, on the one hand, rationalize and legitimize the use of ebonics, or Black English, and, on the other hand, deny Jim and the other slaves in this novel their voices? More specifically, can we ethically defend the training of teachers and the creation of curricula to meet the requirements of ebonics while denying them the right to teach *Huckleberry Finn*? And, finally, how do the proponents of ebonics defend this kind of intellectual hobbling while at the same time arguing against the dialect of the Southern slave under the guise of the terms "minstrelsy," "stereotype," and "Uncle Tomism"? Given the current state of affairs (and to their absolute shock), however, Twain's *Huck Finn* would qualify surprisingly by the standards of the proponents of ebonics as an appropriate book to use to train teachers in this "unique language, thereby putting it on a level with foreign languages." So what has changed, and how did we get here? What are we to do now? And more importantly, who is caring about the young, imaginative minds of students and the creative imaginations and expertise of their teachers?

The nineteenth-century South routinely practiced the punishment of hobbling slaves who tried to run away and were caught or who were constant sources of rebellion. Rebellion included any overt mastery of English—mastery such as Jim and Jack in *Huck Finn* and Roxy and

Chambers in *The Tragedy of Pudd'nhead Wilson* display. But rebel the slaves did, and often through the mastering of English to some extent. Such slaves not only suffered hobbling, but in some cases owners or overseers killed them, for all of them understood the power of language. One has only to read nineteenth- and early twentieth-century African American periodicals to understand clearly that this issue was a real concern. Twain's rendering the slaves' language in their own voice and with their own words not only legitimizes their use of dialect but also reveals within Standard English many levels of stratification while yet revealing basic linguistic constructions of English. For example, Jim and the other African American characters display a solid, working concept of basic sentence patterns as well as an ability to construct more complex ones. Just like many Americans who are wholly unaware of the kinds of sentence patterns they use, they use them. Reading actual slave narratives substantiates this point.

I can remember a time when teachers from all instructional areas, including athletics, believed that it was their individual responsibility to correct any student's use of the English language. The use of slang, hip-hop, and, even a rather pronounced Southern dialect was monitored so carefully that for a student to get away with saying "wuz" for was or "jis'" for "just" always merited on-the-spot correction. The notion of ebonics' creating within students a sense of self-esteem or racial pride was not even an issue. That students would need this linguistic crutch as an explanation for nonmastery of Standard English was a moot point.

But this discussion regarding the use of a Southern dialect and its effects on readers has its roots in the nineteenth century itself. One of the very reasons the Concord Public Library banned *Adventures of Huckleberry Finn* was that the use of Southern dialects and the perceived misuse of Standard English would put children or any well-respected citizen at risk. As one member of the Concord Library Committee stated:

I have examined the book and my objections to it are these: It deals with a series of adventures of a very low grade or morality; it is couched in the language of a rough, ignorant dialect, and all through its pages there is a systematic use of bad grammar and an employment of rough, coarse inelegant expressions. It is also very irreverent. To sum up, the book is flippant and irreverent in its style. It deals with a series of experiences that are certainly not elevating. The whole book is of a class that is more profitable for the slums than it is for respectable people, and it is trash of the veriest sort.

Ironically, what makes the novel so controversial today and has, for instance, precipitated its banning from the library and eradication from the required reading list in Caddo Parish, Louisiana, in 1988, is the very issue that caused the Concord Public Library to ban the novel in 1885—namely, audience sensitivity. The indictments regarding the novel's lack of concern for audience sensitivity have ranged from the novel's blatant burlesque of middle-class philosophies and values to its vulgarization of standard English to racial insensitivity to African American male bashing, or castration. With every protestation and attempted banning, we teachers of English and American Studies have found ourselves rising to the occasion with our traditionally acceptable disclaimer: Mark Twain's *Adventures of Huckleberry Finn* is a recognized American classic—even, according to T. S. Eliot, an epic.

The results of such a ban, of course, are not what the committee member anticipates with regard to the book's or Twain's lasting popularity and vitality. That so many articles and books in addition to discussion groups have continued to examine this novel and that it still creates significant dialogue testify to its continued importance to the social, cultural, and educational scenes.

But how does it impact recent discussions on the pros and cons of ebonics, or Black English? This essay seeks to explore the argument that supports the pedagogical importance of ebonics and the resulting paradox that such an argument creates when *Adventures of Huckleberry Finn* is factored into the equation.

Ebonics, the brainchild of Molefi Asante almost twenty-five years ago, describes this combination of ebony and phonics as the melding of the languages of the West African slaves with their adopted slave language, English. What proponents of ebonics, such as Asante, do not address, however, emerges with the absence of complete and objectively focused information regarding this issue and with the all-encompassing concerns of African Americans. Writer and critic Albert Murray, for example, strongly asserts that ebonics reveals not a separate and distinguishable language at all. Murray states that what many are currently describing as ebonics is nothing more than an amalgam of hip-hop, slang, and a penchant for consciously using incorrect grammar. According to Murray, English does possess distinctive African American traits, but those traits emerge in what he describes as the words and phrases that accentuate and create tonal amplification to Standard English. He further distinguishes language such as that Jim uses as the language of any American who has had to master the use of Standard English aurally rather than formally. Hence, Jim's statement to Huck, "I knows what I knows," reveals not a language distinctive unto itself but a language representative of a time, a period in the United States when survival in part rested on the slave's ability to master a vernacular and tongue deliberately made not his own.

So should we try to explain away Huck's and Jim's many syntactical errors as well as pronunciation problems? And can we delineate so clearly between a negative response to this contemporary usage and a modern rationalization for its use? In the Oakland, California, school district today the proponents of ebonics, such as board member Toni Cook, contend that without the attention they are giving to this form of speech, African American students essentially lack the self-esteem, the cultural legacy, and the ability to effectively gain access to the educational system. This form of speech permeates the linguistic structure so decisively and clearly, according to its proponents, that teachers must also have a working knowledge of it in addition to creating an efficacious pedagogical strategy to meet these students on their levels. Although no one can deny the significance and sincerity of the intent, I am particularly fascinated by proponents' ability to distinguish and qualify between ebonics and the language of Twain's Jim, as well as other Southern slaves.

Teachers and parents must realize that with *Adventures of Huckleberry Finn*, Twain provides a descriptive and often uncomfortable exploration into the lives of two types of Southern slaves—those who decide to run for freedom and those who do not. More importantly, Twain provides for us the journey of an unsuccessful attempt, an approach that was not often explored in such detail during the nineteenth century. Finally, teachers and parents must recognize that Jim in this novel must confront perhaps the most difficult decision any runaway slave would ever face: what price freedom?

The dilemma that Jim's freedom versus his societal enslavement represents is a dialogue that Twain's novel begins and Ralph Ellison's *Invisible Man* continues. What Ellison accomplishes with his novel, in essence, is to complete the hypothesis that Twain posits with *Adventures of Huckleberry Finn*—namely, what does one do with a slave today who as of tomorrow will no longer be an individual denied the American promise of freedom and total equality? Ellison says:

> I am an invisible man. No, I am not a spook like those who haunted Edgar Allan Poe; nor am I one of your Hollywood-movie ectoplasms. I am a man of substance, of flesh and bone, fiber and liquids—and I might even be said to possess a mind. I am invisible, understand, simply because people refuse to see me. . . . It is as though I am surrounded by mirrors of hard, distorting glass. When they approach me they see only my surroundings, themselves, or figments of their imagination—indeed, everything and anything except me.
>
> Nor is my invisibility exactly a matter of a biochemical accident to my epidermis. That invisibility to which I refer occurs because of a peculiar disposition of the eyes of those with whom I came in contact. A matter of construction of their inner eyes upon reality. . . . It's when you feel like this [a phantom in other people's minds] that, out of resentment, you begin to bump people back. . . . He bumped me, he insulted me. Shouldn't he, for his own personal safety, have recognized my hysteria, my "danger potential"? He, let us say, was lost in a dream world. But didn't he control that dream world—which, alas, is only too real!—and didn't he rule me out of it? And if he had yelled for a policeman, wouldn't I have been taken for the offending one?

Jim, Jack, the Wilks's slaves, and the other slaves encountered in the novel are, on the one hand, invisible, while, on the other hand, they gain visibility as the narrative unfolds. But their visibility is limited and qualified, at best, and it is this fact that Twain delivers and explores through their language in *Adventures of Huckleberry Finn*.

In the verbal battle between Huck and Jim on language and Louis the Sixteenth and his possible escape to America, Huck attempts to explain the rationale for the French language and for the value of any language different from English. Jim counters by asking why everyone cannot speak the same language:

> "Dat's good! But he'll be pooty lonesome—dey ain' no kings here, is dey, Huck?"

"No."

"Den he cain't git no situation. What he gwyne to do?"

"Well, I don't know. Some of them gets on the police, and some of them learns people how to talk French."

"Why, Huck, doan de French people talk de same way we does?"

"*No*, Jim; you couldn't understand a word they said—not a single word."

"Well, now, I be ding-busted! How do dat come?"

"*I* don't know; but it's so. I got some of their jabber out of a book. Spose a man was to come to you and say *Polly-voo-franzy*—what would you think?"

"I wouldn' think nuff'n; I'd take en bust him over de head. Dat is, ef he warn't white. I wouldn't 'low no nigger to call me dat."

"Shucks, it ain't calling you anything. It's only saying do you know how to talk French."

"Well, den, why couldn't he *say* it?"

"Why, he *is* a-saying it. That's a Frenchman's *way* of saying it."

This argument ultimately concludes with Jim's asserting that a man must talk like a man and nothing else, regardless of his cultural origins or ethnicity. The focus for Jim is communication.

One critical question we must ask of ourselves is: should we remove certain pieces of literature from students because, as the Concord Library member commented, out of sight, out of mind, and therefore everyone can breathe a sigh of complacent relief? What opponents think they have gained in this sacrifice is significant and substantial attention to racial sensitivity, cultural diversity, ethnocentrism, androcentrism, and gender sensitivity. For example, a recent piece of legislation, House Bill 154, in the Texas legislature, sponsored by Representative Ron Wilson, would require that all curricula include "human rights issues, with particular attention to the study of the inhumanity of genocide, slavery, and the Holocaust." Does not great literature accomplish this objective, plus so many more, without the orchestrated political maneuvering of such legislation? Certainly, *Adventures of Huckleberry Finn* engages the reader immediately in a discourse not only about the issue of slavery, but also about child abuse, greed, illiteracy, pride, honor, religious hypocrisy, loyalty, ethics, and morality—all involving human rights, I should think. Does passage of such legislation guarantee that the teacher will teach the material any differently or that the student's perspective will experience significant transformation? I think not.

It is not legislation, book banning, or curriculum micromanaging that makes for excellent teaching and productive learning. The freedom to be creative and choose what one teaches as well as knowing exactly why, and the security in knowing that one's professional decisions will be honored and trusted—even if questions about classroom value should arise—represent the bond between good literature, the teacher, and the reading student. Can such a transformative relationship be prefigured, and, more importantly, should it be? No. Good literature must communicate, does communicate, and then creates within the reader a desire to know more, to read further, to ask that sensitive question, to listen to the equally sensitive responses, and to engage further in substantive discussions.

The essential distinguishing factor, then, between Twain's opponents and Twain himself lies in Twain's stylistic approach, an approach that allows—even demands—that each individual read and determine for himself or herself the truths and facts as the narrative lays them out with no externally imposed code of behavior and response. That Jim and other slaves speak in their own language further facilitates the novel's relationship with the audience. The teacher provides the milieu in which the student will experience the literary text and context— positively or negatively. Ideally, the teacher is a conduit for Twain as well as for any other writer presented in class. At-Risk, Gifted and Talented, Advanced Placement, Academic, or Regular students all deserve the right to experience great literature in the language that the author deems appropriate.

Fortunately or unfortunately, depending on one's perspective, every person from the nation's chief executive to the average citizen has "the definitive definition" of the problem of literature that is deemed sensitive, particularly because of literature's use and delivery of language, as well as the "quintessential solution" to the problem of the perceived necessary reform. Needless to say, these analyses and solutions have a greater impact on certain departments than on others. Consequently, English departments and their curricula, syllabi, and appropriate pedagogical strategies experience modifications. Never before have Language Arts teachers been under such tumultuous stress and anxiety as they have in the 1990s. The rate of book censorship has increased by 50 percent just within the last two years (1995–96), according to both the

American Library Association and People for the American Way. Those of us who teach at the college level and feel, perhaps, that such attacks could never happen to us and, therefore, have no relevance to us should and must think again. Not only are we subject to that same kind of censorship by the same parents and concerned citizens, but we are most definitely affected by the intellectual quality of the students from the war zones of the never-ending controversy over sensitive books.

The promised effect of censorship actions is always for such reasons as "the protection and moral health of the students" or "the psychological and sociological well-being of African-American students." The concomitant deletions, (re)classifications, and substitutions, we are told, will enhance student learning, critical thinking, social interaction, and value judgments. In Texas, for example, one such concerned citizen contended that eliminating Twain's *Adventures of Huckleberry Finn* and *The Tragedy of Pudd'nhead Wilson* would have absolutely no ill-effect on students, much less on teachers. Jim's language skills particularly disturbed her. This individual sought to ban all of Twain's works from the library and the classroom. How are we to respond to individuals and groups like these with specific regard to Mark Twain and his *Adventures of Huckleberry Finn*? Too often we rely on teachers to do battle alone with irate but concerned parents and baffled school administrators who have not read this novel since they were in high school. And we expect teachers to maintain simultaneously the spontaneity and vivacity necessary to engage attentive students on whom none of this controversy is lost, not even the one involving ebonics. Most often, these students, to their parents' surprise and to their teachers' joy, want the choice and responsibility of reading Twain's *Adventures of Huckleberry Finn* and *The Tragedy of Pudd'nhead Wilson*. Realistically, what is motivating them is not some insatiable, intellectual desire for knowledge as much as it is their recognition of a privilege, an inherent American right, being denied without possibility of appeal. To their surprise and our delight, they do discover Jim and Huck and Tom and Pap and the free Northern Professor, realizing that not only does Twain speak to his own time, but he speaks to an age that most definitely includes them. In students' minds, the language issue becomes one of an inability to comprehend a nineteenth-century vocabulary such as Jim's references to boarding house and nursery to redefine "harem."

As teachers and, of course, being the "trusting souls" that we are, we gather unto ourselves our literature books, lecture notes, and a "dream vision" of what the literature is "supposed" to mean to these students; and we conjoin them with "new and improved and guaranteed" lists and strategic approaches: lists of enabling objectives, lists of performance objectives, and lists of terminal performance objectives, exit tests, and language enhancements (ebonics), if we are high school teachers. If we teach in college, we look at and lament what is happening, but we have no prescriptive solution to educate and debate the opposition.

Parents from the nation's capital to Connecticut to Texas to Arizona to California to New York have expressed identical sentiments about Twain's *Huck Finn*—namely, that it is too difficult to read because of the Southern dialect, too subtle in its message, too expectant that the audience will have a working knowledge of nineteenth-century America. What we most often fail to convey to parents is that these assertions apply to most of the literature which their children read, not just *Huck Finn*. Would students understand without question the following selections?

> My lord, as I was sewing in my closet,
> Lord Hamlet with his doublet all unbraced
> No hat upon his head, his stocking feet
> Ungartered, and down-gyved to his ankle,
> Pale as his shirt, his knees knocking each other,
> And with a look so piteous in purport,
> As if he had been losed out of hell
> To speak of horrors—he come before me. (2.1.77–84)

Or:

> Rearrived on expense account this time you take the limousine to the Battle House not so much remembering the stopover in Atlanta as continuing the interior monologue you began months ago back in Lenox Terrace. . . . As for the pact about being about being a nigger, the most obvious thing about that was that you were nota whicker-bill different like them old peckerwoods were, because you didn't like it and you didn't talk and walk like that and you couldn't stand that old billy-goat-saw fiddle music.

The first, from Shakespeare's *Hamlet*, and the last, from Albert Murray's *South to a Very Old Place*—one Renaissance, the other autobiographically Harlem Renaissance; each encapsulates one facet of this essay's essential argument. Regardless of the students' academic levels, ethnicities, and class and regional differences, they must always navigate a text's language, a language usually different from their own immediate experiences. To expect literature, a great literature, to meet the expectations of a common-denominator audience reveals a naïve understanding of literature's very purpose.

It should not surprise us, therefore, when we ask students to discuss and write about a work's contemporary social implications or modern parallels, and they respond by telling us the "story didn't say anything worth talking or writing about." But these very issues and characters necessitate our continued teaching of *Huck Finn* as well as other racially and culturally sensitive works to all our students.

If we accept the responsibility of teaching *Adventures of Huckleberry Finn*, for example, we must (1) reassess our purpose for teaching it, (2) revise our focus, and (3), most importantly, reevaluate our audience and thereby restructure our teaching strategies. Mark Twain's masterpiece provides the perfect model for this kind of realignment because this novel, since its publication in 1885, has been at the center of a storm of controversy for a variety of reasons. Even in the midst of controversy, this novel yet affirms friendship and sacrifice, thereby rendering the acquisition of human rights framed in adventure. Unfortunately, when all of these approaches fail and our students still look at us askance, we assert boldly, "This novel is good for you, and you'll appreciate having read it later on, when you're older." Such responses worked well on many of us who were in school during the 1970s, 1960s, and earlier. This statement, surprisingly, continues to work on those of us who are destined to become teachers and researchers of literature and literary history. But such statements have failed miserably with today's students—and society at-large—who, like Diogenes of Sinope in the fourth century BC, seek the light of truth and clearer understanding in their own pragmatic, psychosocial reality rather than in our academic world.

So where does effective teaching of *Huck Finn* put us today in relation to our students and their parents? First, we must ascertain whether our purpose for teaching this work now is the same as it was for teaching it to earlier students. And we must honestly and objectively deduce whether we can achieve the same objective with another literary work that is less controversial than *Huck Finn*. In facing these considerations, I assert that our motive for teaching this American classic still echoes what some nineteenth- and twentieth-century teachers, scholars, and critics, such as Frederick Douglass, Andrew Lang, Joel Chandler Harris, Ralph Ellison, T. S. Eliot, Lionel Trilling, Langston Hughes, and many others have contended. Our aim in continuing to include *Huck Finn* in the American literary canon for exploration and close reading by students stems from the following:

–To introduce students to variegated Southern dialects.
–To allow students to examine the psychosocial dynamics of relationships among master and slave, freedman and Southerner, fugitive slave and abolitionist, along with Twain's ironic juxtaposition of "traditional" relationships of family and friends with nontraditional ones.
–To provide students historical and, thereby, contemporary insight into the cultural, social, political, and religious hierarchies of the pre-Civil War United States.
–To allow students who are psychologically, socially, and politically removed to experience a microcosmic rendering of the historical question and paradox of slavery and abolition.
–To provide students with an opportunity to examine such abstract concepts as freedom, democracy, slavery, miscegenation, honor, and loyalty.

Many works by writers of color—such as Harriet Jacobs's *Incidents in the Life of a Slave Girl*; Frederick Douglass's *Narrative of the Life of Frederick Douglass, An American Slave*; Frances Harper's *Iola Leroy, Or Shadows Uplifted*; Pauline Hopkins's *Contending Forces: A Romance Illustrative of Negro Life North and South*; Toni Morrison's *Beloved*; Margaret Walker's *Jubilee*; even Ntozake Shange's *sassafras, cypress, and indigo*—exhaustively explore the depths of slavery and its effects on enslaved and freed African Americans, but they are no less controversial in terms of audience sensitivity.

The primary contemporary issue of complaint and, subsequently, censorship of the novel was established in 1957 with the NAACP's objection to the novel's "racial slurs" and "belittling racial designations." This audience reaction has increased with time and remains the strongest protest with which the novel must contend. In conjunction with this complaint is the most recent psychosocial concern—namely, that Jim's depiction only serves to emasculate young African American males and embarrass young African American females. John H. Wallace, for example, in "The Case Against Huck Finn," asserts:

> [his] own research indicates that the assignment and reading aloud of "Huckleberry Finn" in our classrooms is humiliating and insulting to black students. It contributes to their feelings of low self-esteem and to the white students' disrespect for black people. It constitutes mental cruelty, harassment, and outright racial intimidation to force black students to sit in the classroom with their white peers and read "Huckleberry Finn." . . . If this book is removed from the required reading lists of our schools, there should be improved student-to-student, student-to-teacher, and teacher-to-teacher relationships.

That Wallace's critique focuses on Twain's rendering of Jim is clear.

Another example of this perspective occurred recently in Arizona, where critics of the novel cited Jim as the primary onus to all African Americans. But what such critics fail to acknowledge is that each of the previous works cited, works by African Americans, contains its own unique version of Jim and each work contains the epithet "nigger." To this fact, Wallace responds that while works like these do use "nigger," they were never intended for adolescent audiences. To this assertion I would send the critics to the introduction of Frances Harper's *Iola Leroy*. William Still states, "Doubtless the thousands of colored Sunday-schools in the South, in casting about for an interesting, moral story-book, full of practical lessons, will not be content to be without 'Iola Leroy, Or Shadows Uplifted.' " I would further assert that particularly Morrison's *Beloved*, Jacobs's *Incidents in the Life of a Slave Girl*, and Douglass's *Narrative* have been accepted without significant, if any, protestations. It must also be noted here that most of the works I have cited as well as others like them are far more graphic in language and theme than *Huck Finn*.

While *Huck Finn* might not be the quintessential novel to explore the pre-Civil War United States of the 1840s (although I earnestly assert that it is), the work certainly represents a balanced, focused perspective that circumvents issues which more mature audiences would better appreciate—issues such as miscegenation, random rape, brutal, inhumane punishment and torture, and destruction of the family unit. And it does so relying on the language of its time and characters. It could be further proposed that teaching this novel and exposing students to Jim and Huck with the aforementioned multifaceted purposes can enable and empower students not to avoid what is painful, not to thereby consign to the outer reaches of consciousness what should be confronted directly. Teaching this novel and permitting Jim and Huck to be as Twain allows them to evolve can help students develop their critical thinking about themselves, their country, their past and contemporary history, their perceived and real truths.

With this kind of purpose focused on the novel, we must change our evaluation of our audience. We usually teach *Huck Finn* to high school juniors and seniors and to college undergraduates and graduate students. Many of these students' singular historical and multicultural points of reference rests solely on strong visual and aural images that too often perpetuate the very racial, gender, and cultural stereotypes condemned in *Huck Finn*. In addition to fictional characters, highly persuasive and visual song lyrics, trashy sitcoms, and urban exploitation films further sculpt and define for their young audiences the dominant societal view of minorities and women. And should we doubt this assessment, when was the last (or first) time we explored the question of welfare mothers, "superhuman" athletes, and teenage men in handcuffs charged with violent crimes without thinking "black," and thereby having an immediate image, sound, and imagined picture of action firmly, immediately, and implacably in place?

Again, it is certainly ironic that although many teenagers and twenty-somethings can understand the jargon and slang used by individuals and mediums such as these without the aid of the *Oxford English Dictionary*, when these same students read the first sentences that Huck and Jim speak, they say, "Say what?" These are our honors, talented and gifted, regular, and remedial high school and college students. They are African American, Hispanic, European American, Asian American, Native American, and the forever ambiguous "Other." They span the socioeconomic spectrum. Some have aspirations to further their education. Some hope just to make it to the next level. Some aspire to become entrepreneurs. And some—though we are loath to admit it—intend to become nothing at all. What many of them have in common, however, in the midst of all this diversity is their parents' initial and common abhorrence of *Adventures of Huckleberry Finn*. The students consequently meet Jim and label him a man with a "wimp factor" and Huck as some kind of "guy" with whom they have nothing in common.

What makes today's high school and college audiences even more enigmatic is that each ethnicity brings its own real and perceived historical baggage with it. Nowhere is this phenomenon more prevalent than with young African Americans. Many of these students fit the profile that I described earlier with regard to socioeconomic and entertainment diversity. And because they fit this profile, they tend to tunnel-read so that, to them, Jim alone speaks with a dialect. In fact, many of them miss the fact that the only factor of delineation between Pap Finn and Jim with regard to dialect rests not with race inferiority and race privilege but with literacy consciously refused and societally denied, respectively. Furthermore, African American students tend to ignore the Northern Professor whom Pap Finn encounters and his historical significance in chapter 6. Through this character, Twain introduces his Southern audience, and our twentieth-century one, to a person of color who votes, speaks several languages, possesses proof of his free status, and, more importantly, represents to Southern slaves like Jim and to racists like Pap a persistent reminder of what can happen when individuals control their own destiny.

These students, along with other ethnicities reading this work, if not attended to appropriately and efficaciously, eventually experience what I identify as ethnic isolation. They withdraw from the class and the teacher, not to mention the work, and quietly seethe in frustration and real as well as perceived embarrassment. The problem stems, it seems, from what Ralph Ellison stated as being the failure to identify with "Nigger Jim" or his plight. And, of course, as Kenneth Burke in *A Rhetoric of Motives* asserts, literature and history function more effectively when the audience can achieve rhetorical identification and as a result consubstantiality with the message being conveyed in a piece of discourse.

What must occur, then, is a refocusing and, logically, a restructuring of the pedagogical strategies for introducing and thus allowing Huck's and Jim's voices, and, indeed, the voice of nineteenth-century America, to emerge and evolve. Simply assigning this novel to high school and college students alike and then lecturing on Twain's artistic style, rhetorical motivation and purpose, and scholarly response fail to adequately enable and empower students to assume possession of this piece of discourse. Such approaches further fail to allow comprehensive access to Huck's and Jim's psychosocial realities. Without this kind of empowerment and access, students necessarily experience the novel and its central characters on the peripheries of life rather than at its nucleus.

In addition to these complications, instructors themselves some-times bring gender, cultural, and racial baggage into their classes. The resulting stereotyping—both the benevolent and the radical kinds—ex-acerbates an already sensitive situation. Consequently, what is likely to occur is what Miami-Dade Junior College did in 1969—remove *Huck Finn* from the curriculum, based on the belief that the novel inhibits the learning process because it creates an "emotional block for black students."

To avoid, or at least to ameliorate, these familiar scenarios, teachers who opt to teach this novel must reeducate their audience. They need to use what they know to be preferred vehicles for entry-level knowl-edge acquisition—using actual nineteenth-century documents or re-productions of slave narratives, auction bulletins, bills of sale, periodi-cal reports, and stories from European American and African American periodicals. The impact on students—of all cultures and races—when they see their first rendering of one of the slave ships named *Jesus*, or they see escaped slave Uncle Sandy and read of his self-mutilation to avoid being returned to slavery, or they read of Henry "Box" Brown's having shipped himself to freedom in a box, or they examine the certifi-cate of freedom purchased by Robert Jones, or they read the accounts of those less fortunate runaway slaves whose trek ended in unspeakable mutilation, or they learn of a mother's commiting merciful infanticide and then suicide, without a doubt all these things affect not only the accessibility of the novel and its central characters for students, but their empowerment to confront the sensitive issues presented by the work and, in particular, these characters. Given students' preference for visual materials, incorporating actual documents from the period amplifies and enlivens their immediate and prolonged comprehension.

The next phase of this restructuring of pedagogical strategies would include collaborative teaching and independent student research, each designed to provide students with a holistic approach to reading and comprehending *Adventures of Huckleberry Finn* on its own historical terms. These approaches would result in making the novel and its controversial central characters more relevant and pertinent to con-temporary students and their reality by enabling them to achieve ob-jective distance and empowering them to examine and explore themselves as well as their history objectively and subjectively without fear of recrimination or discrimination.

Ultimately, what students who have experienced the novel and Huck and Jim in the manner described here come to realize is that, as David L. Smith says in "Huck, Jim, and Racial Discourse," Twain uses the narrative discourse between Huck and Jim to reveal the plight and humanity of all African American people, not only Jim. Students also realize that unlike Bernard Bell's concern that "Twain . . . [and, therefore, Huck] never in *Adventures of Huckleberry Finn* does . . . fully and unequivocally accept the equality of blacks," Huck and Jim are the only viable and logical vehicles who have, like Virgil and Beatrice in Dante's *Divine Comedy*, the imagination and vision to lead the audience into the essential dialectic that must occur if reform is the goal.

As teachers of this work, we must realign ourselves with Twain, with the novel itself, with Huck and Jim, and, more importantly, with our new and diverse audience. As readers, we must strive for both the distance and the closeness required by such a sensitive and complex text as *Huck Finn* as well as by such three-dimensional characters as Huck and Jim. We must also be willing, even insistent, with respect to confronting that which makes us uncomfortable and agitated, if we are to be enriched by the sharing not only with Twain, Jim, and Huck, but with each other as well.

When I was teaching high school, and as chance would have it, *Adventures of Huckleberry Finn*, I had an occasion to need a substitute. Upon my return, the substitute's note to me read, "I know that you probably think that you are doing your students a service by requiring their reading of such a racist work as this. Since you have very little understanding of what a work like this means to a black person and, therefore, how much it damages us, please feel free to call me at the telephone number below so that I can explain why you should remove this racist book from your reading list. I would be happy to help you understand the race question and issue." That was in 1978. In 1997 I received the following letter from a man in Tempe, Arizona: "You obviously do not understand that we are tired of the Jims of the world and reject that image. You must not know that we descended from kings and queens and that our home is Africa. We deny and reject slavery and Mark Twain and anybody else who uses nigger, slavery, and all the Jims."

What initially struck me as interesting about the first note was the substitute's sincerity and real desire to help. As for the second message, what struck me was the inherent fear and shame that this man felt from my ancestors. Denying Jim, Jack, and the others to me is to deny the Chadwicks, the Browns, and the other bloodlines coursing through my veins. But what also struck me was anyone's lack of interest in how I was teaching the work, then and now. No one inquired how my students react to the work, nor what my ultimate objectives are for teaching the work. I did call the substitute, and we did talk about the work. I must admit, however, that the tables were reversed when she realized that I, too, was a person of color. I hastened to explain to her my pedagogical approach and strategies as well as my purpose for and intent to continue teaching the work. As for the fellow from Tempe, I called him, went to Tempe and taught classes, instructed teachers, and consulted with groups of parents and school board representatives.

What I have learned and have never allowed myself to forget is that *Adventures of Huckleberry Finn* will always be a touchstone of sensitivity and controversy, and for that very reason those of us who maintain that it and its central characters, Huck and Jim, will prevail must persevere in our endeavors so that students such as the one whose words I include here can perhaps better comprehend their situations or even improve them by being allowed to peer into Jim's and Huck's nineteenth-century world of hypocrisy and paradox. In response to a research survey I conducted regarding students' reading of *Huck Finn*, the student stated:

> I, as a person of mixed . . . background, have had to deal with the prejudice of peers' and teachers' dislike of mixed . . . children. I was exposed to racial conflicts at an early age. I was also raised to dislike certain races, and every day I struggle to avoid judging people on the basis of sex, race, etc. I hope to undo some of the damage that my parents have done in raising me with prejudices, by teaching my children of the harms that such beliefs can cause. [I first thought Jim could have done more, could have just said, "No way! I'm out of here." But reading about other slaves like Jim and what he and they were willing to endure convinces me that like him, I can overcome.] I hope what I have said here will help you.

As I read one student response after another, I found many of them to be echoes of Jim's unrelenting desire and taste for freedom and Huck's acknowledgment of the paradoxical conflict between what he had been taught and what he felt to be his only moral and human recourse. Twain knew that only by distinctively rendering real characters, with real language, would he bring his contemporary and future audiences to fully understand Jim's dilemma. Jim found himself, like all of his African descendants in this country, once again more than a child, less than an adult—only three-fifths of a man by law.

His dilemma began when he said, "*No.*"

As I concluded the article, I immediately thought of a nineteenth-century woman, Ann Plato, a freeborn Connecticut woman of color, and an essay she wrote entitled simply "Education." Plato states that, above all, books must survive in all of their diversity and texture so that future generations will be able to question, reexamine, and discover truths for their own times. And so I, too, conclude with the same conviction and focus of Ann Plato, Mark Twain, Alice Walker, Virginia Woolf, William Faulkner, John Steinbeck, and any other individual who seeks Voice: May the controversy and the ensuing dialectic continue.

The Challenge of Teaching *Huckleberry Finn*

Shelley Fisher Fishkin

Despite the fact that it is "the most taught novel, the most taught long work, and the most taught piece of American literature" in American schools from junior high to graduate school,[1] *Huckleberry Finn* remains a hard book to read and a hard book to teach. The difficulty is caused by two distinct but related problems. First of all, one must understand how Socratic irony works if the novel is to make any sense at all; most students don't. Secondly, one must be able to place the novel in a larger historical and literary context—one that includes the history of American racism and the literary products of African American writers—if the book is to be read as anything more than a sequel to *Tom Sawyer* (which it both is and is not); most students can't. These two problems pose real obstacles to teachers. Are they surmountable? Under some circumstances, yes. Under others, perhaps not.

In this essay I will suggest some practical strategies for addressing these issues. They are not equally applicable to all classrooms. I will use the term "advanced" and "beginner" to distinguish between levels of training, skills, capacity, etc., rather than peg my suggestions to a particular grade level, recognizing that some high school juniors may be more "advanced" than some college seniors. I don't pretend to have any advice that will make teaching this novel—at any level—easy. I suspect that teaching *Huck Finn* will always be—to borrow a phrase Huck himself used in a different context—"interesting but tough."

I

Listen to the talk in the lunchroom of any American high school, observe the conversation in any college lounge, or watch any TV sitcom popular with the young: contemporary students are at home with sarcasm, parody, irony, impersonation, and satire—on a verbal and a visual level.

But during an August 1993 orientation for assistant instructors who would be teaching the freshman composition course at the University of Texas at Austin, "the organizers of one of the sessions recommended that" instructors "*not* teach 'A Modest Proposal' [a selection available in the anthology] because students would not understand Swift's irony." Skeptical of this warning, one assistant instructor taught it anyway, only to find that those who warned her against it had been right.[2]

It doesn't make sense, but it's true. They may laugh uproariously at the satire and send-ups they see and hear on *Saturday Night Live*, but put most students in front of a written text like Swift's and they mutate into hopelessly dogged literalists. According to the rather shaken instructor, the students found Swift's essay "neither ironic nor funny, but horrifying."[3]

The problem seems simple but isn't: how can we get students to understand that the author and narrator are different and may even hold diametrically opposed views? One might reasonably expect that the six years of English classes in secondary schools that most freshmen have behind them by the time they arrive at college would leave them with at least some residual awareness of the Socratic irony that informs virtually any great work of fiction. Unfortunately, that is often not the case. This failing, which may weaken students' ability to grasp the meaning of a range of other texts, is nothing less than fatal when it comes to *Huck Finn*.

It is impossible to read *Huck Finn* intelligently without understanding that Mark Twain's consciousness and awareness is larger than that of any of the characters in the novel, including Huck. Indeed, part of what makes the book so effective is the fact that Huck is too innocent and ignorant to understand what's wrong with his society and what's right with his own transgressive behavior. Twain, on the other hand, knows the score. One must disbelieve (or at least be skeptical about) almost everything Huck says in order to hear what Twain is saying.

Students have great trouble seeing this, in part because Twain makes Huck such an engaging and appealing person, and such a credible narrator. It is not just students, I might add, who have trouble with this distinction. Much of the criticism leveled at Twain every time some-

1

one wants to remove *Huck Finn* from the classroom stems from confusion on this very point. John H. Wallace, for example—who succeeded in getting the novel banned from the Mark Twain Middle School in Fairfax, Virginia—has argued that the fact that no character in the book says slavery is wrong means that Twain didn't think it was wrong either; this failing, according to Wallace, renders the novel "a grotesque example of racist trash."[4] Other critics, writing in a less inflammatory manner, have also conflated Huck's views with Twain's. In a 1991 interview, Ralph Ellison suggested that critics who condemn Twain for the portrait of Jim that we get in the book forget that "one also has to look at the teller of the tale, and realize that you are getting a black man, an adult, seen through the condescending eyes—partially—of a young white boy." Are you saying, I asked Ellison, "that those critics are making the same old mistake of confusing the narrator with the author?, that they're saying that Twain saw him that way rather than that Huck did?" "Yes," Ellison said.[5]

Students who play pickup games of stand-up semiotics in front of the latest MTV video are good at figuring out what messages pictures send.

2

We can use this skill to help them understand the gaps between Twain and his narrator in *Huck Finn*. That is, if we start at the beginning.[6] I do not mean the EXPLANATORY, or the NOTICE, both of which I will come to shortly, I mean the preceding image: the frontispiece photograph of the marble bust of Twain by the sculptor Karl Gerhardt with Mark Twain's signature underneath (figure 1). Why did Twain begin the book with the photograph of the bust? What message does it send? How is the image it projects different from that projected by the Kemble drawing of a grinning Huck in his ragged straw hat and single-suspender pants that appears on the book's opposite page (figure 2)? Why did Twain choose to juxtapose these two images before we read a single word?

Answering questions like these requires students to think about who Mark Twain was and how he viewed himself as an author. Might he have worried that the reader might forget there was a distinguished gentleman (the sort who sits for marble busts) who knew good grammar and proper diction lurking behind this vernacular-speaking street urchin who mangled the English language in his own energetic and ebullient way?

After these two contrasting images and the title page we find the NOTICE (signed "By Order of the Author, G.G., Chief of Ordinance"), whose real effect is to warn the reader not to expect an easy read. No motive, no moral, no plot contained here, the NOTICE states; the message to the reader is "proceed at your own risk." Then follows the EXPLANATORY (signed "The Author"), which tips the reader off that a range of dialects will be used in the text which follows, and that they are differentiated intentionally. Finally, Huck makes his entrance as storyteller in chapter 1.

Ask your students what Twain achieves by preceding Huck's narrative with these two comments in these other voices. This is a good opportunity to introduce the concept of the "frame" in Southwestern humor. (Kenneth Lynn's summary of its function is particularly useful.)[7] In the standard dialect story that one would find in the newspapers of Twain's day, the dialect speaker would be introduced (in a condescending manner) by an educated narrator. On the surface, Twain seems to be discarding the frame completely, letting Huck tell his own tale in his own voice, one of his key innovations in the novel. But as an examination of the pages that precede Huck's first words in the novel reveals, Twain is having his cake and eating it; he is dispensing with the frame on the surface (no educated narrator introduces Huck per se), but he retains it in a de facto manner by reminding the reader not once but *four* times that a respectable author named Mark Twain is the commanding presence behind this rather irrepressible and ungrammatical performance "by" Huck.

The first three instances are, as we have noted, the photograph of the bust, the NOTICE, and the EXPLANATORY; the fourth is Huck's first paragraph:

> You don't know about me, without you have read a book by the name of "The Adventures of Tom Sawyer," but that ain't no matter. That book was made by Mr. Mark Twain, and he told the truth, mainly. There was things which he stretched, but mainly he told the truth. That is nothing. I never seen anybody but lied, one time or another, without it was aunt Polly, or the widow, or maybe Mary. Aunt Polly—Tom's aunt Polly, she is—and Mary, and the widow Douglas, is all told about in that book—which is mostly a true book; with some stretchers, as I said before. (1)

Huck makes it clear from the first time he opens his mouth that there is a distinction between him and the author Mark Twain. The reader knows, of course, that Huck—like Tom and Aunt Polly and the widow Douglas—is Twain's creation. *Huck*'s premise, however, is that he and Twain are distinct from one another.

The tendency on the part of some readers, like John Wallace, to conflate Huck's perspective with Twain's is aided and abetted by a peculiarly "double" aspect of Twain's vision. Samuel Clemens/Mark Twain published the book at age fifty, but he presented it as if it were written by a child—a child who resembled, in some ways, the child Clemens himself once was. Wallace is correct that no character in the novel says slavery or racism is wrong. He would also be correct if he charged that Samuel Clemens failed to condemn either slavery or racism during his own childhood. No one—including Clemens himself—would deny that for the first thirty-some years of his life, Samuel Clemens/Mark Twain failed to challenge the racist assumptions of his society. In his youth, Twain tells us in his *Autobiography*, slavery was never "assailed in any pulpit," but was "defended and sanctified in a thousand." The local churches preached that "the wise and the good and the holy were unanimous in their conviction that slavery was right, righteous, sacred, the peculiar pet of the Deity, and a condition which the slave himself ought to be daily and nightly thankful for."[8] Twain, as a child, accepted without question, as Huck did, the idea that slaves were property; neither wanted to be called a "low-down Abolitionist" if he could possibly help it.[9]

However, between the time of that Hannibal childhood and adolescence and the years in which Twain wrote *Huckleberry Finn*, his consciousness changed. By 1885, when *Huckleberry Finn* was published, Samuel Clemens held views that were very different from those he ascribed to the "fictional" author of his novel, Huck Finn. It might be helpful at this point to chart for your students the growth of the author's developing moral awareness on the subject of race and racism—starting with some of his writings on the persecution of the Chinese in San Francisco (which will be discussed shortly), then moving through his marriage into an abolitionist family, exposure to figures like Frederick Douglass, and his 1869 *Buffalo Express* editorial, "Only a Nigger."

By the time he wrote *Huckleberry Finn*, Clemens had come to believe not only that slavery was a horrendous wrong, but that white

Americans owe black Americans some form of "reparations" for it. One graphic way to demonstrate this fact to your students is to share with them the letter Twain wrote to the dean of the Yale Law School in 1885, in which he explained why he wanted to pay the board of Warner McGuinn, one of the first black law students at Yale. "We have ground the manhood out of them," Twain wrote Dean Wayland on Christmas Eve, 1885, "and the shame is ours, not theirs, & we should pay for it."[10]

Ask your students: why does a writer who holds these views create a narrator who is too innocent and ignorant to challenge the topsy-turvy moral universe that surrounds him?[11] "All right, then, I'll *go* to Hell," Huck says when he decides not to return Jim to slavery. Samuel Clemens/Mark Twain may be convinced that slavery itself and its legacy are filled with "shame," but Huck is convinced that his reward for defying the moral norms of his society will be damnation.

Irony is always risky, particularly when the subject it tackles is one as explosive as racism. Ask your advanced students to speculate as to why Twain chose this particular strategy for exploring this issue. I have found it useful among advanced students to begin with Twain's earliest forays into the use of irony to expose racism, and the reasons why he turned to this technique.

As a young journalist in San Francisco in the 1860s, Twain witnessed an event he considered outrageous. A group of young white hoodlums set upon a Chinese man going about his business and began stoning and beating him while some local policemen looked on in amusement. Twain wrote up the incident for the *San Francisco Daily Morning Call* and looked for it the next day. It wasn't there. His publishers cared more about offending subscribers, who shared the policemen's prejudices, than they cared about the truth. To get into print at all on the subject, Twain found it necessary to turn to irony, writing up his criticisms for national monthly magazines in quasi-fictional satires.

In "Disgraceful Persecution of a Boy," for example, Twain creates a narrator too bigoted to understand the significance of the events he describes. The narrator of the piece (which ran in *Galaxy Magazine* in 1870) is ostensibly motivated to have his say by his outrage at the "disgraceful persecution" of an innocent boy in San Francisco. The narrator is incensed that the boy has been "thrown into the city prison" for an act which strikes the narrator not only as fitting and proper, but as fully sanctioned by the community: on his way to Sunday school, the boy stoned a Chinese man. "What had the child's education been?

How should he suppose it was wrong to stone a Chinaman?" In the heated editorial he writes in defense of the boy, the bigoted narrator reveals much more than he ostensibly realizes about the moral norms of the 1860s San Francisco.

In an effort to prove that the boy was simply responding to signals he had been given by his elders, the narrator drops that San Francisco is a place where mining taxes are impsoed on the Chinese but not the Irish; where many tax gatherers collect the tax twice instead of once; where "when a white man robs a sluice-box . . . they make him leave the [mining] camp; and when a Chinaman does that thing, they hang him" (370). His education taught the boy that "a Chinaman had no rights that any man was bound to respect." Everything in the boy's environment "conspired to teach him that it was a high and holy thing to stone a Chinaman, and yet," the narrator complains, "he no sooner attempts to do his duty than he is punished for it . . ." (380–81).[12] "What a commentary is this upon human justice!," the narrator cries, "What sad prominence it gives to our human disposition to tyrannize over the weak!"

In "Disgraceful Persecution of a Boy," the narrator, too bigoted to understand the import of what he relates, is convinced he is right. In *Huck Finn*, Huck, too innocent to understand the import of what *he* relates, is convinced he is wrong. In both cases, the reader has to understand that the author—Mark Twain—holds a very different attitude. By allowing the reader to see the gap between the author's views and the narrator's views, "Disgraceful Persecution of a Boy" can help prepare advanced students to understand Twain's use of irony in *Huckleberry Finn*.

In *Huckleberry Finn* the time, the place, and the race are different, but the implicit central question remains the same. How can a society that denies the humanity of large numbers of people within its borders think of itself as civilized? How can a society so rife with injustice think of itself as just? Twain requires the reader to ask these questions by preventing any character within the work from asking them. In each case, the gap betwen Twain's awareness and that of his narrator is crucial. It is a major source of the work's power, and also of the problems that are entailed in teaching it. Twain's art requires the reader to learn to read beyond the surface meaning of the text. By presenting a racist society through the eyes of a child too innocent to question its norms, Twain forces readers to judge that society on their own. It is a brilliant strategy, an inspired strategy—and when it works, it works spectacularly well. When it fails, however, it fails miserably. Teachers must decide whether they—and their classes—are up to taking on this challenge.

Close reading, a central dimension of the New Criticism, remains an extremely important skill to impart to our students, particularly when teaching Twain. But I have become more and more convinced that a philosophy of "the text and nothing but the text" is irresponsible and counterproductive when it comes to bringing this book into today's classroom. If we want to teach *Huck Finn*, we have to be willing to teach other works before it and alongside it. Am I saying that if we want to teach this text responsibly, we have to redo the entire American literature syllabus in secondary school and college classrooms? Yes.[13]

Sometimes a work of art can be a lens through which a moment in history is refracted with unprecedented clarity and brilliance. *Huck Finn* is such a work—but only if we allow our students to read it against the backdrop of that history. *Huck Finn* is often the only work on the syllabus that addresses issues of race, and Jim is often the only black voice from the nineteenth century in the classroom. This situation must change. We need to establish for our students, even if only in rudimentary terms, the social, political, and economic contours of the period in which *Huck Finn* was set, and of the period in which it was written. It is not as difficult as it sounds. Here I'll offer some concrete suggestions for ways of doing this on both the beginner and advanced levels.

To help our students understand the nature of antebellum slavery, and also to help them understand the last third of the novel as Twain's satire on the reenslavement of freed blacks in the post-Reconstruction South, we need to teach them the history of these periods. For beginning students, the most effective approach might be lectures by the teacher, geared to the students' level, that synthesize more material than the students could realistically be required to read themselves, combined with readings that would include a handful of clear and effective primary documents. Teachers might assign advanced classes more extensive readings of both primary and secondary sources.

For teachers and for advanced students, secondary sources that are particularly useful include: John Blassingame's *The Slave Community*; W. E. B. Du Bois's *The Souls of Black Folk* and *Black Reconstruction*;

John Hope Franklin's *From Slavery to Freedom*; George Fredrickson's *The Black Image in the White Mind*; Eugene Genovese's *Roll, Jordan, Roll*; Rayford W. Logan's *The Betrayal of the Negro from Rutherford B. Hayes to Woodrow Wilson*; Sterling Stuckey's *Slave Culture*; Kenneth Stampp's *The Peculiar Institution*; Thomas L. Webber's *Deep Like the Rivers*; and Joel Williamson's *A Rage for Order*.

What terror did the prospect of being "sold down the river" actually hold for Missouri slaves? Did slaves' awareness of the dollar value that their masters put on them influence their sense of self-worth? What kind of "freedom" would Jim have encountered in the "free states" had he *not* passed Cairo in the fog? What was happening in the South as Twain wrote the novel (1876–83)? In what ways were the ex-slaves forced, in the 1870s and 1880s, to defer the dreams of genuine freedom and citizenship that they had entertained after the war and during Reconstruction? Historians' accounts (and, for beginning students, teachers' summaries of some of these accounts) can help give students answers to these questions. All of these questions have direct bearing on our understanding of what happens in the novel, and the novel, in turn, elucidates these chapters of history in dramatic and fresh ways. The growing consensus among critics that the imprisonment of Jim on the Phelps plantation suggests the reenslavement of free blacks in the post-Reconstruction South allows us to read the ending as more than an unsatisfying burlesque farce.[14] The more students understand about this chapter of history, the better equipped they are to understand the last third of the novel as a satirical indictment of white society's behavior during that era.

Readings and lectures from historian's accounts can clarify and elucidate aspects of the novel and of the history that it embodies and reflects. But there is no substitute for exposing students to some relevant primary sources as well. Students read about the fake runaway slave advertisement concocted by the king and the duke, but have they ever seen real ones? Why not bring copies of the genuine article into the classroom?[15]

Jim's voice, despite its special strengths, often remains cramped within conventions as confining as the prison shack on the Phelps plantation; he must not be the only African American voice from the nineteenth century heard in our classrooms. To give our students a fuller sense of what slavery meant to the slave, we should have them read accounts from slaves themselves. A primary text that works well for both beginner and advanced students is Frederick Douglass's 1845 *Narrative*. Students who read Douglass's *Narrative* before reading *Huckleberry Finn* will approach the novel with a fuller understanding of the antebellum world in which Huck and Jim move and the challenge of the journey they undertake. Douglass can help give them a new awareness of the significance of Jim's being deprived of his freedom, of the complexity of his decision to run away from his owner, and of the danger he courts every step of the way as he seeks his freedom with Huck in tow. If it is not possible to add a work like Douglass's *Narrative* to the syllabus, it might be possible to at least have students read short selections from collections of slave testimony such as *Bullwhip Days; The Slaves Remember: An Oral History*, edited by James Mellon; or *Slave Testimony*, edited by John Blassingame, or *Before Freedom*, edited by Belinda Hurmence.

Some of the most common problems that surface in the classroom when *Huckleberry Finn* is taught can be mitigated by teaching the novel not only in the historical context outlined above, but also in conjunction with imaginative writing by Mark Twain's African American contemporaries. For example, take the controversy surrounding the pervasive presence in *Huck Finn* of the word "nigger," an offensive racial epithet that remains alive and well in American culture. Historical research reveals that "nigger" is the term that Huck and those around him would have used; to abandon that term would mean giving up all claims to historical verisimilitude. Pointing that out to your students does not lessen the offensiveness of the word; it does, however, allow them to understand why Twain uses it. His African American contemporaries used it, too. Have your students read some stories by Charles W. Chesnutt, a master of irony in his own right, who also felt compelled to show a racist society—warts and all—and who allowed his characters to use the word "nigger" if they would have used it in real life.[16]

As David Smith has observed, "Twain uses 'nigger' throughout the book as a synonym for 'slave.' There is ample evidence from other sources that this corresponds to one usage common during the antebellum period. . . . [The word] connotes an inferior, even subhuman, creature who is properly owned by and subservient to Euro-Americans. Both Huck and Jim use the work in this sense."[17] Smith goes on to cite the famous exchange between Huck and Aunt Sally about the riverboat accident:

"Good gracious! anybody hurt?"

"No'm. Killed a nigger."

"Well, it's lucky; because sometimes people do get hurt." (chapter 32)

In Smith's view, "this exchange is hilarious precisely because we know that Huck is playing on [Aunt Sally's] glib and conventional bigotry. We know that Huck's relationship to Jim has already invalidated for him such obtuse racial notions. The conception of the 'nigger' is a socially constituted and sanctioned fiction, and it is just as false and absurd as Huck's explicit fabrication, which Aunt Sally also swallows whole. In fact, the exchange between Huck and Aunt Sally reveals a great deal about how racial discourse operates" (106). Twain, Smith argues, "takes every opportunity to expose the mismatch between racial abstractions and real human beings" (106). Aunt Sally's—and Twain's—use of this term helps make it clear that even the "good people" in *Huckleberry Finn* are racists, a central premise of the novel, and a central dimension of Twain's critique of antebellum society. It is impossible to probe the dynamics of a racist society without delineating the racial discourse that characterized it.

For advanced students, studying novels such as Chesnutt's *The Marrow of Tradition* or Paul Laurence Dunbar's *The Sport of the Gods* can add much to students' understanding of how Twain's African American contemporaries endeavored to analyze and criticize racism in American society. For beginning as well as advanced readers, Dunbar poems such as "We Wear the Mask" and "An Ante-bellum Sermon" can provide useful points of departure for discussions about the "doubleness" inherent in so much of nineteenth-century African American performance and expression. Dunbar's comments in "We Wear the Mask" and the black preacher's performance in "An Ante-bellum Sermon" can lead into discussions of African American traditions of trickster tales and signifying, both of which left their mark on Twain's art in *Huck Finn*.[18]

Finally, studying Twain's own records of the oral performances of African American speakers whom he knew and admired can further add to students' awareness of the complex multiracial roots of the art with which Twain transformed American prose style (pieces such as "Sociable Jimmy," "A True Story," and "Corn-Pone Opinions" come to mind). For African American speakers (as I have demonstrated elsewhere) helped Twain and a host of twentieth-century writers who came after him learn how to write books that "talked."[19] In *Beyond the Culture Wars: How Teaching the Conflicts Can Revitalize American Education*, Gerald Graff proposes that "teaching the conflicts" can enliven classroom discussions and stimulate a more sophisticated understanding of the issues involved. The debate over the sources of twentieth-century American literature can be just such a teachable "conflict." The denial, throughout most of the twentieth century, of the role that African Americans and African American oral traditions played in shaping American speech and literature is part of the story we need to share with our advanced students.[20]

III

If W. E. B. Du Bois was right that the problem of the twentieth century is the color line, one would never know it from the average secondary school syllabus, which often avoids issues of race almost completely. Like a Trojan horse, however, *Huck Finn* can slip into the American literature classroom as a "classic," only to engulf students in heated debates about prejudice and racism, conformity, autonomy, authority, slavery, and freedom. It is a book that puts on the table the very questions the culture so often tries to bury, a book that opens out into the complex history that shaped it. Much of that history is painful. Indeed, it is to avoid confronting the raw pain of that history that black parents sometimes mobilize to ban the novel. Brushing history aside, however, is no solution to the larger challenge of dealing with its legacy. Neither is placing the task of dealing with it on one book.

We continue to live, as a nation, in the shadow of racism while being simultaneously committed, on paper, to principles of equality. As Ralph Ellison observed in a 1991 interview, it is this irony at the core of the American experience that Mark Twain forces us to confront head-on.[21] Irony, history, and racism all painfully intertwine in our past and in our present. And they all come together in *Huckleberry Finn*.

Because racism remains endemic to our society, a book like *Huck Finn*, which brings the problem to the surface, can explode like a hand grenade in a literature classroom accustomed to the likes of *Macbeth* or *Great Expectations*, works that exist at a safe remove from the lunchroom or the playground. If we lived in a world in which students were adept at reading irony and well-versed in all phases of American history, if we lived in a world in which racism had been eliminated generations before—teaching *Huck Finn* would be a piece of cake. Unfortunately, that's not the world we live in. The difficulties we have teaching this book reflect the difficulties we continue to confront in our classrooms and in our nation.[22]

As educators, it is incumbent upon us to teach our students to read irony, to understand history, and to be repulsed by racism and bigotry. But this is the task of a lifetime. It is unfair to force one novel to bear the burden—alone—of addressing these issues and solving these problems.

Concluding Unscientific Postscript

Leaving the classroom one morning, after we have spent several classes discussing *Huck Finn*, I overhear a student in my undergraduate seminar ask a classmate, "Does all this mean *Huck Finn* can't be the book I loved before I knew all this stuff I know now about it? The romance of the river—the great adventure—is it possible to still read it that way any more?"

I was reminded of that passage in *Life on the Mississippi* in which Twain draws a contrast between the river the passenger sees and the river seen by the riverboat pilot. The passenger, Twain writes, "saw nothing but all manner of pretty pictures in it, painted by the sun and shaded by the clouds, whereas to the trained eye these were not pictures at all, but the grimmest and most dead-earnest of reading matter." When "I had mastered the language of this water and had come to know every trifling feature that bordered the great river as familiarly as I knew the letters of the alphabet," Twain tells us, "I had made a valuable acquisition. But I had lost something, too. I had lost something which could never be restored to me while I lived. All the grace, the beauty, the poetry had gone out of the majestic river! . . . All the value any feature of it had for me was the amount of usefulness it could furnish toward compassing the safe piloting of a steamboat" (95). Was this what my student was trying to say? Had I turned the "poetry" of a book she had loved into the "most dead-earnest of reading matter"? The passage continues, however, as follows:

> I still keep in mind a certain wonderful sunset which I witnessed when steamboating was new to me. A broad expanse of the river was turned to blood; in the middle distance the red hue brightened

into gold, through which a solitary log came floating, black and conspicuous; in one place a long, slanting mark lay sparkling upon the water; in another the surface was broken by boiling, tumbling rings, that were as many-tinted as an opal; where the ruddy flesh was faintest, was a smooth spot that was covered with graceful circles and radiating lines, ever so delicately traced; the shore on our left was densely wooded, and the sombre shadow that fell from this forest was broken in one place by a long, ruffled trail that shone like silver. . . . (95–96)

In these passages Twain is being cagey, as usual. He hasn't lost the river at all, for he has evoked that wonderful sunset *after* he had supposedly "lost" the ability to appreciate it. He may have lost some of his innocent wonder, but he has gained something, too.

Twain tells us that he learned to read the river like a book; so now we have learned to read his book like a river. But we, too, may gain more than we lose, just as Twain gained a new river without really losing the old one. We may know more about precisely what makes the surface shimmer so iridescently, or about why certain dangerous shadows need to be watched with great care. But there is still shimmer. And there is still danger.

Notes

1. Allen Carey-Webb, "Racism and *Huckleberry Finn*: Censorship, Dialogue and Change" *English Journal* 82 (November 1993): 22.
2. The instructor shared this incident with Jean Cole, a fellow assistant instructor who had attended the same orientation meeting. Jean Cole, personal communication, February 1994.
3. A fellow instructor reported to Jean Cole the experience of defying the recommendation not to teach Swift. Jean Cole, personal communication, February 1994.
4. Wallace expressed these opinions on national television when I debated him on *Freeman Reports* on CNN, 14 March 1985.
5. Ralph Ellison, interview with Shelley Fisher Fishkin, 16 July 1991, New York City (unpublished).
6. A facsimile first edition is a must. Fortunately, several editions are available for classroom use, including the Mark Twain Library Edition published by the University of California Press and the Oxford Mark Twain edition published by Oxford University Press.
7. See Kenneth Lynn, *Mark Twain and Southwestern Humor* (Boston: Little, Brown, 1959).

8   Mark Twain, *Autobiography*, ed. Charles Neider (New York: Harper and Row, Perennial Library, 1966), 32.

9   For a discussion of what it meant to be a "low-down Abolitionist" in the Missouri of Mark Twain's childhood, see Shelley Fisher Fishkin, *Lighting Out for the Territory: Reflections on Mark Twain and American Culture* (New York: Oxford University Press, 1997).

10 See Edwin McDowell, "From Twain, a Letter on Debt to Blacks," *New York Times*, 14 March 1984, 1, 16.

11 Advanced students might find it useful to read Wayne C. Booth's *A Rhetoric of Irony* (Chicago: University of Chicago Press, 1974) to understand what irony does and how it works in a range of contexts.

12 While the narrator in "Disgraceful Persecution" is too bigoted to understand the import of what he describes, the narrator of "Goldsmith's Friend Abroad Again" (another satire that works well among advanced students) is too innocent to understand the identical social conditions. Writing at a time when anti-Chinese hysteria was on the rise due to the completion of the transcontinental railroad and the fear that the now unemployed Chinese would take jobs away from whites in the West, Twain attacked the hypocrisy of a society committed to "liberty and justice for all" that was content to grant it only to some. He achieves his end through narrators whose failure to condemn the moral lapses they describe forces the reader to judge the society. In both cases, the reader has to understand that the author—Mark Twain—has a very different attitude from his narrator.

13 Lest this suggestion seem far-fetched, I hasten to add that it is already happening. Recent anthologies such as the *Heath Anthology of American Literature* help facilitate this restructuring. In addition, teachers of nonanthology-based American literature survey courses are increasingly adopting the sorts of changes I suggest here. For example, Cassandra Cleghorn at Williams College had her students in English 208 read Harriet Jacobs's *Incidents in the Life of a Slave Girl* several weeks before she had them read *Huck Finn* in her Introduction to American Literature course during the spring of 1994.

14 For more on this subject, see Fishkin, *Was Huck Black? Mark Twain and African American Voices*, 68–76.

15 This excellent suggestion is proposed by Jocelyn Chadwick-Joshua in her article, "Ethos and Intellectual Freedom: Responsibility and the Function of the Academic," *Texas Library Journal* 107 (Fall 1992): 135–38.

16 See Eric Sundquist's *To Wake the Nations: Race in the Making of American Literature* for an illuminating discussion of Chesnutt and dialect (271–454). At one point, as Sundquist notes, Chesnutt considered using "De Noo Nigger" as a title for a story, but decided against it because "I don't care to dignify a doubtful word quite so much; it is all right for [his character] Julius [to use the phrase], but it might leave me under the suspicion of bad taste unless perchance the whole title's being in dialect should redeem it." Chesnutt quoted in Sundquist, 328.

17 David Smith, "Huck, Jim, and American Racial Discourse," 105–6. See Works Cited for full citation.

18 For a full discussion of these points, see Fishkin, *Was Huck Black?*
19 See ibid.
20 This issue is explored at length in chapter 9. of ibid.
21 Ralph Ellison, interview with Shelley Fisher Fishkin, 16 July 1991, New York City.
22 See Fishkin's *Lighting Out for the Territory*, for an expanded discussion of these issues. Parts of this essay were first published in that book.

Works Cited

Booth, Wayne C. *A Rhetoric of Irony.* Chicago: University of Chicago Press, 1974.

Blassingame, John. *The Slave Community: Plantation Life in the Antebellum South.* New York: Oxford University Press, 1972.

Carey-Webb, Allen. "Racism and *Huckleberry Finn*: Censorship, Dialogue and Change." *English Journal* 82 (November 1993): 22.

Chadwick-Joshua, Jocelyn. "Ethos and Intellectual Freedom: Responsibility and the Function of the Academic." *Texas Library Journal* (Fall 1992): 135–38.

Chesnutt, Charles. *The Marrow of Tradition* [1901]. Ann Arbor: University of Michigan Press, 1989.

Cleghorn, Cassandra. "Introduction to American Literature." Syllabus, Williams College, English 208, Spring 1994.

Douglass, Frederick. *Narrative of the Life of Frederick Douglass* [1845]. In Henry Louis Gates, Jr., ed. *The Classic Slave Narratives.* New York: New American Library, 1987.

Du Bois, W. E. B. *Black Reconstruction in America: An Essay Toward a History of the Part Which Black Folk Played in the Attempt to Reconstruct Democracy in America, 1860–1880.* New York: Harcourt Brace, 1935.

———. *The Souls of Black Folk* [1903]. Reprinted in Nathan Huggins, ed., *W. E. B. Du Bois: Writings.* New York: Library of America, 1986.

Dunbar, Paul Laurence. *Lyrics of Lowly Life* [1896]. Reprint. New York: Citadel Press, 1984.

———. *Sport of the Gods* [1902]. Reprint: Miami: Mnemosyne, 1969.

Fishkin, Shelley Fisher. *Was Huck Black? Mark Twain and African-American Voices.* New York: Oxford University Press, 1993.

———. *Lighting Out for the Territory: Reflections on Mark Twain and American Culture.* New York: Oxford University Press, 1997.

Foner, Eric. *Reconstruction: America's Unfinished Revolution, 1863–1877.* New York: Harper and Row, 1988.

Franklin, John Hope. *From Slavery to Freedom: A History of Negro Americans.* 3rd ed. New York: Knopf, 1967.

Fredrickson, George M. *The Black Image in the White Mind: The Debate on Afro-American Character and Destiny, 1817–1914.* Middletown, Conn.: Wesleyan University Press, 1971.

Genovese, Eugene. *Roll, Jordan, Roll: The World the Slaves Made*. New York: Random House, 1976.

Graff, Gerald. *Beyond the Culture Wars: How Teaching the Conflicts Can Revitalize American Education*. New York: Norton, 1992.

Hurmence, Belinda, ed. *Before Freedom: 48 Oral Histories of Former North and South Carolina Slaves*. New York: Mentor, 1990.

Logan, Rayford W. *The Betrayal of the Negro from Rutherford B. Hayes to Woodrow Wilson*. London: Collier-Macmillan, 1965.

Lynn, Kenneth S. *Mark Twain and Southwestern Humor*. Boston: Little, Brown, 1959.

McDowell, Edwin. "From Twain, a Letter on Debt to Blacks." *New York Times*, 14 March 1984, 1, 16.

Mellon, James, ed. *Bullwhip Days: The Slaves Remember—an Oral History*. New York: Avon, 1988.

Smith, David L. "Huck, Jim, and American Racial Discourse." In *Satire or Evasion? Black Perspectives on "Huckleberry Finn."* Ed. James S. Leonard, Thomas A. Tenney, and Thadious M. Davis. Durham, N.C.: Duke University Press, 1992.

Stuckey, Sterling. *Slave Culture: Nationalist Theory and the Foundation of Black America*. New York: Oxford University Press, 1987.

Sundquist, Eric. *To Wake the Nations: Race in the Making of American Literature*. Cambridge, Mass.: Harvard University Press, 1993.

Twain, Mark. *Adventures of Huckleberry Finn* [1885]. Ed. Walter Blair and Victor Fischer. The Mark Twain Library. Berkeley: University of California Press, 1985.

——. *The Autobiography of Mark Twain*. Ed. Charles Neider. New York: Harper and Row, Perennial Library, 1966.

——. "Disgraceful Persecution of a Boy." *Galaxy* (May 1870): 717–18. Reprinted in Louis J. Budd, ed., *Mark Twain: Collected Tales, Sketches, Speeches, and Essays, 1852–1890*. New York: Library of America, 1992. 379–82.

——. "Goldsmith's Friend Abroad Again" [1870]. Reprinted in Louis J. Budd, ed., *Mark Twain: Collected Tales, Sketches, Speeches, and Essays, 1852–1890*. New York: Library of America, 1992. 455–70.

——. *Life on the Mississippi*. New York: Penguin, 1984.

——. "Sociable Jimmy" [1974]. Reprinted in Shelley Fisher Fishkin, *Was Huck Black? Mark Twain and African-American Voices*. New York: Oxford University Press, 1993. 249–52.

——. "A True Story, Repeated Word for Word as I Heard it" [1974]. Reprinted in Louis J. Budd, ed., *Mark Twain: Collected Tales, Sketches, Speeches, and Essays, 1852–1890*. New York: Library of America, 1992. 578–82.

Wallace, John H. [television debate]. *Freeman Reports*. Cable News Network, 14 March 1985.

Webber, Thomas L. *Deep Like the Rivers: Education in the Slave Quarter Community, 1831–1865*. New York: Norton, 1978.

Williamson, Joel. *A Rage for Order: Black-White Relations in the American South Since Emancipation*. New York: Oxford University Press, 1986.

Huck Finn's Library:
Reading, Writing, and Intertextuality
Anthony J. Berret, S.J.

Adventures of Huckleberry Finn is a collection of books as much as it is a collection of dialects, characters, and localities. From the first sentence, when Huck introduces himself as a character from *The Adventures of Tom Sawyer*, to the last paragraph, when he decides never to write another book, there are explicit references by title, author, or content to more than twenty books, probable allusions or influences from at least twenty more, and many general images of books, reading, and writing. A few of the books mentioned are found and read by Huck himself, some are cited by Tom Sawyer or the king and the duke, and others come directly from the Author, Mark Twain. Huck reacts to these books in a variety of ways. After demonstrating his reading skill before Pap and having his book knocked across the room, he enjoys being free from school and books while under Pap's captivity. Yet he later has "a general good time" reading to Jim out of books that were salvaged from a wreck.[1] Although he balks at Tom Sawyer's efforts to do things "by the book," he wishes that Tom were around when he does something adventurous himself (11, 16, 41, 81).

Besides this variety of reactions to books on Huck's part, there is also a variety in the type of books mentioned (popular and classical fiction, biography, history, drama, sacred scripture), and this forms part of an even wider variety of dialects, styles of discourse (from dialogue to interior monologue, formality to slang), and genres of original writing (letters, advertisements, an oath, an inscription, and a poem). To specify this variety in modes of expression and the different attitudes and functions assumed by them, contemporary critics have adopted the term *intertextuality*. This essay will analyze the intertextuality of books and writing in *Adventures of Huckleberry Finn*.[2] It will also propose exercises in reading and writing that explore the many and diverse effects of the novel's intertextuality.

The most basic reason for including references to books and writing in a written text is that books and writing are the subjects most akin to a written text. A subject that accommodates itself easily to its medium, that fits into the medium without having to undergo some transformation, will be the readiest and easiest subject for that medium. A coat of arms, for example, since it is static and two-dimensional, would make an apt subject for a painting, while a horse race, since it involves motion, would be rendered more suitably by cinema. Neither the coat of arms nor the horse race would lend itself naturally to writing, since writing does not have pictures, at least not directly. A subject that *would* lend itself to writing is dialogue, since words spoken in conversation are closely related to words written on a page. Another subject especially fit for writing is thought. Since words are comparatively abstract—they are not exactly pictures or sounds—they express well the passage of immaterial thoughts through the mind. Finally, along with dialogue and thought, books and other writings are also appropriate subjects for writing, perhaps, in fact, the most appropriate. They are the subjects most akin to what is happening on the written page.

Huckleberry Finn demonstrates this relation between a subject and its medium. About 40 percent of it is dialogue, and the rest consists of the impressions and reflections of Huck himself. There also are numerous references to books and writing, including those that present a written text on the page, like Emmeline Grangerford's poem (139), the posters of the king and the duke (180, 194), the duke's Hamlet soliloquy (179), and Tom Sawyer's inscription (322). One reason why Huck fills his text with these elements and others that are akin to writing would have to be his penchant for what comes easily and handily and is least troublesome. The easiest subject for writing is writing itself. It is likewise comfortable for the reader to be not only reading a text, but also reading another text through the eyes of the narrator. It establishes a kinship between the reader and the narrator, and gives extra support to the act of reading.

Yet the inclusion of books and writing in a text may also be discomforting. A reader may want the words in a text to be transparent, to offer a clear and direct view of the action or thought behind them, to preserve the illusion that something is really happening. When the words draw attention to themselves, when they get in the way of what they are supposed to represent, they distract the reader. They cause the reader to distinguish between the words and what they represent, leading perhaps to doubts about their suitability or fidelity. Constant references to books and writing in a text make the text say, "I am a book, and only a book. I am not real. I am only one version of reality." When such a distinction is made between the medium and the action represented by it, the reader is forced to question the faithfulness and objectivity of the medium.[3]

Mark Twain certainly makes his words draw attention to themselves in *Huckleberry Finn*. He fills Huck's narrative with colloquialisms, grammatical errors, and obvious misinterpretations of fact, causing the reader to see it as just one version of reality coming from a limited point of view and therefore subject to doubts about its reliability. In dialogue, Huck also tells a number of lies to escape from tight predicaments. These lies are meant, of course, to deceive other characters, not the reader, yet the frequent occurrence of them might lead the reader to suspect that Huck is not always telling the truth in narration either. In any case, Huck's narrative intervenes noticeably between the reader and the reality that it is supposed to represent, making the reader aware of its distinctions from that reality and the possibility of inaccuracy in representing it.

References to books, reading, and writing reinforce the distinctness of Huck's narrative. They help make the narrative say, "I am a book, and only a book." Huck's opening reference to *Tom Sawyer* notifies the reader of books from the very first sentence, and it also warns the reader to be suspicious: "That book was made by Mr. Mark Twain, and he told the truth, mainly. There was things which he stretched, but mainly he told the truth. That is nothing. I never seen anybody but lied, one time or another . . ." (1). After this reference, there are the Good Book read to Huck by the widow Douglas, books used as manuals of crime by Tom Sawyer, the book knocked by Pap across a room, and another book kept by him for "wadding" (insulation), pious and sentimental display books in the Grangerford parlor, and an elopement message in a "Testament," books salvaged from a wreck and read by Huck to Jim, one volume of Shakespeare's works owned by the duke and used for his theatrical hoax, and a heavy Bible placed on a dying man's chest. Tom Sawyer writes an oath to be signed by each member of his respectable gang; Huck signs away his treasure to Judge Thatcher "for a consideration" of just one dollar; he also writes a note to Mary Jane Wilks exposing the king and the duke as frauds, and a letter to Miss Watson—reporting Jim's escape and whereabouts—which he later rips up; Tom writes misleading notes to the Phelpses that get him shot and Jim almost hanged; and Huck admits at the end, "if I'd a knowed what a trouble it was to make a book I wouldn't a tackled it and ain't agoing to no more" (362). Aside from the mere presence of these images of books and writing, which itself makes the reader aware of *Huckleberry Finn* as a book—and therefore distinct from the reality that it is supposed to represent and answerable to that reality—there are dubious aspects to most of these images that make the reader extraskeptical about the value of reading and writing. Those two acts seem to be used here mainly for crime, deception, and betrayal.

Simple references to books and writing in a text, therefore, can have contrasting effects. They can make the text feel comfortable, easy, and natural because it is representing subjects akin to itself, or they can disrupt the text, dividing words from objects and forcing questions about the words' reliability. For a reading exercise, choose some paragraphs from *Huckleberry Finn* that have such references and try to determine what effects they have. See, for example, the paragraph beginning "This table" and the ones following it (137–41), or the paragraph beginning "The king got" and those following it (168–70).[4] For a writing exercise, have the students paraphrase or interpret a passage from a written text, then describe an act, a picture, or a piece of instrumental music. What differences are there between writing about something verbal and writing about something nonverbal? Analyze Huck's struggle with this problem in the paragraph beginning "Once I said" and those following (268–71). Which statements had Huck probably heard or read and then simply repeated in his text? Which ones are the result of his grappling with nonverbal events and feelings?

Besides the simple references to books and writing, ample material in *Huckleberry Finn* is taken from the actual content of other books. These influences—"stealings," or "borrowings" in Huck's terminology—fall into three categories, depending on the effects that they produce: burlesque, paradigm, and simple source.

The clearest instance of burlesque in *Huckleberry Finn* is Tom Sawyer's reliance on books as models for boyhood adventures. He bases the activities of his respectable gang on pirate and robber books, makes each member swear to kill the gang's enemies and hack crosses in their breasts—a detail he drew from Robert Montgomery Bird's *Nick of the Woods*—summons the gang by a burning stick that he calls a "slogan" (confusing details from two works of Sir Walter Scott), and raids hog drivers and a Sunday school picnic, claiming that they are really camels and "A-rabs" disguised by "enchantment" as in *Don Quixote* and *The Arabian Nights* (9–12, 14–17).[5] Because Tom is only a boy, his use of literary sources here is cute and comical, although it may raise questions about the effects of violent literature on children. His juvenile imitation of literature, however, is seen by Huck as false, foolish, and unprofitable, even though Huck is sometimes fascinated by it and tries to copy it. Since Tom appeals to books for "authority," for "regular," "correct," and "high-toned" behavior, the reader is prompted to view his exploits as a burlesque on adults who live too much by the book, who depend too heavily on cultural conventions. Huck thinks Tom's adventures are not much different from Sunday school, or, one may add, from the widow Douglas's and Miss Watson's attempts to civilize him. Huck loses interest in Moses because he is dead, and he distrusts formulas of prayer because they will not produce a fishhook. When Miss Watson forces Huck to pray in a closet, she interprets the Bible too literally and amusingly misapplies the Renaissance word *closet* (see Matt. 6: 6). This sort of burlesque shows the comic incongruity that results from applying old and set forms of expression to new and living situations. It exposes the misuse of literature in action or expression.

This misuse is most evident in Tom's handling of Jim's escape at the Phelps plantation. There is less humor here because of the serious issues involved—slavery, emancipation, abolition—and because of the violent outcome: Tom gets shot, and Jim almost gets hanged. Against Huck's plan to free Jim in a simple, economical way, Tom insists on making the deed honorable, mysterious, complicated, prolonged, and troublesome by following the authorities: *The Life of Baron Trenck*, the *Memoirs* of Casanova and Benvenuto Cellini, Dumas's *The Man in the Iron Mask* and *The Count of Monte Cristo*, William Ainsworth's *The Tower of London*, and the *Picciola* (299, 302, 304, 321, 327). He therefore needs a rope ladder, a journal written in blood, case knives to dig a tunnel, an inscription and coat of arms, a snake to tame, frocks for disguise, and anonymous warning notes. He even considers building a moat and sawing off Jim's leg. Again, literature is misapplied to reality, and as a result of this confusion, literature itself is made to appear obsolete, inane, and convoluted. This episode is even more disturbing because of its length (almost one quarter of the novel) and its position— the climax and denouement, when the conflicts of the story are supposedly resolved. Some critics deplore the episode because it does not

Anthony J. Berret, S.J.

match the depth and skill of the episodes leading up to it. But if books and writing are a pervasive subject of the novel, especially as they serve or abuse reality, the Phelps episode, by its concentration on literary models, fits the rest of the story. It may be disappointing that a classic novel ends with an example of the misuse of literature, but this focus makes the reader more critical of the text and of literature in general. It should be evident that the misuse of literature here is part of the Author's strategy, not his failure. Mark Twain wants the reader to object, and he provokes this objection by his limited narrator, his general use of burlesque, and his own unreliable voice, which dares the reader to find a motive, moral, or plot in the book.[6]

Next to Tom Sawyer, the main figures of burlesque in *Huckleberry Finn* are the king and the duke. Their rehearsal of Hamlet's soliloquy and of scenes from *Richard III* and *Romeo and Juliet* resembles many Shakespeare burlesques found in American journalism and show business in the nineteenth century. They also turn popular piety and sentiment into burlesque by their bereavement at the Wilks funeral and the king's fake conversion story at the camp meeting (172–74). Their machinations reveal how literature and social discourse can be used for deception, exploitation, and enhancement of status. Although Huck and Jim doubt their noble ancestry, and the people of Bricksville either spurn or overlook their theater credits abroad, the Wilkses are wholly taken in by their show of sympathy, benevolence, gentility, and professionalism. Classic literature and conventional forms of social discourse can be convincing and persuasive by their own inner merits and long-term use. They do not have to be constantly adapted to reality. They can rest on their laurels, getting by with what has succeeded in the past, and, for this reason, they can be used to dominate and deceive. What the king and the duke attempt and get away with alerts the reader to take a critical view of literary and conventional locution.

Huck himself is involved in several burlesques. By some of his droll comments he enhances the burlesque quality of the books and artwork in the Grangerford house, especially the gloomy drawings and verses composed by Emmeline; but he also tries to write a poem himself as a tribute to her (136–41). When he reads to Jim out of books salvaged from a wreck, he comments on the topics of royalty, books, getting the point, language, and nationality, while Jim expresses concerns about work, money, family, the value of the individual child, and common humanity (93–98). Jim's more basic concerns undercut Huck's pseudo-educated posturings and turn books and their themes into burlesque by making them seem removed from realities. In a later talk with Jim about books and royalty, Huck does not need Jim's remarks to discredit what he says. He does that himself by the clutter of disconnected facts in his own mind. He confuses Henry VIII with three other kings, and relates *The Arabian Nights* to the Doomsday Book and the Boston Tea Party (199–200). This, of course, is more a burlesque of limited book knowledge than of books themselves, but just the same it causes the reader to be critical of what is written. It also clues in the reader to the nature of Huck's mind, which is filled with books—as the novel itself is—but which confuses them with one another and with historical facts.

A good portion of *Huckleberry Finn*, therefore, can be considered a burlesque of books and thus a critique of literature. In burlesque, both literature and other forms of discourse are permitted to become absorbed and carried away with themselves, usually to humorous lengths. This leads the reader to continually question the relation between words and what they are supposed to express.[7]

A second way a book's content can function in a story is paradigm. While burlesque stresses the incongruity between the book referred to and the action of the story, paradigm stresses their compatibility, the book referred to serving as a model for the story. Paradigm is a common trait of classicism, in which certain works and phrases are held to be so perfect and universal that all subsequent works of a similar type should honor them as goals and models of expression. In the realistic period during which *Huckleberry Finn* was written, however, paradigms were viewed as abstract models that needed concrete and original details, even changes and corrections, to maintain their authority, although their presence added prestige and universality to a story. This view seems to characterize the use of paradigms in *Huckleberry Finn*.

Although the Shakespeare rehearsals of the king and the duke have been described as burlesques, they also function as paradigms. The sword fight from *Richard III* is rehearsed and advertised just before the Boggs-Sherburn duel, and performed just after it, although the performance is not depicted in the novel (177–94). In a sense, the performance *is* the Boggs-Sherburn duel, and Shakespeare's scene is a literary rehearsal or draft for it. As pathetic and unnecessary as the duel shooting is, it also has its tragic element, and associating it with Shakespeare's play clarifies this affective complexity. The duel is a tragedy with its own causes, details, and emotions enacted in a particular American setting. It does not copy Shakespeare. His scene is only a rough sketch, but its classic stature reveals and deepens the gravity of the local event. The duel brings Shakespeare's classic up to date and close to home, which is usually what realistic works do when they treat the classics favorably.[8]

The balcony scene from *Romeo and Juliet* has a similar effect on the Grangerford-Shepherdson feud, which occurs just two chapters before the king and the duke rehearse the scene. Shakespeare's plot and theme are localized in a Southern story that has its own distinct touches—the escape of the lovers, for example—but matches or exceeds Shakespeare in its extent of tragic consequence. Even the recitation of Hamlet's soliloquy, occurring as it does when Huck, like Hamlet, is dealing with players, may cause the reader to compare Huck's moral dilemma about slavery to Hamlet's dilemmas concerning revenge and regicide. This comparison would certainly add prestige and universality to Huck's tragic predicament. Finally, the Lear costume, belonging to the king and the duke and worn by Jim while on the raft during the Wilks episode, creates a number of interesting connections with *King Lear*: society's rejection of Huck and Jim; Huck's and Jim's preference for life on the raft; Huck's change of attitude toward Jim while enduring the elements with him; the exposure of the king's and the duke's fraudulence; and the seemingly generous but actually self-serving bestowal of a legacy on the three Wilks sisters. Shakespeare's play is thus translated into the racism and criminal behavior of nineteenth-century America.[9]

Another book with key paradigms in *Huckleberry Finn* is the Bible, although it, too, like Shakespeare, is subjected to burlesque. When the Widow Douglas reads to Huck about "Moses and the Bulrushers," he is "in a sweat to find out all about him" until he learns that Moses is dead. Huck takes no stock in dead people (2). In many ways, however, Huck resembles Moses, and *Huck Finn* often alludes to the Exodus story. Huck is found, like Moses, by a river, and he is raised, not by Pharaoh's daughters, but by the widow and Miss Watson. Like Moses with the Jews, Huck becomes a liberator of Jim from bondage. Hints of the Exodus story reinforce this parallel, from Buck Grangerford's riddle, "Where was Moses when the candle went out?" (135), to the revival preacher's "brazen serpent in the wilderness" (172), to the place names

Cairo, Memphis, and Goshen, which relate the Mississippi to the Nile. The South becomes Egypt, and Huck goes down to Egypt to free the slave.[10]

Another set of biblical images treats the themes of resurrection and rebirth, and these apply more to Huck himself than to his mission as liberator. Several times Huck supposedly dies and comes back to life: on Jackson's Island after escaping from Pap (51), after being lost in the fog (103), and after surviving the Grangerford-Sheperdson feud (154). When Huck arrives at the Phelps plantations and is mistaken for Tom Sawyer, he feels "born again" (282), and when the real Tom Sawyer shows up and thinks that Huck is a ghost, Huck reassures him that he is not; to prove it he says, "You come in here and feel of me if you don't believe me" (283). This is very close to what Jesus says to another Thomas after the Resurrection (John 20: 27). These images could make Huck a Christ figure as well as a Moses figure because he sacrifices himself to free Jim, but they also suggest a baptism or conversion experience for Huck. All through the story Huck invents names and families for himself, but the names change and the families usually perish tragically. It is his helping of Jim and his change of heart toward him that finally cause Huck to be reborn, receive a name and an identity, and join a family. The biblical paradigms bring out the profundity of this experience. They relocate biblical themes in a concrete and modern setting, and they raise and universalize that setting.

One difficulty with these paradigms, and with the burlesques too, is their apparent superiority to Huck's limited mind and point of view. Even though Huck knows the Bible, it is not likely that he would model his own experiences on biblical events. Nor would he be aware of the burlesque in his book talks with Jim, just as Tom Sawyer misses the burlesque in his use of literary sources. To account for these devices, the reader must go over Huck's head and into the mind of the Author, Mark Twain. He is the intelligence behind the novel who juxtaposes things to make them look sublime or ridiculous. And perhaps the reader can go over Twain's head, too. Language and culture are bigger and stronger forces than the consciousness or intentions of one person. When someone speaks or writes, therefore, he or she complies with these forces and may even be controlled by them. Twain used such a theory of determinism to explain literary influences on his own writing. Neither Huck nor Twain may realize the full import of what they say, but careful study should disclose it because it is already in the language and culture that they use to express themselves.

In relation to burlesque and paradigm, several class exercises suggest themselves. A list could be drawn up of books influential on *Huckleberry Finn*, and students could be assigned to read any one of them and analyze its influence in a brief paper, possibly using some critical articles. This exercise would give students a feel for the continuity of literary tradition. Students might also compose original burlesques. For them to seriously undertake this assignment, it would be necessary to have command of an author's style and point of view, so that these can be used for learning and not just for entertainment. Finally, in longer narratives, either fictional or autobiographical, students may be asked to incorporate other works through burlesque or paradigm. This exercise would indicate which past works students rebel against and which ones they ally themselves with. It would help students assemble a usable past and reduce the isolation that they feel in their own time and experience.

Besides Shakespeare and the Bible, other books might serve as paradigms in *Huckleberry Finn*. In recounting the story of his escape, Jim tells Huck that he overheard a conversation between Miss Watson and the widow Douglas about selling him down the river (53). This resembles the scene in *Uncle Tom's Cabin* when Eliza overhears Mr. Shelby's plan to sell Uncle Tom and little Harry. The motive for the sale is the same in both instances—money—and objections to selling are raised by the widow Douglas and Mrs. Shelby. Also, the slave auction after Peter Wilks's death may reflect a similar auction after the death of Augustin St. Clare.[11] More generally, the two movements of *Uncle Tom's Cabin*, the selling into slavery and the escape from slavery, are combined in Jim's "escape" down the river into slave territory. Also, *Uncle Tom's Cabin* constantly uses the Bible as a paradigm, especially the Exodus story and the Passion of Jesus, so it could have influenced Twain in this regard. Jim's often calling Huck *honey* may have come from the similar name that Uncle Remus calls the white boy who listens to his tales. And the subject of many of these tales is the deceit and trickery that the weak must use to defeat or escape from the strong. Huck could have confirmed some of his tactics by these tales.[12] Huck's shock at stumbling onto Jim's campfire may be an echo of Robinson Crusoe's startling discovery of a footprint on the island. On meeting Huck, Jim kneels just as Friday does to Crusoe (48, 51). Like Huck and Jim, too, Crusoe survives on material that he salvages from shipwrecks.[13] Finally, since Huck says that he has read *Pilgrim's Progress* (137), it is tempting to compare his story with Bunyan's. Huck leaves his family, makes a journey, and rejects a corrupt civilization.[14]

The books mentioned above *may* serve as paradigms in *Huckleberry Finn*. Or they may not. To determine which, the question to ask is: does Mark Twain expect the reader to recall the content of these books and compare it to his story? If he does, they are paradigms. If he does not, they may still be literary sources, but not paradigms. A literary source, as it is being defined here, is any literary work that influences an author in writing a book but does not serve, in either the author's intention or the reader's perception, as a paradigm or burlesque in the story. Put briefly, paradigm and burlesque are artistic devices, like metaphors, that induce greater understanding and appreciation of a story, while a source is just a practical aid that an author uses to conceive or develop the tale. While an author expects the reader to recognize a book used for burlesque or paradigm and puts sufficient clues to it in the story, the author may not expect, or even want, the reader to notice a source. In fact, a use of a source may be unconscious on the author's part.

Literary sources are the third way in which the content of other works contributes to *Huckleberry Finn*. Huck himself is certainly a reader, although without much guidance or system. His readings in the Bible, probably forced on him by the widow Douglas, allow him to refer often to biblical personages (Adam, Noah, Moses, Goliath, Jesus) and to discuss Solomon with Jim. Although he must have picked up a number of literary and historical items from Tom Sawyer's reading, he too reads to Jim about "kings, and dukes, and earls and such," especially about Louis XVII, the "dolphin," who was thought by some to have escaped to America (93, 96). This background reading must have helped Huck see through the sob stories of the king and the duke: "It didn't take me long to make up my mind that these liars warn't no kings nor dukes, at all, but just low-down humbugs and frauds" (165). In a talk with Jim after "The Royal Nonesuch" and other scams, Huck says that he is not surprised at the carrying on of the two imposters. All kings are alike; it is in the breed. He cites several kings down through history: Richard III, Henry VIII, Charles II, and others. Although Huck gets his facts confused, he does generally name kings who were "regular rapscallions" (199–201). The historical perspective that Huck gets from his reading allows him to see the king and the duke not as real kings or aristocrats, but as mighty like them. As an alternative way of knowing that is different from experience, reading divides the perception, causing things to be viewed from at least two perspectives—reading and experience—and this process leads to questions about the contents of both and therefore to practice in discerning truth from falsehood.

Far more so than Huck, Mark Twain prepared himself for writing by broad and systematic background reading. He was convinced that literary skill resulted from study and exercise, not simply from genius or inspiration. One area of his reading that influenced *Huckleberry Finn* was moral philosophy. In the middle and late 1870s, when he was writing the first third of his novel, Twain read W. E. H. Lecky's *History of European Morals from Augustus to Charlemagne*, published in 1869. Ideas from this book penetrate Huck's mind and permeate his moral choices.[15] Lecky distinguishes between two sources of moral action, the stoic and the utilitarian. For the stoic, moral choices arise from an innate natural power, while for the utilitarian, they are based on pleasure and pain and training in a code of punishment and reward. Siding with the utilitarian, Twain bases Huck's decisions about lying and stealing, and especially about helping Jim escape, on feelings of pleasure and pain. Helping Jim makes Huck feel trembly, feverish, mean, ornery, miserable, bad, and low. Giving Jim up makes him feel easy and happy at first, but then sick, because he and Jim have spent so much time talking, laughing, and singing together and have made sacrifices for each other, and because Jim has petted him and called him *honey* (124–28, 268–71). Even these good feelings about helping Jim make Huck feel bad, however, because Huck's conscience has been formed by his social environment and training. Although he acts on his private feelings, he cannot trust them as standards of morality when they go against his social conscience.

Another focus of Twain's reading during the years of his work on *Huckleberry Finn* was history, especially the French Revolution. Two books that Twain claimed to have read often were Thomas Carlyle's *The French Revolution* and Charles Dickens's *A Tale of Two Cities*. Details from these books appear in Tom Sawyer's early drawing up of codes for his gang and in the notions about prison life and escape plots that he conceives in his attempt to free Jim. More details appear in connection with the king and the duke, the king claiming to be the escaped Dauphin, Louis XVII. The evils of monarchy and nobility discussed by Huck and Jim and displayed by the king and the duke are drawn from the times and practices of revolutionary France. The savagery and cowardice of the common people, evident in the mob that tries to lynch Sherburn and the crowd that shows up to recapture Jim and would readily hang him, are also illustrated in the works of Carlyle and Dickens. Both authors divide evils between the upper and lower classes, between monarchy and democracy.[16] Although several particular details from their books match incidents in *Huckleberry Finn*, the main effect that these authors have on Twain is the comparison of historical periods that they enable him to make: the common traits of different periods, the use of the past to interpret the present, and the deterministic view that history repeats itself.

Natural and social determinism can also apply to the act of writing. So much writing has been done that when one begins to write, one tends to repeat something that has been written before. In an 1879 speech, Twain called this phenomenon "unconscious plagiarism," and in another place he referred to it as "mental telegraphy."[17] Several incidents in *Huckleberry Finn* seem to have been influenced by other works, yet they are not clearly either burlesques or paradigms, or even results of Twain's deliberate background reading in philosophy and history. They are just plain sources, and most likely unconscious. Pap's abuse of Huck's fancy clothes, reading, and education (23–26) reflects a scene in *A Tale of Two Cities* in which Jerry Cruncher scolds his wife for her piety, and Jim's ridicule of the French language (96–98) resembles that of Miss Pross in the Dickens novel.[18] The way that Mrs. Loftus penetrates Huck's girl disguise (72–73) may have come from Charles Reade's *The Cloister and the Hearth*, and the king's fake conversion story at the revival (171–74) has traits of a Simon Suggs tale, "The Captain Attends a Camp-Meeting," by Southwestern humorist Johnson J. Hooper.[19] Many more incidents in Twain's novel must have been influenced by other sources because Twain read widely, and by his own admission he could not prevent what he read from showing up in his writing, whether he was aware of it or not.

An obvious reading exercise on general literary sources would be to examine Huck's moral reflections (124–28, 268–71) and history lessons (93–98, 199–201) to see if Twain properly fitted these complex ideas to Huck's understanding and style of expression. Students might also explore the general sources of their own ideas and how they have adapted them to their own needs and style. Are there books or other

Anthony J. Berret, S.J.

forms of expression (films, music) whose ideas constantly enter into their talk and writing? Are they aware of this influence, or is it unconscious? Does their writing show either general or particular influences that may be unconscious?

Although these general and simple sources definitely exist in *Huckleberry Finn*, they should not be emphasized in teaching. They are too likely to make students think that a novel cannot be understood or appreciated without knowing something extraneous to it, something that only the teacher knows. Rather, emphasis should be placed on the explicit references to books and writing, the special character of these references (burlesque or paradigm) and their functions in the story. These are the sources that the author uses consciously and expects the reader to recognize. Studying them will add richness and complexity to a text and help students see relationships and coherence in the literary tradition.

Notes

1   *Adventures of Huckleberry Finn*, ed. Walter Blair and Victor Fischer (Berkeley: University of California Press, 1985), 24, 30, 93. Page references to this edition appear in the text.

2   For a readable introduction to intertextuality, with a helpful bibliography, see Thais E. Morgan, "Is There an Intertext in This Text?: Literary and Interdisciplinary Approaches to Intertextuality," *American Journal of Semiotics* 3, 4 (1985): 1–40.

3   This distinction between the medium and the represented reality corresponds to the difference between a signifier and what it signifies (the signified). Structuralists and deconstructionists want this difference stressed, and they see it stressed when signifiers are exposed as signifiers by drawing attention to themselves (as they do here: "I am a book") or by their multiplicity and diversity in a given work (intertextuality).

4   Contemporary critics distinguish between "readerly" texts and "writerly" texts, the latter being those texts that raise questions and need to be corrected and completed (rewritten) by the reader.

5   The Reference Material in the Blair-Fischer edition of *Huckleberry Finn* locates many of the literary sources. For Tom Sawyer's models, see 378, 380. More recent studies include Robert V. Graybill, "Don Quixote and Huckleberry Finn: Points of Contact," *Indiana Journal of Hispanic Literatures* 5 (Fall 1994): 145–60, and John Bryant, "Melville, Twain and Quixote: Variations on a Comic Debate," *Studies in American Humor* 3, 1 (1994): 1–27.

6   George C. Carrington, Jr., argues a position parallel to this one in *The Dramatic*

Unity of "Huckleberry Finn" (Columbus: Ohio State University Press, 1976). He sees drama—the attempt to create order and excitement out of human situations—as the main theme of Twain's book and therefore appropriate to the Phelps episode. Laurence B. Holland discusses the relation of talk, writing, books, and style to action in "A 'Raft of Trouble': Word and Deed in *Huckleberry Finn*," *Glyph* 5 (1979): 69–87.

7   In *Mark Twain's Burlesque Patterns* (Dallas: Southern Methodist University Press, 1960), Franklin R. Rogers studies Twain's background in burlesque writing (chapter 2) and the influence of patterns from this on *Huckleberry Finn* (chapter 4). He argues that Twain, by contrasting literary episodes with real episodes, helps the reader to distinguish between false and true, comic and serious (144–51).

8   For a more thorough study of this and other Shakespeare paradigms in *Huckleberry Finn*, see Anthony J. Berret, *Mark Twain and Shakespeare: A Cultural Legacy* (Lanham, Md.: University Press of America, 1993), 144–78.

9   Other critics who study Shakespeare paradigms in *Huckleberry Finn* are Howard Baetzhold, *Mark Twain and John Bull: The British Connection* (Bloomington: Indiana University Press, 1970), 258 (on *Romeo and Juliet*); E. Bruce Kirkham, "Huck and Hamlet," *Mark Twain Journal* 14 (Summer 1969): 17–19; Paul Schacht, "The Lonesomeness of Huckleberry Finn," *American Literature* 53 (May 1981): 193–96; and Victor Doyno, *Writing "Huck Finn": Mark Twain's Creative Process* (Philadelphia: University of Pennsylvania Press, 1991), 122–23 (on *Lear*).

10 Kenneth S. Lynn notes this parallel in *Mark Twain and Southwestern Humor* (Boston: Little, Brown, 1959), 208, 213, 243; Robert Sattelmeyer finds this and other Old Testament parallels (Adam, Noah, Abraham) in "'Interesting, but Tough': *Huckleberry Finn* and the Problem of Tradition," in *One Hundred Years of "Huckleberry Finn": The Boy, His Book, and American Culture*, ed. Robert Sattelmeyer and J. Donald Crowley (Columbia: University of Missouri Press, 1985). See also Billy G. Collins, "Huckleberry Finn: A Mississippi Moses," *Journal of Narrative Technique* 5 (May 1975), 86–104; Kenneth Seib, "Moses and the Bulrushers: A Note on *Huckleberry Finn*," *Mark Twain Journal* 18 (Summer 1977): 13–14; Joseph B. McCullough, "Uses of the Bible in *Huckleberry Finn*," *Mark Twain Journal* 19 (Winter 1978): 2–3; Kelly Anspaugh, "'I Been There Before': Biblical Typology and *Adventures of Huckleberry Finn*," *ANQ* 7 (October 1994): 219–23.

11 See Harriet Beecher Stowe, *Uncle Tom's Cabin*, chapters 5, 30. Kenneth Lynn sees similarity in the relationships of Uncle Tom with Little Eva and Jim with Huck, *Mark Twain and Southwestern Humor*, 240–41. See also Abigail Ann Hamblen, "Uncle Tom and 'Nigger Jim': A Study in Contrasts and Similarities," *Mark Twain Journal* 11 (Fall 1961): 13–17, and Bong Eun Kim, "Rhetorical Wrestle with Racism: *Uncle Tom's Cabin* and *Adventures of Huckleberry Finn*," *Journal of English Language and Literature* (Seoul, Korea) 41, 2 (1995): 419–35.

12 William J. Scheick makes this point in "The Spunk of a Rabbit: An Allusion to

The Adventures of Huckleberry Finn," *Mark Twain Journal* 15 (Summer 1971): 14–16.

13 See Daniel Defoe, *Robinson Crusoe*, "I Find the Print of a Man's Naked Foot" and "I Hear the First Sound of a Man's Voice." Parallels with *Robinson Crusoe* are noted by Baetzhold, *Mark Twain and John Bull*, 269.

14 Alfred Bendixen argues this point in *"Huck Finn* and *Pilgrim's Progress,"* *Mark Twain Journal* 18 (Winter 1976–77): 21; he also considers Huck's direct, unadorned language realistic like Bunyan's. Sattelmeyer relates Bunyan's allegory to Twain's use of literary allusions and analogues in *Huckleberry Finn*, " 'Interesting but Tough,' " 354.

15 Walter Blair studies this influence in *Mark Twain and Huck Finn* (Berkeley: University of California Press, 1960), 134–44.

16 Blair discusses these influences in "The French Revolution and *Huckleberry Finn,"* *Modern Philology* 55 (August 1957): 21–35; also in *Mark Twain and Huck Finn*, 117–19, 132–34, 178–82, 277–79. Baetzhold studies them in *Mark Twain and John Bull*, 87–94, and he connects the king and the duke with Charles II and James II through Twain's reading of Samuel Pepys's *Diary*, 83–87.

17 See "Unconscious Plagiarism," *Mark Twain's Speeches*, in *The Complete Works of Mark Twain*, Authorized Edition, vol. 24 (New York: Harper, 1923), 77–79; see also "Mental Telegraphy" and "Mental Telegraphy Again," in *In Defense of Harriet Shelley*, in *Complete Works*, vol. 16 (1918), 116–22, 129–30.

18 See *A Tale of Two Cities*, Book 2, chapter 1, and Book 3, chapters 7, 14. Blair cites these influences in "The French Revolution and *Huckleberry Finn,"* 25–27. Joseph H. Gardner finds the model for Pap's abuse in *Our Mutual Friend*, Book 1, chapter 6; see "Gaffer Hexam and Pap Finn," *Modern Philology* 66 (1968–69): 155–56.

19 See Blair, *Mark Twain and Huck Finn*, 129–30, 279–80; see *The Cloister and the Hearth*, chapter 63.

The Relationship of Kemble's Illustrations to Mark Twain's Text: Using Pictures to Teach *Huck Finn*

Beverly R. David

Adventures of Huckleberry Finn has always been America's most revered yet most maligned classic. A few months after *Huck Finn* was published, Joel Chandler Harris praised the work, declaring, "There is not in our fictive literature a more wholesome book."[1] At the same time that the Concord Public Library decided to ban the book, and when *Huck Finn* appeared in *Century*, a school superintendent in South Pueblo, Colorado, wrote to the editor that Mark Twain's writings were "destitute of a single redeeming quality."[2] The controversy continues.

According to today's scholars the problem is in the teaching, not in the novel.[3] Most studies agree that if *Huck Finn* is to be taught in the schools, it should be taken up "under the guidance of a teacher who is aware of the *historical* [emphasis mine] context of the book and author."[4] Unfortunately scholars, critics, and teachers usually ignore a most obvious tool for setting this historical context: the first edition illustrations. And the pictures are useful in many ways other than merely establishing history.

When scanning a picture, people process information differently than when they read a line of prose. Looking at a picture, a reader instantly grasps the artist's idea. The phenomenon is called mosaic formation. When reading lines of text, however, each word, line, paragraph builds separately, slowly, until the complete concept is formed. This phenomenon is called linear processing. Students going through the linear process "build" pictures in their minds; each individual's picture creates his/her personal interpretation of the author's idea. On the other hand, an illustration on a page of text immediately controls a reader's interpretation of that text; it "bends" the message of the linear lines. We all understand this phenomenon. It is the reason why seeing a character in a movie forever shapes our definition of that character when, later, we read the book. For anyone who has seen the 1939 movie of *Gone With the Wind*, Scarlett O'Hara will always be Vivien Leigh, whatever Margaret Mitchell's original intentions may have been. Mosaic formation explains why comic books, splashy magazine ads, and colorful, artfully edited television commercials are so powerful. All give "instant gratification"—no waiting to read the small print.[5]

Literary snobs may still consider "looking at pictures" unscholarly. Yet as early as 1885, Mark Twain knew the power of pictures. He insisted that *Huck Finn* be "fully illustrated." He personally chose the illustrator, Edward Windsor Kemble, approved his sketches, and even directed the placement of the prints in the text. When we also understand how pictures relate to and interpret narrative, we, as teachers, can capitalize on the Kemble illustrations in *Huck Finn* to stimulate today's visually oriented students.

When the use of pictures is encouraged in teaching this novel, it presents some problems. However, in view of the availability of a new and inexpensive reprint of the 1885 Webster Publishing Company edition, the benefits far outweigh the disadvantages. The biggest plus is the power of the Kemble illustrations to immediately establish the book's historical context—the issue that most observers consider crucial. Unfortunately, among the more negative features of the illustrations are the sometime stereotypical views of Jim and other characters. Understanding visual perception can help us explain and compensate for the flawed pictorial components, while, at the same time, we emphasize pictures that relay the messages we, as teachers, want to convey.

The first thing a reader sees when opening the first edition reprint— after viewing the Gerhardt bust of Twain—is the frontispiece. Here is a nineteenth-century Huck with patched pants, a single gallus, and collarless shirt—a hero totally divorced from our contemporary baseball-hatted, Nike-shod, and logo-emblazoned students. The only connection to them is that all are young (see figure 2, on p. 185 in the Fishkin chapter).[6] Huck is seen brandishing an old-fashioned ball-and-cap shotgun, wearing high-top shoes and a sly grin. The picture presents a perfect opportunity for an instructor to illuminate the text by supplying some background on the fashion of a hundred years ago. Kemble's illustrations are ideal to use as examples since all his costuming is authentic. By relating one simple detail about nineteenth-century footwear—the fact that the crude boots of the time were meant to fit either foot, left or right—a teacher can help students understand why Twain's

Huck always preferred going barefoot. "Once upon *another* time" is easily established.

Young women in the class will be interested in Kemble's drawings of the widow Douglas and Miss Watson in the opening chapter (figures 1 and 2). The widow's lacy nightcap and Miss Watson's shoetop-length skirt—authentic features of 1840s' women's dress—leave little doubt as to the time period of Twain's story. These illustrations, along with so many other equally authentic Kemble drawings, evoke a day far removed from Guess, Gitano, and Gap. Male and female students alike, having made the long leap from present-day dress to that of, say, 1840, will have been to some degree prepared for the equally gigantic leap from today's politics and customs—and prejudices—to those of the 1870s and 1880s, when *Huck Finn* was conceived, written, and published.

When the historical groundwork has been fully established, teachers can proceed to examine the novel itself and the more significant aspects of Mark Twain's writing: his wit and biting satire, his irony, and his ambiguous handling of both sex and the race issue. Did Twain intend to include sexual innuendo in his novel? Of course, though he was extremely careful to phrase his narrative to avoid offending a sensitive Victorian audience. Did he control his bawdy, mining-camp humor in his commercially published works? Without a doubt. His 1879 speech, "Some Remarks on the Subject of Onanism," was never published in his lifetime and *Date 1601: Conversation, as it was by the Social Fireside, in the Time of the Tudors,* was "privately printed" in an edition of only fifty for friends in 1882.

Was Mark Twain racist? Certainly. He was born in the 1800s and raised in the South. How could he avoid being a racist? Did he fight against these separatist ideas as he matured? Of course, and ample evidence proves this point, from his helping with the expenses of a black student at Yale to his intercession with President James A. Garfield to prevent the dismissal of Frederick A. Douglass from his government post.[7] Faculty and students must remember that Twain was getting on toward fifty when *Huck Finn* was published—a mature author with a well-established reputation on both sides of the Atlantic. The problem becomes how to help students understand the arbitrariness of the culture in which Twain lived—to understand the Puritanical attitudes of his readers and also to understand, but still not excuse, the racial tensions of 1885.

1

2

— Miss Watson

When studying a novel, what could motivate today's students more than to study the author's sexually suggestive, comic ideas by examining the relationship between the pictures and the prose. With Twain, however, the connections are not always obvious. He was very cagey in his handling of the art/text juxtaposition for *Huck Finn*. For example, Kemble sketched a few original designs for the chapter depicting the pirate/king hugging and kissing young girls, "some of them . . . as many as five or six times." Twain ordered that Kemble's drawings be "knocked out" of the chapter, declaring, " 'It is powerful good, but mustn't go in. . . . Let's not make *any* pictures of the campmeeting. The subject won't *bear* illustrating. It is a disgusting thing, & pictures are sure to tell the truth about it too plainly.' "[8]

In another instance focusing on the king's antics, "The Royal Nonesuch," Twain had both the text and the related picture "toned down." Years later, the author admitted to modifying this episode for his more refined readers: "In one of my books—'Huckleberry Finn,' I think—I have used one of Jim's [Gillis's] impromptu tales, which he called 'The Tragedy of the Burning Shame.' I had to modify it considerably to make it proper for print, and this was a great damage. As Jim told it . . . I think it was one of the most outrageously funny things I have ever listened to. How mild it is in the book, and how pale; how extravagant and how gorgeous in its unprintable form."[9] Obviously, Jim Gillis had pantomimed the "shame" for Twain, acting out in true oral tradition, his gestures adding much to the narrative. Research into The Royal Nonesuch reveals the more vulgar side of the incident. The true basis for the Royal spectacle was a crude campfire story: "Two destitute actors tried to raise money by staging a performance in a small town. One man collected money while the audience gathered (no women were admitted), and when the curtain was raised his partner appeared, kneeling and naked, while his partner introduced the act. 'And now, gentlemen, you are about to see "The Tragedy of the Burning Shame." ' He inserted a candle in the naked man's posterior, and lit it."[10]

A prudent Twain knew that more than just Jim Gillis's tall tale had to be altered. His instructions to his illustrator concerning this and all unseemly passages was to design an illustration that would "deflect the reader's attention away from anything offensive."[11] Kemble's paint-striped, not "naked," king successfully diverted a reader's focus (figure 3). Twain approved, aware that what his "aristocratic audience" saw in the illustration would temper their reading of an otherwise indecent episode.

Similar visual and verbal sexual situations have been investigated. One critic calls Kemble's picture "One of His Ancestors" (figure 4) "carnigraphy," justifying his term by this explanation: "the angle of the warmingpan handle displayed in the illustration suggests yet another, more anatomical kind of handle."[12] Another scholar suggests a Freudian subtext with an analysis of "cross-dressing" since Huck, the king, and Jim, are all seen in women's garb (figures 5, 6, and 7).[13]

One of the less controversial but more blatant depictions of adolescent sexuality, present in both picture and print, appears in the chapter where Tom tries to convince Huck that with the rubbing of a lamp, a genie will appear and aid them in their quest for riches:

> "How you talk, Huck Finn. Why, you'd *have* to come when he rubbed it, whether you wanted to or not."
>
> "What, and I as high as a tree and as big as a church? All right then; I *would* come.
>
> . . . .
>
> I [Huck] thought all this over for two or three days, and then I reckoned I *would* see if there was anything in it. I got out an old tin lamp and an iron ring and went out in the woods and rubbed and rubbed till I sweat like an Injun, . . . but it warn't no use, none of the genies come.[14]

Twain's added emphasis to *have* and *would* before the verb make the reading very clear. When Twain's text is coupled with Kemble's drawing—his positioning of the lamp in Huck's lap (figure 8)—the intent of both author and artist is unmistakable. Kemble's collaborative technique has been referred to as a way of "*re*-presenting Twain's erotic subtext through his [Kemble's] own pictorial sublimina."[15]

Although Twain may have used caution in instances where flagrant reminders of sex were explicit, at other times he delighted in tantalizing his readers. It has been established that the captions to all of the illustrations were approved by Twain and that he changed a good number of Kemble's original ideas.[16] Kemble's working caption for the lamp drawing was literally from the text, "I got an old tin lamp." Twain's revision, RUBBING THE LAMP, supplies the teasing fillip to his narrative, a dimension that would go unnoticed without the picture.

Chapter XXIII

3

4

5

Chapter XI.

6

Chapter XXIV

7

8

Since Mark Twain's novel deals primarily with black/white relationships, the collaboration between Kemble's pictures and Twain's narrative adds an interesting dimension about the race issue not found in unillustrated editions. When studying the illustrated text, do we find that black characters are made to appear more ridiculously funny, more crudely comic, than whites? Are blacks more often the object of derisive laughter than whites? A simple answer is no. However, there is a problem in the first edition illustrations with an inconsistency in the portrayal of Jim. In the early drawings he is not necessarily a sympathetic figure (figure 9).[17] Through the pages his visual persona becomes more distinct, even handsome, and much more likable—in much the same way his character subtly changes in the story. Admittedly, Kemble's Jim is too often drawn with the look of a slack-jawed, cartoon comic; superstition and bewilderment are frequently the focus of the picture. Yet some likenesses are clearly sympathetic (figure 10). In the twenty-eight illustrations of Jim—counting chapter headings where he is almost unrecognizable—there are few derogatory implications. The images are seldom blatantly cruel—the exception being where Jim is dressed by the duke as King Lear in the "long curtain-calico gown." Kemble's figures of Jim in *Huck Finn* are clearly much less derisive than

9

10

11

the predominantly negative "coon" caricatures of the same time period drawn by him and by other illustrators (figures 11 and 12).

Once again, the captions for the illustrations are instructive. For those who are counting, one use of the word "nigger" in *Huck Finn*—though it does not refer to Jim—is seldom considered. Captions for pictures of Jim, though sometimes funny, are never offensive and never use the word "nigger." Usually they refer to him simply as Jim without a modifying adjective. The word does appear in one caption, MISTO BRADISH'S NIGGER (figure 13). In this section of chapter 8, where the word "nigger" is used half a dozen times in the space of little more than a page, it must be noted that it is Jim, not a white person, who uses the word when referring to Mr. Bradish's slave and a number of other black men with whom Jim has had dealings. Incidentally, if the man Kemble has drawn over that caption has the appearance of a sly schemer, it is because the rascal has swindled Jim to the tune of five dollars.

The much-debated narrative "ending" for *Huck Finn* also has a pictorial ending. Long before Rosa Parks sat in the front of the Montgomery bus or Alabama Governor George Wallace stood in the schoolhouse door, Twain was seen as remarkably aware of his nineteenth-century audience's reaction to the issue of racism. He was a businessman as well as an author. Nevertheless, he had inserted as a second-to-last illustration in the first edition a rather contemporary view of Tom, Huck, and Jim. In it, Jim holds the center position, arms draped across the shoulders of his two white companions. The illustration, a "heading" for "Chapter the last"—making it a strategic place to insert this print—has the caption OUT OF BONDAGE (figure 14). Huck's words, "All right then, I'll go to Hell," as he decides not to turn Jim over to the law, coincide nicely with Kemble's drawing of a beaming Jim with a fatherly hand on Huck's shoulder and the other on Tom's.

A market-conscious Mark Twain certainly understood the dangers in the mid-nineteenth century of assigning equal status to his three American heroes. One look at the picture and book sales could plummet. Prudently, he did not sanction using this picture in the sales circular. Yet, even with the possible loss of revenue, Twain approved both Kemble's sketch and the caption.[18] Would a *racist* Mark Twain condone this compassionate view of Jim? Would he consider this picture, with its OUT OF BONDAGE caption, a misinterpretation of his story or of Jim's character? The reader must decide.

E. W. Kemble's first edition illustrations can provide some necessary

12

13

14

tools for teaching *Adventures of Huckleberry Finn*. Kemble's pictures and Twain's story have left a visual and verbal legacy about the repressed sexual climate and the racist mentality during the late 1800s. Both author and artist were taking courageous steps forward when all but the smallest minority was in violent opposition to their views.

Notes

1   Joel Chandler Harris [Letter to the Editor], *Critic* 7 (28 November 1885): 253.

2   Mark Twain, *Adventures of Huckleberry Finn*, ed. Walter Blair and Victor Fischer (Berkeley: University of California Press, 1988), 495–96, n. 160.

3   Here is a sampling of articles concerning the teaching of the novel: Anonymous, "Selling Huck Down the River," *Washington Post*, 9 April 1982, A18; John Head, "It's Absurd to Accuse Twain of Being Racist," *Atlanta Journal and Constitution*, 26 November 1990, A-13 (John Head is a black *Constitution* editorial columnist); Michael Patrick Hearn, "Expelling *Huck Finn*," *Nation* 235 (7–14 August 1982): 117; Nat Hentoff, "Is Any Book Worth the Humiliation of Our Kids?," *Village Voice*, 11 May 1982, 8; Shelley Fisher Fishkin, [television debate] *Freeman Reports* (Cable News Network), 14 March 1985.

4   Dorothy Gilliam, "Banning Huck," *Washington Post*, 12 April 1982, B1.

5   Student retention rates: 10 percent read, 20 percent heard; 30 percent seen; 50 percent seen/heard; 75 percent discussed; 90 percent experienced. Clifford Whithouse, Conference of Association of Instruction for Multi-Media, April 1993.

6   Mark Twain did consider Kemble's Huck as "too Irishy." See letter of Webster to Clemens, 5 May 1884, Mark Twain Project, Bancroft Library, University of California, Berkeley.

7   Edwin McDowell, "From Twain, a Letter on Debt to the Blacks," *New York Times*, 14 March 1985, 1, 16. See also Sterling Brown, *The Negro in American Fiction* (Washington, D.C.: Associates in Negro Folk Education, 1935). Nanelia Doughty, "Realistic Negro Characterization in Postbellum Fiction," *Negro American Literature Forum* 3 (Summer 1969): 57–62, 68.

8   *Mark Twain, Businessman*, ed. Samuel Charles Webster (Boston: Little, Brown, 1946), 260.

9   Walter Kokernot, " 'Burning Shame' Broadside," *Mark Twain Journal* 29, 2 (Fall 1991): 33.

10 Wallace Graves, "Mark Twain's 'Burning Shame,' " *Nineteenth-Century Fiction* 23 (June 1968): 98.

11 Beverly R. David, "The Pictorial *Huck Finn*: Mark Twain and His Illustrator, E. W. Kemble," *American Quarterly*, 26 (October 1974): 337.

12 Tak Sioui, *"Huckleberry Finn": More Molecules* (privately printed, 1962), 9. (For more information on this bad joke, see Norton D. Kinghorn, "E. W. Kemble's Misplaced Modifier: A Note on the Illustrations for *Huckleberry Finn*," *Mark Twain Journal* 16, 4 (1973): 10.

13 Kelly Anspaugh, "The Innocent Eye? E. W. Kemble's Illustrations to *Adventures of Huckleberry Finn*," *American Literary Realism* 25, 2 (Winter 1993): 23. Anspaugh also attributes sexual content to the illustration of "Uncle Silas in Danger," writing that "his phallus is . . . in imminent peril."

14 Twain, *Huck Finn*, 16–17.

15 Anspaugh, "The Innocent Eye?" 21.

16 Beverly R. David, "Mark Twain and the Legends for *Huckleberry Finn*," *American Literary Realism* 15, 2 (Autumn 1982): 157.

17 Kemble was seldom in possession of the whole manuscript and never had the sections in chronological sequence until the last sections of the manuscript. E. W. Kemble to Charles Webster, 2 June 1884, Mark Twain Papers.

18 Twain, 535, n. 362.11.

Using Audiovisual Media to Teach
Huckleberry Finn
Wesley Britton

A plethora of audiovisual materials relating to *Huckleberry Finn* are available for the classroom. Many videos, films, film strips, and sound recordings can be obtained through school libraries, video rental outlets, or retail stores, and many contain material useful in secondary or academic classroom discussions. However, teachers should also be aware of the uneven, erratic, and often downright silly nature of many adaptations of Twain's novel.

In addition, educational film producers have issued useful introductions to the novel, and some provide background on Mark Twain that can supplement lesson plans and add vitality and diversity to class discussions. The following survey of available materials is intended both to assist in choosing what tools to use and to provide suggestions on how to use audiovisual adaptations to initiate class discussions. The choice of materials is largely a function both of personal taste and of pedagogical intention, and new materials will undoubtedly be published in future years, but this guide should save you time by reviewing the most accessible materials and point you to the range of the more useful sources.

Movies and Television

The first adaptation of *Huckleberry Finn* was a silent film in 1919, a rare Morosco-Lasky production. Since then, Hollywood has produced eleven adaptations of *Huckleberry Finn*, some of which are now readily available on home video. These productions were first released in 1931 (Paramount), 1939 (MGM/Loews), 1946 (MGM/Custodians), 1960 (MGM), 1974 (United Artists), 1975 (made for television), 1978 (dir.: Jack B. Hively), 1980 (ABC/Circle Films), 1980 (a New Hope cartoon), 1985 (PBS), and 1993 (Disney). Other animated versions have been released including 1985's *The Raft Adventures of Huck and Jim*. In 1973, Georgian director Georgi Danelia filmed *Hopelessly Lost* in Moscow— the darkest and, by far, the most adult version available on video. And in 1992, Disney televised *Return to Hannibal: The New Adventures of Huck Finn and Tom Sawyer*, a non-Twain story reuniting Huck, Tom, and the novel's other characters fifteen years later.

Most big studio versions have attempted to appeal to a wide family audience, emphasizing folksy, Midwestern characterizations with laundered dialogue as whitewashed as Tom Sawyer's fence. The phrase "politically correct" has frequently been used to describe Disney's 1993 version, but older versions are rarely any more faithful to the original text. As *Magill's Survey of Cinema* notes, most versions "focus on the novel's colorfully picturesque moments, scenes of human stupidity, bigotry, and intolerance." However, scripts, settings, and photography are typically prettified, scrubbed clean and lightly comic, and most characterizations are broadly played and rarely in the spirit of Twain's intentions.

Another appropriate complaint is noted in *Magill's* 1993 review of the Disney version, observing that most film versions, including the Disney adaptation, are flawed by attempting to tell too much story in too little time, lacking the emotional spirit Mark Twain intended. So, since classroom time too is limited, use of media should be carefully and judiciously thought out. It is often not time-effective to screen entire movies in the classroom; however, because of the variety of treatments of the novel, showing specific scenes can lead to profitable discussions of the novel's ending and to characterizations of Huck, Jim, the king, the duke, and other characters. One example of a usable scene is the "Raftsmen passage" reenactment in the PBS 1985 television version. The scene is a showcase of keelboat dialect and the Mississippi brag. Purists will have to forgive the addition of the raftsmen painting Huck blue for spying on them, but viewing this section does provide some of the flavor Twain captures in the text. The rest of the four-hour miniseries offers a standard, if expanded, treatment of the main characters. Viewers will be struck by the degree to which Jim, though not as indignant as in the 1993 Disney version, is clearly speaking with a twentieth-century accent.

Disney's 1993 version provides much more usable material, particularly where Jim's character has been modernized as an extremely intelligent and morally outraged spokesman against slavery far different from Twain's more realistic, dialect-speaking, deferential slave. Some of the movie's speeches make for sharp contrast with Twain's less politically correct character, and classroom comparisons would point to the differing perspectives of the nineteenth and twentieth centuries.

Another notable change can be seen at the film's outset when Jim declares slavery is wrong, Huck agrees with him, and therefore much of Huck's moral dilemma is lost in the filmscript. While Huck's "I'll go to hell" climax does occur onscreen, its impact may be lessened by his earlier actions. Students, of course, may have a different interpretation; either way, insights into racial perspectives would result from compare/contrast essay assignments.

Other films have varying degrees of useful material. Director Norman Taurog's black-and-white eighty-minute 1931 release was the first major motion picture adaptation, using essentially the same cast as the previous year's *Adventures of Tom Sawyer*, both films emphasizing the relationship between Huck (Junior Durkin) and Tom Sawyer (Jackie Coogan). Jim (Clarence Muse) is only a minor character, and most of the film bears only superficial resemblance to Twain's text. MGM's 1939 release, directed by Richard Thorpe (also black and white, running for 90 minutes) stars Mickey Rooney as Huck, Rex Ingram as Jim, and William Frawley as the duke. According to *Magill*, this is a "weak adaptation," although, on the positive side, the emphasis has shifted from the Huck/Tom relationship to Huck and Jim's misadventures on the raft. MGM's highly touted second *Huckleberry Finn* (1960), directed by Michael Curtiz, runs for 107 minutes and was the first color version (Metrocolor). *Magill* is largely correct when it praises the production values but pans the broad acting. The film stars Eddie Hodges as Huck and ex-boxer Archie Moore as Jim, but the film's emphasis on Tony Randall as the king and Mickey Shaughnessy as the duke makes this film a showcase for those characters played as lovable ruffians. Useful comparisons can be drawn between Hollywood's treatment of the con men, Twain's descriptions, and, if possible, the characterizations in the Russian *Hopelessly Lost* adaptation in which a ruthless king and duke dominate Huck and Jim.

In 1974, United Artists released a color, 118-minute musical version. Directed by J. Lee Thompson and starring Jeff East as Huck, Paul Winfield as Jim, and Harvey Korman as the king, the film would probably only be useful in a classroom setting if instructors chose to focus on dramatic interpretations of Twain's characters. "If you choose to bring musical treatments of Huck into your discussions, the 1985 Roger Miller Broadway musical *Big River*, not yet filmed, has been issued as a soundtrack album with songs that may demonstrate points about popular culture rather than the novel itself." The 1975 made-for-television *Huckleberry Finn* (74 minutes)—directed by Robert Totten and starring Ron Howard, Donny Most, Antonio Fargas, Merle Haggard, and Jack Elam—is fun at times; Ron Howard is especially good as Huck. Another 1970s offering, the 1978 *Adventures of Huckleberry Finn* (97 minutes), is directed by Jack B. Hively and stars Forrest Tucker, Larry Storch, and Brock Peters; it rates as one of the less memorable versions of Twain's novel.

Disney's 108-minute 1993 Technicolor version, being the most recent, may prove the most useful Hollywood version for the classroom. Director/screenwriter Stephen Sommers chose to emphasize the racial aspects of the novel, focusing on the relationship between Huck (Elijah Wood) and Jim (Courtney B. Vance), excluding the antics of Tom Sawyer altogether. While Twain scholars largely dismiss the film, some film critics look on Sommers's "noble attempt" more kindly. *Magill*, in a generally favorable treatment, notes that Sommers tries to blend the novel's "sobering ingredients into the film's more boyishly adventurous exploits." Some episodes are clearly more topical than earlier treatments, such as the outcome of the Shepherdson-Grangerford feud, which highlights the violence of American society, both then and now. As *Magill* observes, the "illogical horror" of the outcome of the episode is one of the film's most effective moments.

The ending, without Tom Sawyer's romanticized adventures, is worth comparison with the ending in *Hopelessly Lost* (with Huck and Jim still trapped on the raft with the king and duke) or that of the four-part PBS television version. It too considerably shortens the novel's protracted youthful insensitivity to Jim's feelings. As this section of the novel is typically one of considerable interest and controversy, moviemakers' attempts to "improve" Twain's original ending may spark provocative student insights. Sommers's version, for example, has Mary Jane Wilkes save Jim from a lynch mob, a rather less than satisfying reworking of Colonel Sherburn's speech. *Magill* describes the ending as "sadly lacking in believability and emotional fervor"—so perhaps Twain's version is not as bad as some have proposed. But perhaps the most useful films were not produced for Hollywood. Georgi Danelia's *Hopelessly Lost* (dubbed in English) is far more naturalistic in tone and content than any other feature-length version, and it is certainly the most appropriate for college-level audiences. This film has been available on video (although it is now out of print), most often packaged as *The Adventures of Huckleberry Finn*, and is worth considering for either a complete or abridged viewing.

Some adaptations and background films were created with the classroom in mind, the newest and most useful being the Learning Channel's hour-long documentary, "The Adventures of Huckleberry Finn." The film is a detailed introduction to the novel, with a variety of perspectives including commentary by Twain scholars Justin Kaplan and Vic Doyno, along with observations by Nat Hentoff, Garrison Keilor, and John Wallace. The film also includes scenes from film adaptations of the novel, including the rarely seen silent versions, along with new readings and enactments from the book. Narrated by Donald Sutherland, produced by Dale Minor and Gordon Hyatt for Discover Productions, this installment of the Great Books series won a Cronkite Award in 1994. The project contains more useful material than any other audiovisual aid currently available, although the editing is occasionally confusing and the last fifteen minutes wander.

Other made-for-classroom tools include Syracuse University's 1956 short version of the novel for National Educational Television that can be useful if available in your school library. In 1965, Britannica Educational Corporation released *Huck Finn and the American Experience* for classroom use, emphasizing *Huckleberry Finn*'s universality as an example of classic literature. The film is pointedly geared for high school readers, although lower-level college readers can also benefit from viewing it as part of discussing the novel in a larger context.

Some extremely useful material discusses Mark Twain the author rather than Huck Finn, adding illuminating insights into the novel's creator. In the fall of 1994 the Learning Channel aired a well-constructed, hour-long biography of Twain on its *This Century* series, a film NBC originally produced in 1989 for its *America: A Look Back* series. Narrated by Tom Brokaw, the documentary emphasizes Twain as a cultural figure and observer of his times, ignoring his literary output. While the film touches on many underdeveloped points, it is well illustrated with photographs and art of the era, emphasizing styles and fashions of Twain's lifetime.

The 1960 series *Mark Twain's America* (not to be confused with Disney's fanciful series of the same name) provides historical background, and 1980's *Mark Twain: Beneath the Laughter* (available on film) is a one-hour candid look at Mark Twain's life and trials. Numerous other, shorter biographies are available on film, video, and filmstrip, and instructors should consult their media library catalogues to see which are accessible. (A detailed listing of these educational aids is in my *Mark Twain Encyclopedia* entry, "Media Adaptations of Mark Twain's Works.") New products regularly are issued; at this writing, for instance, a three-hour biography of Mark Twain is being developed for PBS. Instructors may wish to keep abreast of these productions and adopt them when appropriate. (Note: My periodic "Media Updates" are published both in *The Mark Twain Circular* and online on *The Mark Twain Forum*. The first installment in the *Circular* appeared in 9.3 [July/September 1995]: 7–9; the second appeared in 11.2 [April-June 1997]: 1–4.)

Recordings

Hal Holbrook, the most famous contemporary Mark Twain impersonator, has recorded two very effective readings from *Huckleberry Finn* on two Columbia long-playing (LP) discs, "Mark Twain Tonight" (not to be confused with "Mark Twain Tonight: Highlights from the CBS Television Special") and "More Mark Twain Tonight." At the beginning of side two of each LP, Holbrook-as-Twain introduces the novel, providing details about what inspired Twain to write it. Then he reads passages from the novel in a tour de force performance of Twain-as-Huck, acting as an old man imitating a young boy's voice. The acting is superb, with comic pauses and excellent vocal characterizations. Both readings are abridged and condensed passages from early in the novel, including Pap Finn's diatribe and Colonel Sherburn's episode. Either recording provides excellent flavoring for the classroom. Each reading gives students insights into both the characters and the writer, and other parts of the LP reveal much about Twain's background and ideas. While playing these recordings has long been a tool for classroom use, instructors should be aware that the selection on "More Mark Twain Tonight" contains Pap Finn's racist diatribe, including use of the offensive term "nigger." Depending on your situation, it may prove wise to edit onto tape a presentation cutting the offensive word (which is easily done), or perhaps you may choose the other reading. In either case, students benefit from hearing Huck's dialect spoken aloud, which may help some readers with the nineteenth-century diction and the depth of characterization that showcases Huck's emotional nature. These vinyl recordings are available in many school libraries or might be tracked down in larger secondhand record stores. They are also available, in a form that will probably be more convenient for most users, as a two-cassette set from Audio Partners.

Other sound recordings are available, but may prove less satisfying in the classroom. *NBC Radio Theater*'s one-hour radio drama of *Huckleberry Finn* from 1949 has long been available on cassette tape, but its usefulness would be limited to classes planning to dramatize the novel. Other condensations of the novel have been produced as audio Cliff's Notes, including releases from Cram Cassettes, Comprehensive Communications, Audio Language Studies, and many others. Full-length taped versions are available on loan for handicapped students either from Recordings for the Blind or from Readers Services for the Library of Congress. Disabled students can call these agencies' toll-free numbers to borrow the tapes.

For Further Reading

Haupt, Clyde V. *Huckleberry Finn on Film: Film and Television Adaptations of Mark Twain's Novel, 1920–1993.* Jefferson, N.C.: McFarland, 1994. Haupt's overview is uneven but valuable for the amount of information it contains as well as its insights into the adaptation process.

Mark Twain Forum. This is a valuable resource for all things Twainian, including many reviews of new Mark Twain media projects posted at the Forum website: <http://web.mit.edu/linguistics/www/forum/twainweb.html>.

Rasmussen, R. Kent. *Mark Twain A to Z: The Essential Reference to His Life and Writings.* Foreword by Thomas A. Tenney. New York: Facts on File, 1995. Contains much information on Twain media not listed in the *Mark Twain Encyclopedia*, including film synopses, cast notes, and lengthy analyses.

High-Tech Huck: Teaching Undergraduates by Traditional Methods and with Computers
David Tomlinson

My mind to me a kingdom is . . .—Sir Edward Dyer

Stone walls do not a prison make
Nor iron bars a cage;
Minds innocent and quiet take
That for an hermitage.—Richard Lovelace

"Turn him loose! he ain't no slave; he's as free as any cretur that walks this earth!"—Tom Sawyer in *Huckleberry Finn*

"When I read about Huck free on the raft, free on the river, everything here just fades away; and I am there too, away from all the messy things I have to do," the student said, visibly relaxing at the memory of the mood. For years I disregarded such comments, thinking that students were telling me what they thought I would like to hear; but I disregard them no more. I have decided that such observations not only are solid tributes to Twain's art but also signal that the teacher's job can begin.

The fact that *Adventures of Huckleberry Finn* has so reliably caused my students to make such observations keeps bringing me to it over and over again as a staple in our basic English course at the U.S. Naval Academy. The plebe (freshman) courses, required of all entering students are accurately titled "Rhetoric and Introduction to Literature." That is, the courses teach writing skills and introduce students to various literary genres including, in the second semester, the novel.

Huckleberry Finn allows me to acquaint students with standard techniques of fiction writing. Many of them meet terms like "picaresque," "bildungsroman," and even "first-person narrative" for the first time. The course allows them to see the intricacies and difficulties of plot and its relative lack of importance in a novel. The course's main gift, however, is offering me a rather wide opening to introduce them to the life of the mind.

Mark Twain and Computers

Since 1988 the Academy has required each midshipman to purchase a computer on entrance. The school chooses the machine, arranges for mountains of software to be loaded onto it, gives each student a port to connect the machine to the school network, and arranges some minimal instruction for the software packages being used. The computer is, then, as much a tool in the educational process at the Academy as is the pencil. In turn, I can and do require that my students hand in their compositions on disk. I copy the computer files, take them home, correct the work using a set of macros I have created for standard errors, insert comments specific to the individual writing, and send the corrected materials back to my students by modem from home.

Would Mark Twain approve? In any real sense, the question is irrelevant, of course. Nevertheless, I feel better knowing that Twain embraced the technology of his own time wholeheartedly even if sometimes foolishly. He early submitted his manuscripts in typed form; and his dalliance with mechanical typesetting is well-known. Though his daughter Susy claimed that he had little mechanical knowledge and less mechanical ability, Twain admired and championed the innovation that these machines represented; and he did so with the typesetter, though obviously unintentionally, to his own financial disadvantage.

Whether the feeling is warranted or not, then, I believe that Twain would have approved of my using the computer to help teach others about *Huckleberry Finn.* I make use of the machines in three ways: (1) with the program *Exploring the Novel* to introduce the genre in general and *Huckleberry Finn* in particular; (2) requiring that students submit their assignments on Twain's novel as WordPerfect files; (3) occasionally producing a mock newspaper from the students' work on the novel.

Using Exploring the Novel

The hypertext program Exploring the Novel[1] is given to each student in my plebe classes at the beginning of the spring semester. Using IBM's Linkway and funded by a Naval Academy instructional development grant, I was able to put together a grab bag of information for my students. The package—using an IBM clone, EGA/VGA graphics, and a mouse—enables the student to view a wide range of information, including some very specific information about *Adventures of Huckleberry Finn*. The student determines how much information will be viewed and in what order the items will be presented. The initial menu of the program organizes the information under five headings:

1. The novel: searching for an acceptable definition.
2. Kinds of novels: a glossary of literary terms.
3. Character, plot, and technique: an overview.
4. Examining two important novels: *The House of the Seven Gables* and *Adventures of Huckleberry Finn*.
5. Chronologies of the History of the Novel in England and the United States.

While a student begins by choosing one of these five areas for study, hypertext buttons in one area allow jumping to linked information in the others at will.

When we begin our study of *Huckleberry Finn*, I ask my students to view that information specifically. They may study sections dealing with the publication of the novel, with character development, or with setting. There is a discussion of the kind of novel that Twain has created and a consideration of plot. In addition, students may access information about Twain's life and two bibliographies, one containing works in the Academy's Nimitz Library written by Twain and another of works about Twain.

The colorful screens are illustrated with Kemble's drawings from the first edition of the novel and with pictures of Twain from cartoons drawn by a Baltimore artist in 1907.

The program gives access to valuable information while saving class time. I no longer must take an hour to review the events of the author's life, nor must I give basic background about the novel. The program contains these things. I can devote classroom time to discussion of the book itself and to the students' writing about the book.

Eliciting Interesting Student Writing

At the beginning of our classroom discussion of *Huckleberry Finn*, I tell my students that they will be doing one of their eight major out-of-class writing assignments about Twain's novel. I have seen more than enough student speculations about the ending of the book and too many amateurish critical appraisals of facets of the author's performance to want to see others; and I have begun dimly to suspect that such assignments do not teach undergraduates as we suppose they do, either. Instead, I choose to build on the imaginative spark that Twain reliably awakes in most readers. I discard the usual freshman essay form entirely.

I tell my students that I would like for them to pretend to be nineteenth-century newspaper reporters or editors. Though I know very well that they will have some trouble discarding the trappings of our own century for the previous one, I believe the exercise helps them both in understanding this novel and in knowing what to do to put themselves in a proper frame to understand any historical period besides the present one.

They are, I tell them, to write a news story, an editorial, or a feature article either about events related in *Adventures of Huckleberry Finn* or about characters or events introduced in the novel but not followed to completion. That is, the less creative of them may satisfy the assignment by merely making a news story out of the facts Twain supplies. I let them know, however, that what brings a story to life (and what, incidentally, will earn the highest grade) is furnishing the details about every matter of interest. In this case, since the only facts we know are those Twain has related, they may make up any additional information, any additional characters, and any additional dialogue they need so long as they do not contradict Twain in any way. In short, they are urged to be highly imaginative.

I provide them with a list of incidents in the novel from which they might make fine stories. The following list, drawn from the main action of the book, is typical:

1. The robbers and the Sunday School picnic.
2. Huck sells his fortune to Judge Thatcher.
3. Huck makes his escape from Pap look like murder and mayhem.
4. Flood on the Mississippi.
5. Huck masquerades as a girl under mysterious circumstances.
6. The wreck of the *Walter Scott*.
7. Story of the baby in the barrel.
8. The Shepherdson-Grangerford feud.
9. The Shepherdson-Grangerford elopement.
10. The Royal Nonesuch.

11. The murder of Boggs.
12. Colonel Sherburn eludes a lynch mob.
13. The showmen are run out of town.
14. The Duke and the Dauphin unsuccessfully pose as brothers of Peter Wilks.
15. Jim is sold.
16. Huck, mistaken for Tom Sawyer, visits his aunt. (Small town papers often used to print notices of those visiting relatives.)
17. Jim attempts to escape from the Phelpses' farm.
18. Jim has been freed.

Clearly, the list is merely a starter. I ask them to take two days, thumb through the novel, note the incidents they find that have the most potential, and come back to class with short proposals for three stories and the angles they would take with those stories to make them come to life.

In class, we sift through the proposals, choosing one as the best for each student. Obviously, having them make three choices instead of a single one permits me both to select for quality within the individual student's list and to screen for repetition in the class as a whole.

What the Students Produce

The students produce a riot of imaginative material about the novel. Like latter-day Tom Stoppards producing their own versions of *Rosencrantz and Guildenstern Are Dead*, these students excitedly depict events that might have surrounded Twain's novel. The difficulty for them in producing such writing is to meld Twain's ideas with their own. They cannot violate the terms of the novel. That is, they must be true to the situations and characters that Twain created. They must also be true to the nineteenth century in fundamental ways.

Some intriguing possibilities strain credibility. For example, one student has Mary Jane Wilks falling in love with Huck and fleeing with him by steamboat (and presumably some overland conveyance) to Idaho. And in trying to imagine a situation in the mid-nineteenth century, my students sometimes miscalculate which modern inventions were available at what time. For example, one of them has a sheriff warned by telephone about the shenanigans of the Duke and the Dauphin. While Alexander Graham Bell demonstrated the first telephone apparatus in 1876, nearly a decade before *Adventures of Huckleberry Finn* was published, the action of the book is set before the Civil War. Such mistakes may keep the story from ringing true; but they become useful teaching tools. Individual or class discussion of them helps student get a better grasp on events and enjoy looking for chronological howlers.

The best of the student stories show imagination in form and in content. One editorial by Clint Tracy mourns the loss of Huck Finn in much the same sentimental style that Twain has Emmeline Grangerford use in her poems. It begins, "Grief has fallen brutally on our hearts upon the tragic loss of our beloved Huckleberry Finn. We can never forget the joy and happiness he contributed to Hannibal. We must avenge his death by apprehending the scoundrels who hideously murdered an innocent boy with an axe. Our duty as law-abiding citizens is to bring the guilty party to the gallows." There follow anecdotes and reminiscences about Huck and a call to "focus our efforts on the task of bringing the fiends who robbed us of our Huck to justice."

Michael Gibson asked to produce a newspaper advertisement for a scam that Twain had not imagined. It is titled "Advertisement: Become an In$tant Millionaire" and begins, "The Duke serves as France's Foreign Minister of Finance, and to prove how lucrative this plan is, he has brought his royal Highness The Dauphin with him to America. Across the world millions of people have responded to this one chance only opportunity to make millions with no work, no sweat and no effort. You too can live a life of luxury—before your eyes the initial investment you make will grow into millions." The unwary victims are invited to invest in a get-rich-quick scheme involving trade between France and "the far east." The advertisement is fanciful all around, of course, and fun to boot. Its fun is in continuing the kind of scam the two bamboozlers Twain created are famous for. It has Louis XVI still sitting on the throne about half a century after he was beheaded. Of course, the dauphin was lost originally because he was supposed to have escaped the riotous mobs that imprisoned and later killed his father and mother. The scam artists, however, never worry about their story's being accurate. They rely on the gullibility and ignorance of the people around them. What fools the mortals reading the ad would have to be to believe it. On the other hand, what fools they were to believe anything those two did in *Huckleberry Finn*.

Usually the student writer of such a piece is well aware of what he is doing. That is, he knows the history well enough to realize what a distortion he is having his characters make of it. A classroom discussion of a bit of writing like this one allows the class to question the events and to review for themselves the bit of history involved. The teacher rarely has to get involved as an authority in this discussion.

One of Twain's techniques the students invariably imitate is the use of whimsy. In describing what he imagined a sheriff would find on board the *Walter Scott*, Johnnie Caldwell described the bodies and went on to provide the rap sheet of Jake Packard: "Packard was wanted in Hazard County where he stole three chickens, a horse and a pecan pie." Another popular technique is re-creating the informal conversation Twain uses in *Huckleberry Finn*. My students do not get the accents right; but the air of informality gets captured perfectly.

Also, some are imaginative enough to give characters whom Twain created a history and some motivation for their actions in the novel. For example, Douglas Bates, in an item titled "Gunfire Kills Samuel Boggs," not only reports newspaper-style on the Sherburn-Boggs encounter, but he also provides a history of the bad blood between the two:

> In 1820 the two men enlisted in the United States Army and were stationed together at Fort Anne, near Memphis, Tennessee. They were both held in high esteem as soldiers despite their differences in nature, Boggs had an affinity for the bottle while Sherburn was a church going man. One day the two privates were out on a training patrol. One of their recruits died during the exercise. An Army investigation ensued. Boggs, found guilty of negligent supervision, was discharged from service. Private Sherburn was found not guilty of all charges and continued his career, eventually receiving a commission as an officer, retiring with the rank of Colonel. Sources involved with the investigation say, "Sherburn was guilty of the negligence, however, his testimony placed the blame on the drunken Boggs."

The attempt to imagine ordinary language use, the attempt to imagine circumstances that might have provoked Sherburn to shoot Boggs, and the attempt to understand the mourning of a small town for one of its less-than-illustrious citizens are all part of the enterprise of growing up. The misunderstanding about army life in 1820 is merely factual and easily remedied. Often in my classes some military history buff will accurately detail the conditions of such early nineteenth-century service.

Going One Step Further

As rewarding an exercise as the writing of newspaper articles, editorials, features, and advertisements has proven for me and my students, the computer makes one spectacular finishing touch possible when time permits: publishing an actual small paper containing the student stories. To all the advantages that the writing fosters—use of imagination, careful study of the text, keeping a watchful eye on actual practices of another era, and enjoying the initial reaction of an audience—this kind of publication adds one more: pride of authorship.

There are problems in doing the desktop publishing, of course. My students live by a strict schedule, so no time and no software are available for them to do the actual publishing themselves. I must do all that work. Often I cannot accomplish it as soon as both they and I would like; but the reaction to it is inevitably the same no matter when the mock newspaper is finished: a flourishing pride of authorship.

I must sacrifice more than time to make the paper a successful production. I cannot, for example, make it a true paper of the 1840s. Those papers, for the most part, consisted of long columns of small type with tiny headlines and no pictures. I compromise on historical authenticity to print something that my students find eye-catching but with the flavor of something old. First, I choose modern versions of traditional typefaces. I print the *Mississippi Times* on 11" × 17" paper, which allows four 8½" × 11" pages to be printed on one sheet. Folding the large sheets appropriately makes the production look more professional than having separate 8½" × 11" sheets stapled together.

Each story has a byline bearing the name of the student who did the work; and authentic nineteenth-century pictures are used, although all come from around the time of the publication of Twain's book rather than from the period depicted in the story. Most often, I use the illustrations from the first edition of *Huckleberry Finn*, which I capture with a hand scanner. When I need a picture that Kemble did not draw, I find a suitable illustration in the *Century Magazine* from the 1880s or 1890s and create a label to make it appropriate to the accompanying story. Thus, the picture of Samuel Boggs on the front page of the *Mississippi Times* is purloined from the *Century*.

Of course, the stories produced by the students catalogue adventures happening over a number of weeks and in a string of locations. The paper ignores these differences, putting the news of Huck's presumed murder, his masquerade as a girl, and his part in helping Jim escape all in the same issue. Not only does the paper ignore the differences of time and place, but the students do the same, accepting the premise of the *Mississippi Times* that it prints "all the collected flotsam and jetsam of the mighty muddy waters."

Weighing the Advantages

In a school like the Naval Academy, where military discipline reigns supreme, students do not have freedom of movement. That is, when they are not in class, they must be on parade or taking care of company business or attending a military lecture. Their private time is strictly limited. But many of my students discover that even in this highly disciplined world, there is a real freedom in the life of the mind.

Adventures of Huckleberry Finn proves a particularly important book for the plebes in my classes because just reading the text gives them that sense of freedom of mind in full measure. I try to extend that experience by giving them assignments such as viewing a hypertext program in which they may make the choices about which information route to follow. Obviously, the assignment of writing a newspaper article offers them a measure of creative freedom as well.

Many of my students show such joy in discovering this freedom that it is infectious. Soon, others join in. The discovery that their minds are kingdoms which can bring them delight may seem merely a way of escape from the present; but it is not. It has utility. It has power. The writing, when it is shared through reading in class or through the mock newspaper, helps them realize that the creative power of the mind can be shared. It can bring delight and insight to others.

Although they seem to learn other lessons as well from the assignments presented here, if they learned just this one with the force that personal realization gives it, I would be more than satisfied. Not only has Mark Twain given Jim freedom and Huck knowledge in the *Adventures*; he has, more than a hundred years after the writing, given my students a powerful measure of the same.

Note

1   Teachers who desire to see or use *Exploring the Novel* can obtain a free copy by sending a DOS-formated high-density disk to David Tomlinson, English Department, U.S. Naval Academy, Annapolis, MD 21402-5044. The program requires DOS 3.3 or, later, 2.0 megabytes of hard disk space, an EGA or VGA monitor, and a mouse.

III   Playing to the Audience

The Innocents Abroad Travels to Freshman
Composition
Tom Reigstad

Mark Twain's bestselling travel book *The Innocents Abroad* (1869)
is customarily studied in upper-level college literature courses or in
graduate seminars on Twain. However, I have had some success using
the book to enhance the reading, writing, and research skills of college
writers in a freshman composition course. It provides entertaining,
lively reading about issues that are still relevant today, offers count-
less models of exemplary prose, and serves as a departure point for
personal narratives and research paper topics generated by freshman
writers. Furthermore, by examining selected excerpts from Twain's
notebooks and *Alta California* dispatches, and comparing them to their
Innocents Abroad counterparts, students gain valuable insights into
Twain's composing process—and, hopefully, more carefully consider
their own acts of revision.

Before the course begins, I chart a reasonable schedule for reading
The Innocents Abroad and devise an accompanying reading guide. I
usually suggest that my students complete the book in phases over a
five-week span. Accordingly, my reading guide consists of five install-
ments to help preview material contained in each segment of our reading. First, the reading guide suggests a handful of general tips for inter-
acting with the text:

1. Look for how Twain ridicules parochialism (small-town-mind-
edness) and the typical tourist mind-set of his fellow travelers.
2. Watch for ways in which Twain makes homey, folksy connections when describing exotic details so that American readers will
better understand what he is saying.
3. Observe how Twain satirizes the most revered subjects: holy
relics, the Old Masters, etc.
4. Look for examples of Twain's personal biases and prejudices.

5. Watch for two specific strategies in Twain's writing style: (a) how he builds an idea around contrasts and incongruities (often based on the discrepancy between expectation and reality); (b) how he constructs key passages that lead marvelously toward a gag line or "snapper" at the end, usually for comic purposes.

Then, before each weekly reading and discussion, I distribute a new reading guide to each student. In a highly subjective way, I attempt to alert my freshman writers to essential elements of the text. On the reading guides I highlight central passages that illustrate Twain's social criticism, his descriptive skills, and, above all, his comic devices. I provide page cues (we use the Signet Classics paperback edition, 1980), identify some vocabulary terms, and occasionally recommend that they compare the *Innocents Abroad* text with Twain's original *Alta California* newspaper letters. The reading guides reflect my own reading and pedagogical idiosyncrasies, but students have responded favorably to the guides in course evaluations at the end of the semester. On one guide that accompanied the last stretch of reading (chapters 53–61), I wrote this as a research incentive: "The first student who can find and explain the pun alluding to a famous incident in American history (appearing on page 455) will be exempt from one of our six required essay assignments." Needless to say, I was pleased when an enterprising freshman identified Twain's line about tourists resisting Egyptian beggars, "it was millions for defense, but not a cent for baksheesh," as a clever twist on U.S. Ambassador Charles C. Pinckney's 1797 motto— "Millions for defense, but not one cent for tribute"—in response to Talleyrand's demands in the XYZ affair. My student dug through several sources before eventually nailing down the reference by consulting his former high school social studies teacher.

Here is an example of the guide that I recently prepared for the second reading phase of *The Innocents Abroad*, from chapters 17 through 28:

Things to Look for in Pages 115–222
–Criticism of holy relics (119; 129; 162).
–Description of "The Last Supper" (136–40) and Old Masters (169–73; 218–21).
–Comparison of lake of Como to Lake Tahoe (144–47).
–Mocking of American travelers who adopt foreign accents (167–68).

–Getting a shave in Venice (173–74).
–Criticism of the church (183–87); compare this from an *Alta California* letter: "It takes three hundred flabby, greasy vagabonds in holy orders to run this awful ecclesiastical swindle" to 184 of *IA*.
–Note the exquisitely exaggerated summing up of Civita Vecchia (last paragraph of chapter 25, 189).
–Humorous account of Coliseum and sports card (198–205).
–Treatment of guide in Rome (211–13).
–Compare episode on Columbus and Genoan guide (210–11) with the corresponding passage [provided to students] in an *Alta California* letter.
–Words: "geegaw" (128)—a showy trifle, a bauble, a trinket; "barouche" (140)—a four-wheeled carriage.

We then follow up on items from *The Innocents Abroad* reading guides in our weekly in-class discussions of concepts and writing techniques. For example, students generally respond favorably to Twain's revision of the doctor's encounter with the Genoan guide and recognize that *The Innocents Abroad*'s comic effect is improved because Twain heightens the humor of miscommunication and closes with an amusing pun.

In addition to a chronological reading and discussion of the book, I encourage freshmen to look for devices that Twain uses to enhance his comically satirical viewpoint of an American abroad. Twain relies on exaggeration and is adept at pacing his humorous passages; in "How to Tell a Story," he describes the posture of a deadpan narrator tricking an innocent audience into listening to a rambling, disjointed story that closes with "a nub, a point, or a snapper" (Twain, 1962, 239). One episode in *The Innocents Abroad* illustrates this technique when the narrator visits the ruins of Pompeii (Twain, 1980):

> But perhaps the most poetical thing Pompeii has yielded to modern research was that grand figure of a Roman soldier clad in complete armor, who, true to his duty, true to his proud name of a soldier of Rome, and full of the stern courage which had given to that name its glory, stood by his post by the city gate, erect and unflinching, till the hell that raged around him *burned out* the dauntless spirit it could not conquer.
>
> We never read of Pompeii but we think of that soldier; we cannot write of Pompeii without the natural impulse to grant to him

the mention he so well deserves. Let us remember that he was a soldier—not a policeman—and so praise him. Being a soldier, he stayed—because the warrior instinct forbade him to fly. Had he been a policeman, he would have stayed also—because he would have been asleep. (240–41)

My freshmen study this passage, noting the slow, seriocomic buildup leading to the delivery of the punch line. Then we compare it to the tame, bland version Twain sent in as correspondent for the *Alta California* (McKeithan, 1958): "In a stone sentry-box, just outside the city wall, we saw where the gallant mail-clad soldier stood his fearful watch that dreadful night, till he died, scorning to desert his post till he heard the relief call which was never more to sound" (81).

This version, devoid of humor, helps students see the care that Twain put into his revision of the scene for book publication. We also discuss possible reasons for Twain's changes. Twain's use of snappers is only one of several effective contrastive cues that he employs to convey comic disillusionment on his journey. I tie in our study of Twain's contrastive devices to a chapter from Ken Macrorie's *Telling Writing* (1985). Macrorie advises inexperienced writers to "make it a habit to look for oppositions. You will find suddenly that you are wiser than you thought. Do it automatically. If you find yourself putting down *hot*, consider the possibility of *cold* in the same circumstances. . . . The result is tension" (71–74). In *The Innocents Abroad* Twain's encounter with the Parisian barber masterfully uses the "opposition" of expectation versus reality. Again, the scene is deliberately set up to heighten the hilarious letdown of his high expectations (Twain, 1980):

From earliest infancy it had been a cherished ambition of mine to be shaved some day in a palatial barbershop in Paris. I wished to recline at full length in a cushioned invalid chair, with pictures about me and sumptuous furniture; with frescoed walls and gilded arches above me and vistas of Corinthian columns stretching far above me; with perfumes of Araby to intoxicate my senses and the slumberous drone of distant noises to soothe me to sleep. At the end of an hour I would wake up regretfully and find my face as smooth and as soft as an infant's. Departing, I would lift my hands above that barber's head and say, "Heaven bless you, my son!" . . . I said I wanted to be shaved. . . . Then there was an excitement among those two barbers! There was a wild consultation, and afterwards a hurrying to and fro and a feverish gathering up of razors from obscure places and a ransacking for soap. Next they took us into a little mean, shabby back room; they got two ordinary sitting-room chairs and placed us in them with our coats on. . . . I sat bolt upright, silent, sad, and solemn. One of the wig-making villains lathered my face for ten terrible minutes and finished by plastering a mass of suds into my mouth. . . . Then this outlaw strapped his razor on his boot, hovered over me ominously for six fearful seconds, and then swooped down upon me like the genius of destruction. The first rake of his razor loosened the very hide from my face and lifted me out of the chair. I stormed and raved. . . . (84–85).

About this time I ask students to think of an event that they have looked forward to—a concert, a dinner, a dance—and to try their hand at a brief account, patterned after a Twainlike contrastive opener. Here are leads by two students that forecast clear, contrastive cues:

> *Student 1:* When I was asked to go to the prom I was so happy. I ran out to find the perfect gown. Not just any gown would do. It took me a while, but I found the most beautiful dress in the whole world. My date wore a tux that matched me to a tee. My spirits were so high when I walked out of my front door, but they were soon to be let down lower than low. As I was walking down the steps of my porch, my date stepped on the back of my gown. I kept walking, but my gown didn't. . . .
>
> *Student 2:* All through high school I dreamt about going down to Florida during Christmas vacation. I could just see the beaches now. The sun would be shining. It would be hot, but not warm enough to sweat in. I would lounge on the beach all day not doing anything more than lifting the tropical drink to my mouth. Of course, everywhere you looked there would be beautiful women. Every hour or so some beautiful women would offer to rub my back with suntan lotion. This would be a great week of rest and relaxation. . . .

Along with writing exercises like these, where students practice Twain's stylistic gimmicks in their own firsthand personal narratives, they also write in-depth analytical, text-oriented pieces in response to their reading of *The Innocents Abroad*. They produce research papers based on prompts, such as: read a travel book (I provide a list by authors such as Paul Theroux, Joan Didion, William Least Heat Moon, and Jonathan Raban) and write a detailed paper comparing it to *The Innocents Abroad* in terms of audience, purpose, voice, critical acceptance, and popular appeal; compare *The Innocents Abroad* to either *Life on the Mississippi* or *Roughing It*; compare *The Innocents Abroad* to *The Ugly American*, a 1958 novel by William Lederer and Eugene Burdick; choose a book from the current *New York Times* nonfiction bestseller list and compare its subject, style, and appeal to *The Innocents Abroad*—which is generally thought to be America's first nonfiction bestseller; or compare *The Innocents Abroad* with another late nineteenth-century nonfiction bestseller.

I also require students to write a timed essay-exam in class in response to *The Innocents Abroad.* I distribute the following two essay questions one week before the exam and ask students to select one to write on during the 75-minute class meeting:

> *First Essay Exam Question:* Several published reactions to *The Innocents Abroad* in 1869 were less than complimentary. Mark Twain was pictured as an ignorant, raucous frontiersman romping through venerable lands, sneering and laughing at everything foreign. A British critic found the book "offensive, . . . supremely contemptuous, . . . ostentatiously and atrociously vulgar," while the *New York Tribune* deplored its "offensive irreverence." Discuss specific features of *The Innocents Abroad* that readers (including you) may find distasteful. And explain why Twain's attacks on the church and classical art especially may have been so disagreeable.

John's response to this exam question reveals independent critical thinking about what he saw as Twain's provincialism, a narrative characteristic that annoyed John as a reader: "I think Twain failed to see the real culture of Europe. His criticism toward the church was offending. . . . He traveled to Europe with his eyes seeing only what he wanted to see. . . . I think that Twain acted like the average American going through Europe and comparing everything to what he sees in America."

> *Second Essay Exam Question:* H. R. Haweis once observed, "Put Mark Twain on to mountain, lake, storm at sea, a prairie fire, or a

volcano, and you need not pull out your photographic apparatus." Select five significant scenes from *The Innocents Abroad* in which Twain describes vividly the natural beauties of the Old World and discuss why these descriptive passages create such effective word pictures.

This question elicited several perceptive comments by freshmen who clearly admired Twain's descriptive skills. Some responses were innovatively phrased; still others were eloquent. This is how Marilyn expressed her admiration for Twain's photolike verbal skills: "Twain carried us there in his suitcase. . . . He often uses the word 'picture,' as in, 'from my window here in Bellagio I have a view of the other side of the lake now, which is as beautiful as a picture.' . . . In contrast . . . he describes Palestine as unpicturesque. Palestine is even drearier than Jerusalem, as though situated 'in sackcloth and ashes.' Boy, what an UGLY picture he paints. . . . I feel like I got my film developed and it came back." Patricia singled out concrete descriptors and action words as chiefly responsible for Twain's success in writing about scenes: "Twain uses adjectives and verbs but not just everyday ones. He uses words that help readers see in their minds pictures such as 'nestled,' 'stately,' and 'gliding.' " And Lynn discussed how Twain effectively builds on the familiar in order to stress what is unique about a place: "Turning something like the Rock of Gibraltar into a 'gob of mud' is quite typical of Twain's technique throughout the book. Twain uses short phrases like this that catch the reader by surprise."

I was particularly delighted by an exam response from Adam, who argued in an original way that Twain overused the "contrastive" gimmick and employed an overblown prose style much like that for which Twain later criticized James Fenimore Cooper. "The use of the anticlimax can be powerful and funny, but Twain abuses this. Every time he begins to speak of expectation, you know not to expect it. His disappointment with the Turkish baths or his blighted hope upon seeing Jerusalem make use of this tiresome technique. . . . Twain also often uses clichés and travelese. In his account of Lake Como, 'syrupy' words infest Twain's stale and unimaginative text; phrases like 'picturesque pinnacles,' 'handsome country,' 'fancifully adorned,' and 'voluptuous scene.' "

And evidence that some of Twain's breezy, engaging prose style may have rubbed off on freshman writers existed in Patty's charming introduction. It demonstrated that, perhaps, Twain had inspired her to take a risk and follow the impulse of her natural writer's voice—even under exam conditions, where freshmen usually choose a safe, voiceless, almost frozen, point of view:

> Have you ever been invited to a friend's house for dinner only to be bored with vacation stories or, worse yet, slides? The trip becomes even more deadly and foreign to you. Travel books can have the same alienating, deadening effect. The author should speak in a personal manner, creating a common ground, giving the reader something to relate to. It takes skill to write about travels, a secure personality to recognize and relay human flaws, and an excellent wit to put the two together. Mark Twain had this ability and used it well in his travel masterpiece, *Innocents Abroad.*

The Innocents Abroad can challenge the intellects and stimulate the writing skills of students at all levels, including college freshmen. By carefully developing activities that evoke written responses both connected to the text and using the text as a point of departure, teachers of freshman composition can use Twain's book to make students better thinkers, readers, and writers. An insightful endorsement of the timeless value of studying *The Innocents Abroad* in freshman composition was supplied by one of my students on a course evaluation form: "Although I'm sure that things have changed where Twain once traveled, the experiences through his eyes will always be informative and funny to new readers."

Works Cited

Macrorie, Ken. *Telling Writing.* Portsmouth, N.H.: Boynton/Cook, 1985.
McKeithan, Daniel. *Traveling with the Innocents Abroad.* Norman: University of Oklahoma Press, 1958.
Twain, Mark. "How to Tell a Story." *Selected Shorter Writings of Mark Twain.* Ed. Walter Blair. Boston: Houghton Mifflin, 1962. 239–43.
——. *The Innocents Abroad.* New York: Signet, 1980.

On Teaching *Huck* in the Sophomore Survey
Victor Doyno

I begin to talk to colleagues, to fellow professionals, about my teaching of *Huck* fully aware of several attitudes. I recognize that it is probably considered somewhat off-beat to talk about actually *teaching* the novel. A general college and university attitude assumes that a professional presentation, in lecture or article, should have almost no relation to the classroom, but the prevailing attitude does not declare that the classroom is sacrosanct, privileged, or inviolate. No, instead it seems to assume that teaching is often so easy, or so natural, that it would be somehow moronic or, at most, sophomoric to take teaching seriously, as an activity that can bear up under intellectual scrutiny. These attitudes I oppose.

It seems that I have an opportunity here to reconcile both meanings of the word *sophomore* (knowledge and fool) since I'm still foolish enough to offer some knowledge about my actual teaching practices in print. But I also trust that Twainians, or "Twainiacs," do form a voluntary intentional intellectual community. Although it seems risky and intimidating to imagine this readership actually visiting my classroom for four or five classes in sequence, I shall offer information as one practicing teacher to other practicing teachers.

First, it is necessary to set an educational context. At SUNY, Buffalo, I teach *Huck* at every level, from freshman seminars to graduate seminars, but today I shall concentrate primarily on how I teach *Huck* in our sophomore American literature survey, Major American Writers II, English 242. At SUNY, Buffalo, our average incoming freshman has a combined SAT score of 1106 and a high school average of 91. More important, in my opinion, about 55 percent of our students are the first generation of their families to attend college, as I was. And a high percentage of their parents did not even finish high school. Many are commuters who live at home. Many of our students seem utterly pragmatic in their approach to a university education, thinking of college as a place to get a technical certificate that will perhaps, if they are lucky, qualify them for employment. Many students work fifteen to twenty-five hours per week, and some attempt to work thirty-five to forty hours weekly while also carrying a full-time course load. Some report that it is easier in Buffalo than in their hometowns to get work, and some send money home to their families. Accordingly, it is relatively optimistic or delusional to think that students willingly or routinely fulfill the Carnegie unit of two to three hours of homework for each class hour.

About student trust and rapport: it is my intuitive experience that students at some more expensive schools tend to trust themselves first, then their fellow students, then the teacher. But at Buffalo, our students tend to trust the teacher first, then notice smart fellow students (sometimes with envy), then trust themselves later, if at all. One of my goals is to establish my classroom as a place where it is okay and admirable for my students to be smart, and where it is safe to take an intellectual chance.

The last contextual information is that some, but not all, have read *Huck* before and, accordingly, do not wish to read it again. For example, some engineering students, burdened with math and physics courses, think it is "inefficient" to commit time to a "pass-fail" American lit course, especially if they have read *Huck* in high school.

So, within this less than ideal (but manageable) context, what do I do? Usually I teach *Huck* in about two or two-and-a-half weeks (six or seven fifty-minute periods on MWF, or five eighty-minute classes on Tuesdays and Thursdays). By this time in the semester they are trained to come to each class with a question and an insight.

In the first class, students are to write for five to seven minutes, with two or three tasks: I ask them to write down any questions for a passed-around, anonymous question bag, and I also ask, as an option, those who have read *Huck* before to write down what they remember about the book.

The main writing task is for them to write, for their eyes only, about a time in their childhood when they felt badly treated or felt ignored or confused. "What did it feel like, smell like, taste like, etc.? Please use three or four senses." If the student finishes writing early, he or she is asked to reread the opening chapter, listening for a voice. The purpose is to center on the text and to permit an easy linkage with their individual experience. My goal is to engage and enable, and ultimately to educate, their sympathetic imagination.

My lecture begins with the well-known opening, and I coax, coach, and encourage my students "to listen eloquently," to infer as much as possible about Huck's life, mind, past experience, self-esteem, etc. I try to train them to think in terms of "observation/inference/interpretation, leading to a generalization," and I wish them to link my and their statements or insights to a piece of evidence, a quotation or passage from the text. Certainly I alert them to themes or motifs—like the Moses/water journey/passover/liberation motif. Because my students have somewhat limited attention spans, I intersperse, for example, two established theories or approaches with four questions from the question bag, which I answer, then two more theories and four questions, etc.

The questions are pulled out of the bag in random order, and this action gives the students an early sense of anonymous "ownership," participation, and unpredictability. No one knows exactly what will happen next. In response to their questions, I usually can offer much information about slavery, punishments, lynchings, the word "nigger," pre- and post-Civil War living conditions in Missouri, Black Codes, and the Reconstruction failures. When the information comes up in response to student questions, they seem to pay better attention. The established theories remind the students that there is a shared body of thought about a masterpiece. And I explain that they will have to apply or transfer the theories to the text in the next several classes. These theories usually include the picaresque tradition, the naïve narrator, the American Eden, the search for the father, the River God and rivershore dichotomy, the Machine in the Garden, the realistic social criticism of Mississippi Valley life, Huck's development or lack of development, and the male bonding (white male / male of color theory). All of this explanation of available literary theories is fairly conventional (but not necessarily familiar to the students), and I explain that I want them to know enough to become "part of the conversation."

By the middle of the second class I usually put on the board my version of Bloom's taxonomy of intellectual skills, listed in order of increasing difficulty (figure 1). Of course, I as a teacher walk into my classroom wishing to begin by talking and questioning at the synthesis and evaluation level; but when I do begin that way, I often get the dead-fish-eye stare and evasive eye movements—messages which say, "Don't

Creativity

Evaluation

Synthesis

Cause and Effect

Analysis

Exemplification (illustrations/examples)

Comparison and Contrast

Transfer

Application

Description

Narration

Figure 1   *Source:* Adapted from Benjamin Bloom's *Taxonomy of Educational Objectives* (New York: Longmans, 1956).

call on me"; or I observe frantic "purse diving" or "page turning" or, in a graduate seminar, "pipe stuffing." Accordingly, I've learned to warm them up by beginning at "the bottom of the stairs" of intellectual difficulty and working upward.

Usually I tend to give narration short shrift because it is easy to follow, but on my infrequent best, patient days, I ask a "C" and an "A" student to narrate—retell chronologically—the same part or segment of the novel, and I nonjudgmentally let both versions stand. Then I ask "C," "B," and "A" students for character descriptions of Pappy Finn, of Tom Sawyer, of Widow Douglas, of Miss Watson, of Jim, and of Huck.

Then, at the end of the second class, I ask them to think about some applications or transfers of the established theories to the texts. Obviously, the discussion in the third class gets more open-ended. Comparisons and contrasts clarify dramatic conflict: "How would you compare and contrast Pap, Boggs, and Jim as fathers?" Later I can ask, "What traits do the King and Tom Sawyer share?" and "How would you compare and contrast the Grangerford-Shepherdson feud with the king and duke's *Romeo and Juliet*?" Time flies; their minds get lively. It can be a bit like taking thirty-five or forty kangaroos on a stroll. And I gradually get them to understand Twain's oddly duplicative, duplicitous way of repeating the same patterns of action in comic and tragic ways. In all the classes I read some passages aloud, using different voices and tones.

I also make them read some passages to themselves, making them move their lips and hear their own dramatizing voices, urging them to change their voices as the speakers change. Hear the pauses; hear the silences. "Listen eloquently!"

If time permits, I put a list of tones on the board (e.g., naïvely approving, laconic, enthusiastic, wistful, puzzled, etc.) and ask them to find examples. But usually I assign that as a homework task because it is time-consuming. Then, in class, I have them pair up to read and teach a passage, with tonal variations, to each other.

When they think they know what will happen next, I suddenly say, "Please take out a piece of paper and write down six to ten things Huck does well." And about one minute later I say, "Now please turn it over and write down—for your own eyes only—ten to fourteen things that you can do well." Oddly enough, the room usually gets quiet. Then I ask them to take another sheet and divide it vertically and horizontally, into heredity on top and environmental influences on the bottom half, with disadvantages on the left and advantages on the right. "Please write for your own eyes only your personal limitations and advantages." This process takes about four to six minutes. "Has everyone put six to eight items in each quadrant?" "Have you ever done this before?" "How can you make the most of your list?" "Please fold up your two sheets and put them into your pocket to be read at least twice during this and next week." This experience makes them much better readers of Twain's treatment of Huck's thoughts about his heredity and training. Moreover, the exercise helps my usually astonishingly nonreflective students to gain some resonance.

Usually at several points I will ask the students to write, for their eyes only, about something they understand or perceive now that they did not understand or perceive thirty minutes ago. Such interim recapitulation helps them think, and it keeps them attentive. Or I may ask them about ten or twelve minutes before the class ends to write down four or five important points. Then I prep them with some questions for the next class. One week *after* we conclude *Huck*, they will have to hand in their essay folder with a three-to-five page essay analyzing a passage, accompanied by draft versions.

I do not wish to have to read plot summaries or paraphrases, which are usually reductive and boring. So I devote some class time to discussing the process of preparing the paper, saying early on that I fail a plot summary or paraphrase; instead, I shall try to teach each student how to write a factor analysis, based on a stylistic analysis of how Twain's language actually works.

Usually I teach analytical close-reading to prepare them for this paper-writing by picking some rather ordinary passage (or I let the class pick one or flip pages to get one by chance). I develop a factor analysis of these already defined literary devices on the board:

Stylistic Devices or Literary Techniques

Setting	Selection of details (evidence
Characterization	for inferences; showing vs.
Imagery (similes/metaphors)	telling language)
Image patterns	Repetition
Narrator's tone	Juxtaposition
Dramatic conflict	Symbolism
Vitality of tones	Metatextuality
Variety of tones	Humor
Allegory	Dramatic irony
Irony	Foreshadowing
Persona	Contradiction
Iconic images	Holes or omissions
Figure/ground relationships	Interaction of stylistic devices
Synecdoche, metonomy	

How are these literary devices used in this passage? I assign the factors: "This row read for setting and irony; this row read for characterization and imagery," etc. First, I evoke and note on the board the insights on each topic, such as imagery. Then I get *two* outlines up on the board—dramatizing, enacting—the message that there is no one inevitable, right, perfect outline, but asking them to ponder choices. What order should they use for paragraphs on each factor? (Least important to most important, or most obvious to least obvious, etc.). And, of course, the most important factor is always the interaction of the factors listed above, which demands a summative metaanalysis. For this paper, they pick any passage and decide which four to eight factors are most revealing. Some students cannot think that complexly and need to rewrite. I insist that students hand in at least three and preferably four drafts in their folders, by saying, "I read my own first drafts; I read our children's second drafts; I read your third or fourth draft." The paper should be three to six pages.

I even tell the students, who absolutely have a fixation on grades, what factors I will use to grade their papers. I tell them that I am lazy and just wish to fill in the grades F, D, C, B, A:

Analytical organization —
Paragraph development —
Inclusion of evidence —
Extraction of all possible thought/meaning from evidence —
Clarity of observation/inference/interpretation/generalization process —
Insight —
Editing —
Optional Criteria: [often used later in the semester]
   Memorable phrasing —
   Authoritative, lively, intelligent tone —
   Variety of sentence length and structure —
   Lively verbs (very few uses of "is, are, was, were")

This analytical factor grading gives them some goals, and I can double or triple some factors. If a paper has a lot of grammar problems or typos, I can write, "Please write down 'Editing' three times for your next paper." Usually in the sophomore class I ask that they write in the left margin which paragraphs are derivative of class discussion or secondary reading and which paragraphs present an original insight.

Over time I have learned that clear, forthright expectations and pre-announced criteria work better for our students. They seem to thrive on explicit, focused requirements. In a junior-senior honors course I might phrase an assignment vaguely—e.g., "Please read around in Twain's short stories." But such vagueness is just ignored or is confusing or anxiety-producing in a sophomore class.

At some point I explain some other theories I've developed, such as the nationalist, postcolonial, antinobility, anti-European approach, the psychological development theory, the role of universalism and defiance of hell, the reflections on books and literacy and the act of reading, the importance of cheap European fictions and the lack of international copyright, the convict-lease system and Jim's imprisonment, and the structural use of $40 changing hands.

Recently, as I've been practicing genetic criticism by working with the newly rediscovered manuscript, I've begun to form some new theories, which I test out with my students, attempting to determine if the theories hold water, are explanatory, or can be contradicted. Here's how I do that. I bring in early manuscript versions of some passages. In the genetic process, I call attention to usually nonemphasized aspects of the novel. These topics were in the text but have been mostly ignored, but now in the 1990s they deserve more attention. (Some of the manuscript pages I use can be found in the 1996 Random House edition of *Huckleberry Finn.*)

First of all, Huck is actually a homeless child, except for the short period of regulated safety in the widow Douglas's house. In the original manuscript version his homelessness received a bit more emphasis. Twain originally had Huck speak more about food, and you can infer what his norms were. In the first chapter Huck originally referred to what he had eaten in terms appropriate for hog food, but this was revised to "in a barrel of odds and ends, things go better and the juice sort of swaps around." Huck and his father had been living in the hog yard, competing with and snatching garbage-like food from the animals. Perhaps you have a gagging reaction, as my rural students do, to the juice swapping around.

The adaptation of a homeless child to the society around him fascinates some modern students, and this emphasis helps all students reevaluate the picaresque approach and understand much more sympathetically Huck's great, favorable emphasis on his food while with Jim and at the Wilkses' and Phelpses' homes. In another developing approach, I emphasize that Huck is the child of an alcoholic, with a great desire to compromise or mediate to keep the peace, a great fear of anger and violence, and a great ability to read moods. I also point out how Twain revised to create Pappy Finn's frightening domestic violence. This approach can help some of my students reach important new self-understandings, thanks to the novel. Our changing recent times now permit us to recognize aspects of this masterpiece that some earlier generations did not and could not discuss.

Huck is also a novel that deals with child abuse. I find that my students are relatively ignorant about historical standards and cultural differences with respect to child abuse. In the original manuscript, Huck mentions three times that his father would whip him with a whip made from untanned leather. I've learned that in Missouri in 1845 such whips were cheaply made, with untanned strips of cowflesh, soaked in a salt brine and braided together with chunks of rock salt to retard putrescence. I infer that the salt brine and rock salt would have increased the hurt that Huck felt whenever his father whipped him.

But Twain apparently decided to revise his original phrasing to a "cow-hide." Fashions change, and by 1885 the original phrasing meant, surprisingly, a tanned upper-class buggy whip that was partially covered with brown and white horse hair, and cost about double what a "cowhide whip" cost. My students learn a little about changing word meanings and realize that child abuse does not refer to compulsory farm planting by the entire family or to their having no choice about sending money earned at college home to their parents.

Huck can also seem to be quite contemporary because this fictional child is a witness to a traumatic event. Apparently in our supposedly civilized but recently vandalized country, on an average day about fifty children see someone shot. Seeing someone shot isn't as it usually appears in movies or on television; instead, the child may witness begging, pleading, screaming, writhing, and finally, at death, the involuntary release of the victim's sphincter muscles. Twain wrote very carefully and revised very carefully about Huck's reaction to the shooting of Boggs and the shooting of Buck Grangerford.

Huck witnesses Buck Grangerford's last few minutes from a cottonwood tree a few feet above his friend. As I work through the original version and the revisions with my classes, I ask them to imagine how a contemporary child about twelve to fourteen years old would react in the parallel circumstance of an urban drive-by shooting. And I read the portion of the book, in Huck's laconic voice, about his tormented dreams and burying Buck. Two minority students have confided to me after such discussions that they felt fearful about returning, during summer vacation, to their old neighborhoods. As a consequence, summer school registration was arranged for them. These two students had no difficulty with the intellectual skills of applicability or transference, and I like to think that Clemens would have been pleased to know how Huck spoke to those young men.

Of course, Huck does survive; in fact, his personality structure is that of a survivor, a person who can come through numerous severe, damaging traumas without going belly-up. What are the traits, the coping skills, of a survivor? My college students, with moderately inquisitive minds, desperately need to know. This approach explores the new findings on the traits of resilient children. A partial list of Huck's survival traits would include the stamina to withstand fatigue; the ability to cope with apprehension, anxiety, and dread; self-reliance; a recognition of his own successes; planning; adaptability; psychological compartmentalization; a pragmatic ability to stay focused; a realistic acceptance of his situation; and a refusal to feel singled out by bad fortune. Huck never whines, "The world is doing X to me," but instead he thinks along the lines of "X is happening to the world. What should I do?"

As I indicated, most of my students are astonishingly nonreflective, but I do challenge them to ponder their own moments of doubt and moral crisis. For example, I may ask them to write for their eyes only, for four minutes, about a time when they committed an act that some-one from home would criticize as immoral, some act that would disappoint someone who loved them. Then I distribute, on one sheet, Twain's first draft of Huck's feelings after he conceals Jim from the slave-hunters. After discussion about the early characterization of Huck and his values, I permit them to read the corresponding passage from the finished novel. They see the difference between the absolutist, low self-esteem of the early version and the shift to individual judgment in an early form of situational ethics. Our discussion is usually detailed, emotionally considerate.

Usually I conclude my treatment of *Huck* with attention to how a certain artistic text, a masterpiece, can keep revealing new aspects of itself as the eras or times change. And I ask them to think about other, yet undiscovered ways that this text could be read, ways this novel could be a distant early warning system about topics not yet fully known, but topics that will be prominent in the years leading up to 2000. Some students have suggested that soon people will learn to read *Huck* as a "care-giver" novel, a novel about how two disadvantaged outsiders cope and intermittently care for each other.

Usually students do not end up resentful about having to reread this masterpiece. They become interested in a book that seems to change; it is not the book they once read. For some, the book can become a correlative self-measurement, an indicator of their own intellectual, emotional, and ethical growth, perhaps a bookish version of the yardstick height measurements made at home on the back of their bedroom door.

I conclude with the definitions of and distinctions between the words "authoritarian," "authoritative," "authorial," and "author." After attempting to engage and educate their sympathetic imaginations, I urge them to attempt to take an authorial role toward their own lives, as Huck did. They can claim, assert, or maintain some authority over their own lives by being articulate.

Later, when I hand back their *Huck* papers, I read aloud or photo-copy some or all of the most insightful three or four papers and provide time for everyone to read over his or her own paper and make notes about what could be improved. "Is that paragraph well-developed?" "Did this paragraph have good use of quotations as evidence and a clear, explicit interpretive process?" "How could you strengthen your own paragraph?"

I find teaching to be both exhausting and exhilarating. There are times when everything clicks in class, when I am teaching "in a zone," when the jokes work, when the emotional and artistic sensitivity clicks, when the historical background and connections become searingly relevant. The best reward for those days is the walk to another class and a wave or thumbs-up from a former student.

To Justify the Ways of Twain to Students:
Teaching *Adventures of Huckleberry Finn*
to Culturally Diverse Students in an
Urban Southern Community College
Joseph A. Alvarez

Reading *Adventures of Huckleberry Finn* in white Southern schools
and colleges before desegregation apparently posed no racial problems
either in the use of the word "nigger" or in the portrayal of Jim. No
doubt, the idea that the novel might resonate with racism or might
demean African Americans did not surface in discussions. Now, more
than thirty years after desegregation in the South, both issues must be
addressed, in part to defend inclusion of *Adventures of Huckleberry
Finn* in the school and college curriculum (and even on optional reading lists or in school libraries). Another obstacle in the Bible Belt South
involves Twain's insistent and merciless satire of religious hypocrisy
permeating the book. As one who has taught *Huckleberry Finn* in
English composition and American literature (1800–1900) courses in a
culturally diverse urban community college, I have faced both issues
and survived to tell about the experience.

Instead of a magic bullet, I have several suggestions for colleagues,
along with some student responses to gauge the results of attempts to
navigate between the Scylla of race and the Charybdis of religious
satire (from experiences in the hometown of Billy Graham and the
adopted region of Jim Bakker). Instructors must prepare themselves
and the class if they wish to stay afloat and not founder on those con-
tentious (bed)rocks. Instructors should prepare themselves by checking their own attitudes about race and, to a lesser extent, religion, and
by reading (yes, *reading*) some of the recent dialogue about race in
Mark Twain's works and in American literature as a whole. If you as an
overworked instructor—whether at a community college, university,
four-year college, or high school—hear that last statement as a death
knell, let me suggest to you that a few hours of critical reading will help
extricate you from that "close place" where you find yourself when you
attempt to deal with these issues in the classroom. I have included a

recommended reading list, much of which your college library may already own. If, however, your library does not have some of the recent works, plead with your acquisitions librarian to purchase them as soon as possible. Municipal libraries often collect books related to popular works like *Adventures of Huckleberry Finn* because of their heavy traffic in the high school student research paper trade. Even resort to buying one or two (or several) for your personal library. Instructors should also prepare the students by foregrounding the discussion of the novel with assignments and discussion of works about and by African Americans, at least, and perhaps works about and by individuals from other ethnic groups as well.

That we concentrate on the issues of race and religious satire does not deconstruct the "other" *Huckleberry Finn*. The instructor should situate the novel in at least some of the by-now traditional thematic contexts: freedom, lying and gullibility, civilization as malignant, the symbolic river journey, superstition, loneliness, the inhumanity of the "damned human race," the picaresque, and the bildungsroman. This last theme fulfills Twain's intention "to run" one of his boy characters into manhood—"on through life (in the first person)"—as enunciated in a letter to William Dean Howells in 1875. Not surprisingly, many of these traditional thematic streams empty into or intersect with either the race river or the religion river. David L. Smith has situated the race issue in the context of satiric punches at other American institutions: "Slavery and racism, then, are social evils that take their places alongside various others which the novel documents, such as the insane romanticism that inspires the Grangerfords and Shepherdsons blithely to murder each other, generation after generation. . . . No other nineteenth-century novel so effectively locates racial discourse within the context of a general critique of American institutions and traditions."[1]

Assessing Jim's character in the novel, Shelley Fisher Fishkin notes that Ralph Ellison says that he and his brother Herbert both identified with Huck rather than Jim, perhaps because "Jim's voice retains enough of minstrelsy in it to be demeaning and depressing."[2] This comment emerges from the context of Fishkin's assertion that European American and African American voices have crossed over racial boundaries to influence writers of both races. For example, she asserts that Huck's voice echoes Jimmy's from Twain's 1874 *New York Times* sketch about a young African American boy, "Sociable Jimmy" (as well as Jerry's voice from Twain's posthumously published "Corn-Pone Opinions"), and, therefore, is also "black." Fishkin—among other scholars—flatly states the need to incorporate other African American voices when using books like *Adventures of Huckleberry Finn* in all classrooms, desegregated or not:

> Jim's voice is, ultimately, a diminished . . . voice with which any student, black or white, whose self-esteem is intact would not choose to identify with for very long. Yet it is often the only black voice on the syllabus.
>
> . . . Jim must not be the only African-American voice from the nineteenth century that is heard in the classroom. . . . The only way to counter the demeaning experience of encountering Jim's voice is by adding others, by exposing students to the eloquence of Frederick Douglass and W. E. B. Du Bois, to the "signifying" wit of Charles Chesnutt and Paul Laurence Dunbar, to folktales and folk sermons, to the rhetorical power of Sojourner Truth, to the lucid anger of Ida B. Wells.[3]

In the post-*Brown v. Board of Education* environment the racial elements of *Huckleberry Finn* (and the religious satire) have proved vulnerable to attack and censorship in the public schools and even, in 1969, at Miami-Dade Community College.[4] An English instructor may read the novel as the "noble and beautiful" book seen by Twain, but the students may read it as demeaning to them personally or as offensive to their religious beliefs.

In our former English Composition II (before the sequence was reconfigured in 1990, leaving English Composition II without a novel), students read and wrote about short stories and a novel. I typically assigned—and still do, even now without the novel—several of the following stories by and about African Americans or Jews: Arna Bontemps's "A Summer Tragedy," Langston Hughes's "On the Road," Alice Walker's "Everyday Use," James Baldwin's "Sonny's Blues," Richard Wright's "The Man Who Was Almost a Man" or "Big Black Good Man," Ralph Ellison's "Battle Royal" or "King of the Bingo Game," Kate Chopin's "Désirée's Baby," Eudora Welty's "A Worn Path," Jamaica Kincaid's "Girl," Philip Roth's "Defender of the Faith." I also assigned some international stories such as Julio Cortázar's "We Love Glenda So Much," Gabriel García Márquez's "A Very Old Man with Enormous Wings," Albert Camus's "The Guest," and Frank O'Connor's "Guests of the Nation." Those who know these stories recognize that most, if not all, dwell on themes of race or religion or both (e.g., Hughes, Bontemps, Roth, Walker, García Márquez, Cortázar, and Ellison). It does not take a Twain scholar to see that students in my English Composition II course had to confront the issues of race and religion as seen in literature if they wished to survive, never mind succeed in, the course.

Some students tried to waffle on the issues, but most addressed, if not confronted, them. They did so in three ways: informal reader-response journal entries, class discussion, and formal essays and research papers. As a result of these assignments, students dealt with, if not assimilated, the idea of "the other" in literature and, by extension, in reality. They were more likely to try to understand the racial issues in *Huckleberry Finn* than if they had read a more traditional set of stories on their way to the novel. Perhaps you object to this multicultural reading list because you think your students are different from mine or for some other reason. If so, and that little objection simmering in the back of your mind boils over into hostility, look at your students. They come from different racial and ethnic backgrounds almost everywhere in the South (and in the North). Even in the rural areas untouched by the economic prosperity that has concentered in the urban South, a significant percentage of the students are, most likely, African Americans, Mexican Americans, Cuban Americans, Vietnamese Americans, or Chinese Americans. If your classroom is still not very ethnically diverse, demographers tell us that it soon will be if current population trends continue. Very few scholars would argue against the inclusion of the stories I use on the grounds of merit. Each one can hold its own against the canonical fiction, and each one challenges the students to view ideas from different perspectives.

Students' essays and reader-responses in these English composition classes—after discussion of the evolving Huck-Jim relationship—addressing a topic that invited them to attack the novel as racist or to defend it, uniformly supported the notion that both Twain and Huck survive the charge. One white female student (Michelle Reedy) entitles her essay "Nigger Is Not a Naughty Word" and defends its use historically: "Given the fact of the cultural setting of the time of this novel, the term 'nigger' is justified. Granted the entire era of slavery was inhumane cruel, and unnecessary, it was common in the South and accepted. Mark Twain should not be criticized or have his novel censored because of historic truth." That same quarter an African American female student (Andrea Brevard) generally agrees that the novel rises above racism; but she feels the sting of the term "nigger," as she notes in her reader-response journal:

> I feel that this novel was not racial but that during that time period, Mark Twain wrote what he saw and perhaps experienced. Racism is a very sensitive word to me because of the way of life so many blacks were forced to live in. I can not understand how any human being would or could ever continue to live with himself or herself knowing that they are treating another person as a four-legged animal. On the other hand, I really wished the word "nigger" was not stressed throughout the entire story. I know this was a term that was used during the time of the story, but that doesn't make it right.

Other responses from African American students divert the issue somewhat by spending more time on Jim's positive portrayal and on the humor than on the negatives. Sharon Mills writes that "nigger" has been a negative way of labeling African Americans "over the past four hundred years." She continues:

> Though the main African-American character is titled "Nigger Jim," and the novel exhibits some stereotypical thoughts, it is Jim who is chosen by Twain to play an extremely important role in Huckleberry's adventures. Jim is undoubtedly placed in a positive light. From the relationship that Huck develops with Jim, it is evident that Twain is not using Jim as a tool to promote racism, but as a tool to show us that two races can come together, despite the times in which they live.

Most white students appreciate the growth they find in the Huck-Jim relationship and applaud Huck's efforts to see Jim as a human being. Further, most students—African American, European American, and other ethnic American—agree that for the time and for his background, Huck's apprenticeship in humanism under the tutelage of Jim leaps forward rather than falling backward toward Pap, or perhaps to Miss Watson and the Phelpses, in whom the contradiction between slave ownership and devout Christianity seems most tortuous.

Research in recent years, especially by African American scholars in books like *Satire or Evasion? Black Perspectives on "Huckleberry*

Finn" (1992) and by Shelley Fisher Fishkin in *Was Huck Black? Mark Twain and African-American Voices* (1993), can help teachers sort out the issues of race and racism. The imperative to set a context for *Adventures of Huckleberry Finn* by including the study of, or at least reference to, texts by African Americans helps focus appropriate critical attention where it belongs: on the ideas and merits of *Huckleberry Finn.* Of course, race looms large as a major theme in the book.

In the American literature (1800–1900) course that I teach, we study Melville's "Benito Cereno" and excerpts from Stowe's *Uncle Tom's Cabin,* Douglass's *The Life and Times of Frederick Douglass,* and Harriet Jacobs's *Incidents in the Life of a Slave Girl* before reading *Huckleberry Finn.* I also point out, as we read and discuss their works, the abolitionist views of Thoreau and Emerson, Whitman's advocacy of the Free-Soil movement (against extending slavery into new territories), and Hawthorne's lack of sympathy for abolition. Students (and harried instructors with little time to prepare for classes?) generally do not know that Thoreau in "Civil Disobedience" does not simply oppose the Mexican War as a war; he opposes the inevitable extension of slavery after the war. They do not know that Whitman's departure from his position as editor of the *Brooklyn Daily Eagle* stemmed from the very same reason as Thoreau's opposition to the war. Whitman's early and vigorous identification with the nationalistic notion of "manifest destiny" gave way to his increasing support of the Free-Soil movement as embodied in the Wilmot Proviso of 1846.[5] He, like Thoreau, saw in the Mexican War a blatant grab for new slave territory, which would eventually strain the relative balance of free states to slave states since states formed from the newly acquired territory would most likely enter the Union as slave states and tip the balance toward a permanent sanction of slavery. Neither do students know that Hawthorne wrote Franklin Pierce's campaign biography, and that Pierce's (and Hawthorne's) party in its 1852 presidential campaign supported the Southern plantation aristocrats against the abolitionists. Traditional nineteenth-century American literature courses tend to pay little or no attention to the most divisive political and social issue of the time, as if the authors themselves lived outside their time and place. Twain, almost alone, stands out and, therefore, makes an easy target. Of the traditional authors and texts—Poe's poetry and short stories, Emerson's essays and poetry, Thoreau's *Walden,* Hawthorne's *The Scarlet Letter,* Melville's *Moby-Dick,* Whitman's *Leaves of Grass,* Dickinson's poetry, Twain's

Huckleberry Finn—only *Huckleberry Finn* directly addresses the issues of race and slavery.

As in the English composition class, students in American literature write reader-responses and have to answer short essay questions such as, "Explain your agreement or disagreement with the idea that the novel is racist because of the use of the term 'nigger' and because of the portrayal of Jim," and, "Explain *both* Pap Finn's *attitude* toward slaves and free African Americans and *its effect* on Huck, if any."

Students' reader-responses should precede class discussion; often they do, but sometimes they are turned in after class discussion has made it safe to agree with the instructor or other students. The first of Asian American Shital Patel's two required *Huckleberry Finn* responses reflects her genuine response to the race issue (but after having read only "the first fifty pages" (chapters 1–9):

> The word nigger was used quite often by the characters, esp. Huck. I don't think though Huck meant any ill will by using it. He was just ignorant and had never been taught better. The connotation & denotation of nigger had eluded him. I can understand why Twain would employ the word nigger. To him it was part of the dialect. I'm not saying that was the sole reason because it can never by truly proven.
>
> Though I can see why people would be upset with Twain. Nigger enforces stereotypes and since many impressionable children read *Huck Finn* they do not understand the literal meaning behind nigger. Nor can they understand Twain's reason behind employing nigger.

A white male (Michael Connell) writes a response defending the novel and expressing sadness "that a generation may never read it because *Huck Finn* is not politically correct." He ends his response by noting the positive aspect of race in the novel: "I would encourage people of all races to read *Huck Finn*. It demonstrates that people of all races can be good or evil. It shows us how our upbringing can influence our views, and it shows us that people of all races can be friends." Another white student (Louis Pratt) connects Jim's action to Frederick Douglass's refusal to be beaten by Covey, the slave-breaker: "Throughout the novel Jim is not scared of slavery or the consequences of being captured because if he was he wouldn't have fled for the beautiful journey down the Mississippi into the heart of slavery. I sensed Frederick Douglass's motive of having to take things head on to obtain what you rightfully want and believe in." Seemingly on the opposite side, African American Vanessa Hemingway expresses the historical perspective but obviously guards her feelings:

Jim was viewed as being superstitious and ignorant and inferior to the Euro-American. Jim was thought of as being inhuman, with a mentality not equal to Huck. . . . Even then he [Huck] still didn't fully accept Jim as a human being equal to himself. Because Huckleberry said "I knowed he was white inside." Why not black inside, as black as his skin, this goes to show that the given time the word "Nigger" was a great pastime. So Huckleberry's trickery is not surprising it's only the trend of the society as a whole during this time period, therefore, with that thought in mind I can accept *The Adventures of Huckleberry Finn* as a great work or great masterpiece.

Even though these students' testimony resonates around my advice to treat the issue of race candidly and in a context of other voices, including those of Frederick Douglass and Harriet Jacobs, themselves former slaves, you may need a few more rounds of ammunition to prepare for the assault against *Huck Finn*. A commonly noted feature of the "darky" stereotype portrayed at times through Jim has to do with Jim's apparent foolishness or ignorance because of his superstitions. I suggest you disarm this attack by comparing Jim's reaction when he first sees Huck on Jackson's Island (chapter 8) to Tom Sawyer's similar reaction at the Phelps Plantation (chapter 33). Jim's reaction plays to the stereotypical exaggerated fear of ghosts (recall that Huck startles Jim, who thinks he's alone on the island, at "gray" daybreak): " 'Doan' hurt me—don't! I hain't ever done no harm to a ghos'. I alwuz liked dead people, en done all I could for 'em. You go an git in de river ag'in, whah you b'longs, en doan' do nuffn to Ole Jim, 'at 'uz alwuz yo' fren'.' "[6] The key superstition relates to the reality of ghosts and what they do to the living. But if Jim's reaction paints him as an ignorant, superstitious "darky," how do we account for Tom Sawyer's similar reaction later (in broad daylight on his way to his aunt and uncle's plantation)?

and his mouth opened like a trunk, and stayed so; and he swallowed two or three times like a person that's got a dry throat, and then says:

"I hain't ever done you no harm. You know that. So, then, what you want to come back and ha'nt me for?"

The two scenes compare almost to the exact words, except that, as the scenes continue, Tom, the educated, middle-class white boy, needs more evidence that Huck is indeed alive than does the "ignorant" slave, Jim. Coupled with a few descriptions of Huck's own superstitions (e.g., at the end of chapter 1), this comparison repels the attack on that portion of the racial issue—superstition as prima facie evidence of degradation. All the major characters display their own superstitions—even the pious Widow Douglas and her sister (Jim's owner), Miss Watson, whose "superstitions" extend to holding a mercilessly satirized belief: one can own slaves and be a good Christian.

The religious satire seems to offend a relatively smaller percentage of students, although the Bible Belt sensibility still informs most of the urban areas of the New South. Where I teach, a large number of students hail from other regions of the country, even though some of them were drawn there for the religious atmosphere (hence, the earlier allusion to Jim Bakker, whose PTL television program attracted many thousands of people). So I address the issue directly by analyzing the religious satire in appropriate episodes, particularly near the beginning with the two versions of Providence signified by Miss Watson and the Widow Douglas, in the Grangerford-Shepherdson episode near the middle, and in Huck's decision to "go to Hell" to free Jim from the Phelps farm.

In each of these cases, the issue of slavery accompanies and constitutes a major part of the satire, again splicing what appear to be mutually exclusive beliefs: devout Christianity (including "brotherly love") and slavery. Sometimes the satire works in a subtle way, as in chapter 1 when Huck observes, "By and by they fetched the niggers in and had prayers, and then everybody was off to bed." One has to wonder what the slaves pray for. Frederick Douglass and Harriet Jacobs answer resoundingly: freedom! Would Miss Watson say to the slaves what Huck reports she says to him before he prays for fish line and hooks (chapter 3): "pray every day, and whatever I asked for I would get it"?

Probably the best synechdochal link between race and religion occurs in the much maligned "evasion" sequence. Twain conflates the two issues into a joke about Silas Phelps (chapter 33), which he sets up by making Silas naïvely accept Huck's deception about how fast a worn-out horse can travel: "He was the innocentest best old soul I ever see. But it warn't surprising: because he warn't only just a farmer, he was a preacher, too, and had a little one-horse log church down back of the plantation, which he built it himself at his own expense, for a church and a school house, and never charged nothing for his preaching, and it was worth it, too." Not content to expose one naïve soul's hypocrisy, Twain indicts the South as a whole for its religious hypocrisy, signified by simultaneously condoning slavery and preaching Christian values: "There was plenty other farmer-preachers like that, and done the same way, down South."

Alternative and new readings of *Adventures of Huckleberry Finn* continue to appear. I have heard credible readings of the book as a parody of contemporary travelogues (Gretchen Beidler) and of Huck himself as child of an alcoholic parent (Elizabeth C. Prioleau). Another critical vein extending back at least to the early 1980s identifies *Huckleberry Finn* as having attributes similar to those of the slave narrative (Lucinda MacKethan and William L. Andrews). The 1990 discovery of the lost manuscript pages has already opened up questions and possibilities. Victor Doyno has shared a significant emended episode from the manuscript when Jim and Huck are talking about ghosts. Jim launches into a story about a medical school cadaver that acts like a ghost. We have no evidence explaining why Twain crossed out the whole story—perhaps because it would further inscribe Jim as a minstrel show "darky." We can look forward to other imaginative readings and further insights from genetic criticism because scholars now have access to a portion of the manuscript in the 1996 Random House edition of *Huckleberry Finn* and to the entirety at the Buffalo-Erie County Library. At least Doyno will most certainly provide new perspectives as he proceeds to revise and supplement the findings of his 1991 *Writing Huck Finn* in light of the manuscript evidence.

Using *Adventures of Huckleberry Finn* in a culturally diverse community college classroom (or university, four-year college, or high school) can work, even in the face of attacks on the novel related to racial epithets and religious hypocrisy. In spite of these attacks and bans from required or optional reading lists, high school students continue to read *Huckleberry Finn*. But reading and studying the novel in a college setting with an instructor informed by the recent scholarship changes the students' perspective from their examination of the book in high school. One cannot and should not sidestep the issues of racism and religious satire in the novel. To do so would not necessarily emasculate the novel's impact, but it would suggest a retreat from academic discourse about issues important in Twain's day, and in our own. The suggestions I have provided here are a few ways by which I try to turn the study of *Adventures of Huckleberry Finn* into a meaningful and useful confrontation with, rather than an evasion of, the pertinent issues.

Notes

1 David L. Smith, "Huck, Jim, and American Racial Discourse" (1984), rpt. in *Satire or Evasion? Black Perspectives on Huckleberry Finn*, ed. James S. Leonard, Thomas A. Tenney, and Thadious M. Davis (Durham, N.C.: Duke University Press, 1992), 116.

2 Shelley Fisher Fishkin, *Was Huck Black? Mark Twain and African-American Voices* (New York: Oxford University Press, 1993), 107.

3 Fishkin, *Was Huck Black?* 107.

4 " 'Huck Finn' Not Required," *New York Times*, 15 Jan. 1969: 44, qtd. in Peaches Henry, "The Struggle for Tolerance: Race and Censorship in *Huckleberry Finn*," in Leonard et al., eds., *Satire or Evasion?*, 26.

5 For more details about the relationship between Whitman's views on these issues and his dismissal from the editorship of the *Brooklyn Daily Eagle*, see Joseph Jay Rubin's *The Historic Whitman* (University Park: Pennsylvania State University Press, 1973), 173–80; Justin Kaplan's *Walt Whitman: A Life* (New York: Simon and Schuster, 1980), 124–36; and Philip Callow's *From Noon to Starry Night: A Life of Walt Whitman* (Chicago: Ivan R. Dee, 1992), 142–51.

6 All *Huck Finn* quotations come from *Adventures of Huckleberry Finn* (Berkeley: University of California Press, 1985).

Recommended Reading

Budd, Louis J. *Mark Twain: Social Philosopher*. Bloomington: Indiana University Press, 1962. One of the first books to treat the issue of race.

Doyno, Victor. *Writing "Huckleberry Finn": Mark Twain's Creative Process*. Philadelphia: University of Pennsylvania Press, 1991. Uses genetic criticism to show how Twain composed his masterpiece, including speculation about intentions. In the process of revision since the discovery and authentication of the long-lost first half of Twain's manuscript.

Ellison, Ralph. *Shadow and Act*. New York: New American Library (Signet), 1964. Important early essays about African Americans and Twain.

Fishkin, Shelley Fisher. *Was Huck Black? Mark Twain and African-American Voices*. New York: Oxford University Press, 1993. Groundbreaking research about African

American models for Huckleberry Finn, multicultural voices in the novel, and the cross-fertilization of European American and African American literature.

Kaplan, Justin. *Mr. Clemens and Mark Twain: A Biography.* New York: Simon and Schuster, 1966. At times frustrating because of what one learns about Samuel Clemens, but still one of the most authoritative biographies.

Leonard, James S., Thomas A. Tenney, and Thadious M. Davis, eds. *Satire or Evasion? Black Perspectives on "Huckleberry Finn."* Durham, N.C.: Duke University Press, 1992. Includes fifteen essays, six of which are original. The others are revised from their original publication in the *Mark Twain Journal* (1984, 1985). The only source with this many different African American views on *Huckleberry Finn* in one volume.

Leonard, James S., ed. *Mark Twain Circular.* Newsletter of the Mark Twain Circle of America. Published four times a year. Includes short articles about Twain and his works, abstracts of Twain scholarship, and announcements of Mark Twain Circle-sponsored sessions at Modern Language Association and American Literature Association annual meetings, as well as other conference notices and calls for papers.

Morrison, Toni. *Playing in the Dark: Whiteness and the Literary Imagination.* Cambridge, Mass.: Harvard University Press, 1992. Revised versions of three William E. Massey, Sr., Lectures in the History of American Civilization given at Harvard University in 1990. The second, "Romancing the Shadow," speaks particularly about *Adventures of Huckleberry Finn.*

Pettit, Arthur. *Mark Twain and the South.* Lexington: University Press of Kentucky, 1974. Early and fairly thorough treatment of race and slavery. One of the first suggestions of the "evasion sequence" as a parody of Southern Reconstruction.

"Pretty Ornery Preaching": *Huckleberry Finn*
in the Church-Related College
Stan Poole

The frequency with which *Adventures of Huckleberry Finn* has been the target of censors in recent years has been disturbing to many people who view the book as an American classic. Such objections to the novel, however, at least indicate that readers have experienced and responded to the book's powerful representation of racial tensions in American culture. As an instructor at a church-related liberal arts college where many of my students take their religious faith seriously but few have critically examined their own religious traditions, I have sometimes longed for some indication that my students are disturbed by the book. Perhaps because they have been taught to revere it as a masterpiece or because they read it primarily for entertainment, few of my students respond to the subversive elements of the novel until prodded to do so.

The problem is not that Christian students reject Twain's criticism of the religious establishment for its approval of slavery. Even those students whose own religious traditions are closest to the Southern evangelicalism that Twain satirizes quickly label the religious characters in the novel as villains and Huck Finn as the good "bad boy" who defies social convention and religious teaching in helping a runaway slave. Moreover, they often find confirmation for their views in the critical commentary on the novel, much of which has described the moral dynamics of the book in oppositional terms such as nature vs. civilization, raft (or river) vs. shore, vernacular vs. "official" values.[1] Initiated by Twain himself when he described Huck's dilemma as the conflict between "a sound heart and a deformed conscience" (Blair, 143), such oppositions may suggest the broad outlines of Twain's moral intentions, but they obscure his more subtle ironies and tempt us to indulge in the kind of moral complacency that James Cox has called "the pleasure of principle" (403). Armed with these convenient moral categories, students can distance themselves from the cultural attitudes that Twain satirizes. By simply dismissing the religious characters in the novel as hypocrites for supporting a system of slavery that so obviously contradicts Christian ethics, they can accept Twain's critique on a superficial level without allowing it to challenge their own unexamined assumptions about the connections between religious belief and ethical behavior.

One of the most effective ways I have found to move students beyond this simplistic view of the novel is to introduce them to the historical context of Southern religion in the nineteenth century. The work of historians such as Donald Matthews, Bertram Wyatt-Brown, Samuel Hill, and John Boles offers a rich cultural background against which Twain's critique of evangelicals emerges with striking clarity.

Historians have shown that in the three decades before the Civil War, religious leaders in the South spent a great deal of energy developing theological and ethical arguments to support slavery.[2] Most students are vaguely aware of this fact, but they are often surprised to learn that an antislavery movement arose among Southern evangelicals between the Revolutionary War and the War of 1812. Although the movement never gained widespread appeal, both its existence and its decline clarify the relationship between evangelical religion and the social context in which it developed. Donald Matthews in *Religion and the Old South* attributes the development of this abolitionist movement in the South to the nature of evangelical piety, with its emphasis on conversion to a life of "stern self-discipline and personal holiness" (70). Despite its individualistic orientation, Matthews argues, evangelical conversion "borders on a radical moral heroism, which, had it been taken seriously, would have had social results. Individuals could not brood over moral failings and eternal obligations without including perforce their relationships with other people" (70). That a similar evangelical fervor was one of the strongest sources of abolitionist activity in the North seems to confirm Matthews's point. Why, then, did this radical potential within Southern evangelicalism ultimately fail to overturn the proslavery ideology of the South? How was the antislavery rhetoric of some evangelicals in the early part of the nineteenth century converted to proslavery apologetics by mid-century?

Historians have argued that Southern opposition to slavery died out at least partially because contradictions within the belief system of evangelicals undermined their attempts to apply the ethical implications of their faith to social issues. Besides cultivating moral intensity, the emphasis on conversion also promoted ambitious goals for evangelization. Baptists, Methodists, and, to a lesser extent, Presbyterians adopted the methods of the revival and made spectacular gains in the South throughout the early decades of the nineteenth century. Interpreting this rapid expansion as evidence of God's favor, they were unwilling to jeopardize their gains with an antislavery message that would alienate slaveholders, the most economically and politically powerful group in Southern society. Their commitment to evangelism and their desire for a stronger position of influence within Southern society came into conflict with their antislavery impulses. As John Boles has pointed out, "The Baptists and Methodists, realizing that their stance toward slavery might seriously hamper their ability to spread their version of the gospel, chose to make their racial attitudes conform more closely to the slaveholders' ethos" (28). Thus, evangelicals suppressed the social dimensions of morality and channeled their moral energy almost exclusively toward personal holiness.[3] By the 1820s, the radical potential for social justice implicit in the evangelical belief system had been crushed by accommodation to the cultural realities of the South. During the same period, evangelicals were gradually transforming themselves from what Boles describes as a "despised, at times persecuted minority" (25) to the culturally dominant religious group in the South.

This history of evangelical experience does not negate the familiar oppositions with which we have framed the novel's moral concerns, but it does help students begin to see the complexity of Twain's moral vision in *Huckleberry Finn*. Rather than simply opposing a corrupt religion to natural goodness, Twain's narrative explores the contradictions within evangelical religion and their implications for Southern culture. The novel exposes the limits of a morality of personal holiness, but it also illuminates resources for moral renewal implicit in the evangelical belief system. Although Twain may have been reluctant to acknowledge it, his alternative to evangelical ethics—the moral sensitivity represented by Huck in his best moments—is derived in part from the very belief system he is attacking. To trace this process of representation, criticism, and adaptation of the evangelical ethos, I ask students to examine more carefully the character who both embodies and challenges our assumptions about evangelicals—the Widow Douglas.

In the opening chapter of *Huckleberry Finn*, the widow is the target of one of Mark Twain's favorite satirical strategies—exposing conventional piety to the logic of hardheaded common sense. One by one, the widow's projects for reforming Huck are undercut by Huck's pragmatism: her attempt to teach Huck the biblical story of Moses falters since Huck "don't take no stock in dead people"; her ritual of saying grace before each meal only makes Huck wonder why she "grumbles over" food that is perfectly good; and her restriction on smoking inspires resentment rather than repentance since the widow herself takes snuff (2–3). The widow's "dismal regular and decent . . . ways" and her vigilant religious teaching are clearly out of touch with Huck's actual experiences.

As the narrative progresses, however, Twain begins to qualify this negative view of the widow. Introducing Miss Watson as a counterpart to the widow, Twain displaces some of the negative qualities of evangelicalism onto Miss Watson, making the widow a more sympathetic character. In contrast to the widow's gentle prodding, for example, Miss Watson lays down strict rules: "Don't put your feet up there, Huckleberry. . . . Don't scrunch up like that, Huckleberry—set up straight. . . . Don't gap and stretch like that, Huckleberry—why don't you try to behave?" (3). Determined to reform Huck by forcing him into the conventions of polite society, Miss Watson makes no distinction between manners and morals. Although the widow shares Miss Watson's aim of "sivilizing" Huck, she sympathizes with him and intervenes on his behalf when Miss Watson makes things unbearable. By emphasizing the compassion of the widow, Twain begins to develop distinctions within his overall critique of the evangelical ethos.

The most important of these distinctions is revealed in the contrasting notions of prayer held by the two women. While Miss Watson asssures Huck that if he prays every day, he will get what he asks for, the widow urges Huck to pray for "spiritual gifts": "I must help other people, and do everything I could for other people, and look out for them all the time, and never think about myself" (13). With his typical pragmatism, Huck sees no advantage in the widow's advice "except for the other people" and decides to just "let it go" (14). But a crucial distinction has been established. The widow rejects Miss Watson's view that personal piety entitles one to special blessings from God; instead, she insists that prayer is an acknowledgment of one's selfishness and one's need for the spiritual gifts of humility, self-sacrifice, and concern for others.[4] For the widow, an individual's relation to a

God of mercy necessarily entails an ethical responsibility to other human beings. Ironically, as many readers have noted, this is precisely what Huck Finn practices, though he claims to have rejected the widow's teaching as impractical. Confronted later by moral choices involving Jim's freedom, Huck is guided by a sense of responsibility to Jim, and regardless of how instinctive Huck's generosity may seem, it has been reinforced by the widow's teachings. Huck himself acknowledges this influence when he compares his concern for the gang of murderers on the *Walter Scott* to the widow's concern for "rapscallions and deadbeats."

The widow's motives, however, have been called into question by critics who link her notion of respectability to the ideology of slavery. Richard Poirier, for example, has argued that the widow's religious teaching has the same dubious status as the romances that inspire Tom Sawyer's fantasies; both are lies that serve to socialize Huck and replace his instinctive goodness with the corrupt cultural norms of Southern society (182). The only way Huck can preserve his virtue, according to this view, is to seek refuge in communion with nature. This argument seems plausible so long as we interpret the novel within the framework of a simple opposition between nature and civilization, but when we place the widow's efforts to reform Huck in the historical context of the antebellum South, her instruction takes on a different tone and significance. The widow's concern for respectability reflects in part the efforts of evangelicals to overcome disruptive tendencies both in their own religious experience and in the larger cultural context.

Probably the single most important factor in the development of nineteenth-century evangelicalism was its revivalistic orientation.[5] With its particularly volatile form of religious expression and its tendency to undermine class distinctions by affirming the equality of all people before God, revivalism was potentially a disruptive social force. Highly individualistic, subjective, and emotional, evangelical religion lacked the traditional restraints of institutional authority provided by the old established churches. As Donald Matthews has pointed out, "The danger of allowing the convert to evaluate his own experience and acts was obvious. Christians of all eras had dealt with Antinomians, who believed themselves free to act in any way they chose" (61). In order to counteract such potential disorder, evangelicals emphasized "personal holiness." Their preoccupation with order and self-discipline as marks of sanctification thus worked to control the powerful forces unleashed by revivalism's subjective religious experience.

Twain seems to have recognized the potential danger of evangelical religious experience when not adequately ordered and controlled by self-discipline. Huck's description of the camp meeting at Pokeville emphasizes the emotion of this style of worship. As the intensity of the meeting rises to its climax, emotional expression overwhelms rational understanding: "You couldn't make out what the preacher said, any more, on account of the shouting and crying. Folks got up, everywheres in the crowd, and worked their way, just by main strength, to the mourners' bench, with the tears running down their faces; and when all the mourners had got up there to the front benches in a crowd, they sung, and shouted, and flung themselves down on the straw, just crazy and wild" (172). Huck is clearly uncomfortable with such uncontrolled outbursts of emotion, though he makes no explicit judgments regarding its authenticity. The king's affectation of the conversion experience and his success in working the crowd for money, however, suggest that such emotional experiences are easily counterfeited. Moreover, such powerful emotions seem to take the crowd to the brink of unseemly sensuality. As Huck reports, "every little while the prettiest kind of girls, with the tears running down their cheeks, would up and ask [the king] would he let them kiss him, for to remember him by; and he always done it; and some of them he hugged and kissed as many as five or six times" (173). Twain apparently found this sensuality repulsive. He decided to delete his illustrator's drawing of "the lecherous old rascal kissing the girl at the campmeeting" and told his publisher that "It is a disgusting thing, & pictures are sure to tell the truth about it too plainly" (Blair and Fischer, 410). Compared to the emotional excess of the camp meeting, the widow's emphasis on self-discipline and respectability seems healthy.

Besides this internal threat to order, however, evangelicals also had to contend with what W. J. Cash has called the South's "hedonistic temperament," which was in part a product of its class structure: "In that void of pointless leisure which was his, the poor white turned his energies almost wholly to elaborating the old backcountry pattern of amusement and distinction. . . . To stand on his head in a bar, to toss down a pint of raw whisky at a gulp, to fiddle and dance all night, to bite off the nose or gouge out the eye of a favorite enemy, to fight harder and love harder than the next man, to be known eventually far and wide as a hell of a fellow—such would be his focus" (51–52). Evangelicals constantly struggled with this hedonistic tendency in their efforts to create moral and social order out of a relatively unsettled and chaotic frontier. If their strictures against drinking, smoking, gambling, and dancing seem prudishly repressive, they also can be understood, given the daily battle they waged against real social problems caused by this pattern of excess in Southern culture.

In this context, the widow Douglas's efforts to make Huck respectable seem less an attempt to brainwash him with the corrupt values of society than an extension of her genuine concern for a homeless boy destined to grow up under evil influences. Donald Matthews's explanation of what "elevation" meant to evangelicals illuminates the widow's motivations: "Elevation" was not mere social mobility—although for many people it was surely that—but the conversion from illiteracy, ignorance, and powerlessness to learning, power and self-respect" (94). In this sense, acquiring respectability was essentially a democratic process that provided a means for empowering marginalized people. Respectability was open to anyone, provided he or she was willing to conform to evangelical discipline. Is this, however, the value that Twain places on respectability in the context of the novel? In some obvious ways it is not. There is no doubt that Huck's recoil from the widow's stuffy ways is intended to satirize the restrictive and artificial conventions by which evangelicals defined respectability. But the satire cuts both ways, as Twain playfully exploits Huck's naïve faith in superstition, his ignorance of common cultural knowledge, and his sometimes crude behavior. More importantly, the effects of the widow's efforts to make Huck respectable seem less pernicious when we consider the only alternative for Huck—living with Pap Finn.

When Pap returns to St. Petersburg to claim Huck, he immediately confronts Huck about the trappings of respectability he has acquired under the influence of the widow. After discovering that Huck really can read, Pap demands that he drop out of school and warns him, "Now looky here; you stop that putting on frills. I won't have it. I'll lay for you, my smarty; and if I catch you about that school I'll tan you good. First you know you'll get religion, too. I never see such a son" (24). Pap's linking of education and religion here is no accident. For Pap, as for the widow, education and religion are related means of acquiring respectability, but Pap feels betrayed by Huck's elevation in society and his acceptance of its values. A prime example of Cash's Southern hedonist, Pap encourages Huck to steal, indulge his vices, and otherwise spurn the expectations of polite society.

This counterpoint between the widow Douglas and Pap Finn as competing models for Huck does not easily fit the moral categories we have applied to the novel. Rather than reducing moral questions to such clear-cut oppositions of instinct and civilization, freedom and repression, Twain represents social reality in more complex terms. His affirmation of vernacular values such as freedom from social convention and pragmatic individualism is qualified by his recognition that they often find expression in anti-intellectualism, moral insensitivity, and self-indulgence. His condemnation of the official values of the social and religious establishment is tempered by his recognition that, despite its hypocritical tendencies, the evangelical emphasis on self-discipline and education can improve the prospects for the South's poor, illiterate, backwoods people.

Twain thus locates more precisely and subtly where a society with good intentions goes wrong and illuminates far more cogently the source of corruption within the dominant culture. What Twain understood—and *Huckleberry Finn* implicitly suggests—is not that evangelical religion exercised too much influence on society, but precisely the opposite: it too easily accommodated itself to existing cultural values and restricted its ethical concerns to matters of personal piety. Although the widow's interest in Huck is genuine and her values of respectability and order are not in themselves corrupt, her advice to Huck to "help other people, and do everything I could for other people, and never think about myself" rings hollow given the fact that she and Miss Watson "fetched the niggers in and had prayers" (4) every night. Her acts of piety, regardless of how genuine, blind her to the reality that she exploits the slaves for her own economic interests. Similarly, the Grangerfords and Shepherdsons go to church and hear a sermon "all about brotherly love" (147), only to slaughter each other the next day. The satire is directed not toward their theology, but toward their failure to turn theological reflection into ethical practice. In yet another example, Twain invites us to share Huck's admiration for Silas Phelps, a farmer-preacher who built "a little one-horse log church down back of the plantation . . . at his own expense" (285), but Silas's belief that his paramount Christian duty is to return Jim to his proper owner illustrates the failure of Southern evangelicals to act on the best insights of their faith. In each case, the potential for a radical social ethic—implied by the widow's advice to Huck, the sermon about "brotherly love," and Silas Phelps's self-sacrifice—is undermined by a narrow preoccupation with personal holiness. Thus, Twain's sensitivity to the basic goodness and decency of many of his religious characters underscores the tragic failure of their religious commitment to create a genuine desire for social justice.

Besides clarifying Twain's representation of his religious characters, this account of the history of evangelical experience helps students better understand Huck Finn's crucial decision regarding his ethical responsibility to Jim. When I ask my students to compare Huck's moral dilemma with that of Southern evangelicals, they begin to see that the decision he faces in chapter 31 recapitulates the choice faced by evangelicals early in the nineteenth century. In his internal debate over whether to turn in Jim or not, Huck attempts to conform to evangelical standards of personal holiness:

> I about made up my mind to pray; and see if I couldn't try to quit being the kind of a boy I was, and be better. So I kneeled down. But the words wouldn't come. Why wouldn't they? It warn't no use to try and hide it from Him. Nor from *me*, neither. I knowed very well why they wouldn't come. It was because my heart warn't right; it was because I warn't square; it was because I was playing double. I was letting *on* to give up sin, but away inside of me I was holding on to the biggest one of all. I was trying to make my mouth *say* I would do the right thing and the clean thing, and go and write to that nigger's owner and tell where he was; but deep down in me I knowed it was a lie—and He knowed it. You can't pray a lie—I found that out. (269)

The language here, as Henry Nash Smith has noted, is clearly that of evangelical confession, and its preoccupation with the inner state of sinfulness overwhelms the sense of ethical responsibility that Huck has developed toward Jim (120–22). As his thoughts move away from his inner life and back to his experiences on the raft, however, Huck's concern for Jim resurfaces and powerfully overturns his desire to do the "right" thing. The crucial moment when Huck rejects the evangelical conscience by saying to himself, "All right, then, I'll *go* to hell," has been the key to many interpretations of the novel. What has not been recognized, however, is that in Huck's battle with his conscience,

Twain has created a remarkable dramatization of the conflicts within evangelicalism itself. Huck's dilemma mirrors that of evangelicals early in the century who were faced with a choice between entrenched cultural values and a radical sense of justice. While their moral zeal had indeed generated antislavery sentiment, "the social realities of slavery and the psychological realities of racial prejudice simply could not be counterbalanced by religious commitment" (Matthews, 70). By the time that Huck started his journey down the Mississippi, evangelical leaders in the South had abandoned their earlier abolitionist activities. In the 1830s, they had begun to channel their energy into articulating a humane slaveholding ethic—"Bible slavery," one writer termed it—and justifying slavery on the grounds that it brought the message of Christianity to the slaves.[6] Huck's rejection of a single-minded preoccupation with personal holiness realizes the possibility of moral heroism implicit in evangelicalism before it capitulated to the ideology of slavery. Twain thus affirms the moral imperatives at the heart of evangelical Christianity—the humility, self-sacrifice, and concern for others expressed by the widow Douglas—in repudiating its practices.

What are the pedagogical benefits of approaching the novel from the perspective of evangelical history? First, as students become attentive to the novel's interaction with its historical context, they become more sophisticated as interpreters, discovering that the subtleties of Twain's irony and the complexities of his characterization cannot be reduced to simplistic moral formulas. Perhaps even more importantly, introducing students in the church-related college to the history of evangelicalism encourages them to identify more closely with Twain's religious characters and thus to see their personal experience reflected in the novel. Like Huck responding to the Grangerfords' minister, they begin to find this book "pretty ornery preaching" when they allow its ironies to penetrate their assumptions about the connections between religious beliefs, personal morality, and social justice. No longer simply a masterpiece to be revered, the novel prompts in some students a profound reexamination of the ethical dimensions of their own religious traditions. In many cases, they begin to see how their religious training has defined ethics narrowly in terms of personal holiness and ignored the radical social implications of Christian faith. Applying the lessons of *Huckleberry Finn* to more recent history, for example, they cite the failure of white Southern churches to support desegregation in the 1950s and 1960s. *Huckleberry Finn* becomes for these students not only a powerful indictment of the ideology of slavery but a prophetic work that continues to address issues of social justice in a world where religious institutions have often abdicated their moral authority by embracing the cultural values of the status quo. Such a response is valuable in any context, but it is particularly appropriate in the church-related college, where students are sometimes tempted to substitute a superficial piety for the hard work of authentic moral reflection.

Notes

1 Under Works Cited, see, for example, Tanner, 161–65; Trilling, 83–84; and Smith, 113–37. More recently, Victor Doyno has examined this issue with greater subtlety by giving some attention to the historical context of nineteenth-century religion, but his chapter title, "Christianity in Conflict with Morality," indicates that he still formulates the novel's moral aims in oppositional terms.
2 The rationale developed by Southern evangelicals is explored at length by Matthews (136–84) and Wyatt-Brown (155–82).
3 Samuel Hill, Jr., in *Southern Churches in Crisis* confirms this individualistic orientation toward morality, although he attributes it not to conflicts over slavery but to inherent qualities of evangelical piety (103–15).
4 In a related issue, Edgar M. Branch has insightfully examined the contrast between the "two Providences" of the widow and Miss Watson, but to my mind he overstates the extent to which the novel affirms a providential order.
5 The discussion of revivalism that follows is based on several sources: Ahlstrom, 521–32; Hill, 65–70; Matthews, 34–38, 58–64; and Miller, 3–35.
6 Both Matthews (136–84) and Wyatt-Brown (155–69) discuss the development of the evangelical response to slavery. The original source of the quotation is R. G. Grundy, "Thoughts for the People—No. 9," Memphis *Bulletin*, 1862 October 19 (quoted in Wyatt-Brown, 162).

Works Cited

Ahlstrom, Sidney E. *A Religious History of the American People.* New Haven, Conn.: Yale University Press, 1972.
Blair, Walter. *Mark Twain and Huck Finn.* Berkeley: University of California Press, 1960.
Blair, Walter, and Victor Fischer. Explanatory Notes. *Adventures of Huckleberry Finn.* By Mark Twain. Berkeley: University of California Press, 1985. 371–422.
Boles, John B. "Evangelical Protestantism in the Old South: From Religious Dissent to Cultural Dominance." In *Religion in the South.* Ed. Charles Reagan Wilson. Jackson: University Press of Mississippi, 1985.

Branch, Edgar M. "The Two Providences: Thematic Form in *Huckleberry Finn*." *College English* 11 (1950): 188–95.

Cash, W. J. *The Mind of the South*. New York: Knopf, 1941.

Cox, James M. "A Hard Book to Take." *One Hundred Years of Huckleberry Finn: The Boy, His Book, and American Culture*. Ed. Robert Sattelmeyer and J. Donald Crowley. Columbia: University of Missouri Press, 1985.

Doyno, Victor A. *Writing "Huck Finn": Mark Twain's Creative Process*. Philadelphia: University of Pennsylvania Press, 1991.

Hill, Samuel S., Jr. *Southern Churches in Crisis*. New York: Holt, Rinehart and Winston, 1966.

Matthews, Donald G. *Religion in the Old South*. Chicago: University of Chicago Press, 1977.

Miller, Perry. *The Life of the Mind in America from the Revolution to the Civil War*. New York: Harcourt, 1966.

Poirier, Richard. *A World Elsewhere: The Place of Style in American Literature*. [1966.] Madison: University of Wisconsin Press, 1985.

Smith, Henry Nash. *Mark Twain: The Development of a Writer*. Cambridge, Mass.: Belknap Press of Harvard University Press, 1962.

Tanner, Tony. *The Reign of Wonder: Naïvety and Reality in American Literature*. Cambridge: Cambridge University Press, 1965.

Trilling, Lionel. Introduction. *Adventures of Huckleberry Finn*. By Mark Twain. New York: Rinehart, 1948. Reprinted in *The Liberal Imagination: Essays on Literature and Society*. New York: Viking, 1951.

Twain, Mark. *Adventures of Huckleberry Finn*. Ed. Walter Blair and Victor Fischer. Berkeley: University of California Press, 1985.

Wyatt-Brown, Bertram. *Yankee Saints and Southern Sinners*. Baton Rouge: Louisiana State University Press, 1985.

"When I read this book as a child . . . the ugliness
was pushed aside": Adult Students Read and
Respond to *Adventures of Huckleberry Finn*
Michael J. Kiskis

Most college-level instruction is traditionally aimed at eighteen to
twenty-one year olds warehoused in on-campus housing and enrolled
in semester-length or quarter-length courses of study with two or three
class meetings per week. I am now back in that environment after
spending five years as an administrator and instructor for adult, non-
traditional students. From 1988 through 1993, I taught at Empire State
College (one of the colleges that form the State University of New
York). ESC tailors its program to adult learners—students who come to
higher education later in life or, more often, return after they have
attempted traditional ways of earning a living.[1]

During August 1993, I completed a term (twenty-four weeks) teaching in ESC's Forum program, which employs a mix of individualized
learning, group meetings at three weekend-long residencies, and distance education to make it possible for corporate managers to complete baccalaureate degrees (the majority of students complete degrees
in management, though not all students focus so tightly on professional studies). Students enter the program with a wealth of learning
in the practices of business; however, few have either the theoretical
background in management or the breadth of learning in nonbusiness
topics (especially within the humanities) needed to meet degree requirements.[2] The program provides direction and instruction designed
to broaden the students' experience with interdisciplinary thought.[3] It
also attempts to ease their reintroduction into the academy and to
support them as they face the prospect of not being the expert when
they walk into a room (a particular challenge for professionals, several of whom handle budgets larger than those of midsize liberal arts
colleges).

That introduction brings me to my experience and this attempt to
tell the story of a journey that brought my students both pleasure and

pain. Students found various levels of pleasure within the prospect of moving into a different and unexplored part of their national culture and with reading (and at times rereading) stories that are often taught as tales meant for children. They found various levels of pain not only in the demand that they read a series of fictional and autobiographical texts (several students admitted that they read little other than technical, job-related materials) but also in the variety of ideas, images, and themes that emerged from their reading. It is a journey marked by my students' words more than mine, and I will let them speak for themselves as appropriate. Some of their words will help to shed light on my own journey and how their work prompted me to explore and question my own agenda and goals as a teacher.

When I started to think about all this, I was drawn to a statement written by one of my students: "When I read this book as a child . . . the ugliness was pushed aside." The author is Brian Condon, a mid-level manager for NYNEX in New York City. His simply worded statement encapsulated the experience of many of my students who returned to *Adventures of Huckleberry Finn* after some years. While they recalled the joy of Huck's adventure, the physical and psychological violence that flows through the tale became increasingly disturbing; they were surprised and appalled that they had read past the brutality and the abject and resolute prejudice when they first met up with Sam Clemens's adolescent storyteller. I had hoped to give my students an opportunity to learn about Clemens, his times, and the influences that played upon his creative work; they thought they were going to get the "real" story (the tabloid version) about Mark Twain. I am still not quite sure that we managed to find a common point of agreement.

One of the premier challenges of working with adult learners is the fashioning of a study that offers a twist. Faced with a choice of studies, adult learners often gravitate toward topics that are more familiar. Familiarity breeds contentment. Familiar topics are safe: you already know what to say; you do not face as great a risk when you offer an opinion; you maintain a little of the expertise that brought you professional success. American literature is usually not among these students' favorite topics. Also, adult learners are demanding; they expect to be presented information that is useful (though that is far too often used to criticize adults) and are looking for possible relationships between their "school" work and their professional and personal lives. Adult learners are not shy: "So," they ask, "what exactly *does* Mark

Twain have to do with management?" A quick response—"Well, I can show you how *not* to go bankrupt" or a rather ephemeral "Management is often managing people not things. What better way to understand people than to read Twain"—will not be enough. A humanist tendency to argue vaguely for culture and appreciation of tradition and context will often fall flat. Ironically, one of the more effective arguments for the humanities is that they offer intellectually challenging vacations from professional thought and study. I ask, "Do you want to be so beaten down by Organizational Behavior and Managerial Economics that you can't lift your head? Think about taking topics so different that they let you escape. Shift gears completely." It often works.

I hoped my study for the term—"Mark Twain's America: A Confluence of Western Idyll and Racial Tension"—would shift some gears. As I designed the study, I confronted several disturbing questions, not only about the material I was expected to present, but about my primary goals as a teacher.

Let me deal with each question. First, the material, the reading list. My experience with adult learners has taught me the risks in thinking that adults are able to handle complex questions of canon or research methodology simply because they are adults (age is not the primary determinant of intellectual sophistication or the ability to think critically). Many students are drawn to tradition because it is what they think *should* be taught. They want to make sure their time and money are spent gaining what they believe college learning should be. That attitude can set up resistance to reading material or combinations of material that deviate from preset (and perhaps anachronistic) expectations. One option, then, was to send students off to read extensively in Mark Twain's works. Another was to season a list with stories by Twain's contemporaries (I had thought, for example, of including works by William Dean Howells, Marietta Holley, Stephen Crane, Henry James). Again, adult learners might take each plan as a version of what they missed earlier and ask no questions about the design and foundation for the study. But would they be attracted to it? I wanted to do something else to challenge students and to entice them to join the group.

I decided to focus on *Adventures of Huckleberry Finn*. I asked students to read *Huck* first so they could meet Twain at one of his more successful and more controversial points. If we start with Twain's comment that he wrote not for children but for adults who had been children, *Huck Finn* did seem a better place to begin than the more child-like *Tom Sawyer.* Starting with *Huck* would let us jump immediately into the critical questions that now surround that book and to use those questions to move back into Twain's canon to explore *The Adventures of Tom Sawyer, Life on the Mississippi, Pudd'nhead Wilson, Tom Sawyer Abroad, Tom Sawyer, Detective,* and the autobiography.[4] These formed the nucleus of the Mississippi writings and established the first half of the study's subtitle—the focus on western idyll. So far, students were going to get what they expected—a lot of Mark Twain, and a lot of Mark Twain on the Mississippi.

I felt it important, however, to introduce students to a deeper appreciation of the discussion and controversy that has grown around *Huck* and the question of racism. This approach had little to do with any obscure notion of political correctness; instead, I was most interested in placing issues that define and build culture before my students so that they could engage questions which link past and present—both within the general culture and within their own families. Some of my students had children either in high school or in college, and I suspected the controversy would make its way into their homes before long (I was eventually proved right). I also felt it increasingly important to encourage students to join the critical discussion so that they felt a part of the debate that was shaping their culture. Throughout my preparations for the study, I was influenced by R. W. B. Lewis's notion of culture in *The American Adam*—"a culture achieves identity not so much through the ascendancy of one particular set of convictions as through the emergence of its peculiar and distinctive dialogue" (2).[5] I wanted to introduce students to both the contents and the process of that dialogue.

To be active participants in that discussion, students had to have some appreciation not only of the discipline's approach to reading but of both nineteenth- and twentieth-century voices that combine to shape the critical debate. For an introduction to the discipline, I asked students to read David E. E. Sloane's *"Adventures of Huckleberry Finn": A Student's Companion to the Novel;* for nineteenth- and twentieth-century voices, I asked them to read two slave narratives, Harriet Jacobs's *Incidents in the Life of a Slave Girl* and Frederick Douglass's *My Bondage and My Freedom* (for firsthand accounts of slavery and for additional experience with the rhetorical strategies for addressing audiences) and selected essays from Leonard, Tenney, and Davis's *Satire or*

Evasion? Black Perspectives on "Huckleberry Finn." Incidents, Bondage, and *Satire?* formed the second half of the course's subtitle, the focus on "racial tension."

But what students would be attracted by this scheme? How would they react to the tensions that weaved through the study? In the end, ten students signed up (the average number is twelve per group).[6] There were five men and five women; one was an African American student. The students were all mid-level managers in New York state corporations. Some were beginning their first term in the program; others were in their second or third term. Each came to the study with a slightly different motivation: most needed to complete a humanities study to balance against their professional credits; most were also interested in reading more of Mark Twain and learning about him. A couple of students were attracted to the study because of the mix of Twain and African American writers; two of them came along despite that mix. All, I think it is safe to say, were more than a little apprehensive, both because of the workload and because they simply were not sure what was going to happen; they did not have a clear idea of what I would expect of them.

As I said, students who enter this program gravitate toward topics that grow out of their workday experiences (such topics are easier because they are not so alien). These ten students, however, were taking a chance. Their backgrounds were varied and rich; however, they were walking into an uncertain, even threatening, environment. They did not know a lot about Twain. Some had read several of his books as children, but they had set all of that aside. They all knew of my interest in Twain (faculty profiles were published in the bulletin describing the studies for the term). They were, as a group, motivated and ready, but also uncertain and skeptical. None of them were hostile. One, Brian, was brash and good-naturedly rebellious. He prefaced his first paper to me:

> Michael, I must admit that I began this course with a jolt of energy, a surge of adrenalin, "What?! A hundred bucks worth of books?!!" But hey, I did luck out when you sent that free postcard so now I consider things equal, that is, compared to all those other 4 credit courses with about forty dollars in books, but without the postcard. Don't misunderstand—I like the postcard, very much so; this

is just a pitiful attempt to distract you from the fact that I am cheap, and will never again pick a course without pricing the book list.

It was neither the last nor the most strenuous reminder these students gave me about workload and choice of books. After all, they worked within a business climate buffeted daily with downsizing and budget tightening—something that had clear implications for some students who were not always sure about job stability or security.

I asked the group to read *Huck* and to send in their first response papers by the time we met for our first residency (week 4 of the 24-week term). Their first papers offered a broad range of comments in a variety of styles and voices. Let me offer samples of their comments here to show the kind of reactions (sometimes very emotional) they were having to the reading and to the discussion. First, a comment on Huck as a boy: "Huck is a street-smart kid who is rebelling against gentrification. But he pays a heavy price for his rebellion. By his very acts of rebellion and his rejection of the widow's standards, he is forced to confront the veracity of his beliefs which no longer apply to the world in which he finds himself." This focus on the boy and his rebellion and on the companion notion of *Huck* as a boy's book would come up again for another student:

> I brought my own bias to this book, that of the story written with a target audience of twelve year old boys. How far from the truth that prejudice was!
>
> In reflecting on the work I viewed it as a quest for freedom— Huck's freedom from a drunken abusive father and from the respectable ways of the widow, and Jim's freedom from slavery. Huck and Jim on their raft float through a tough American world. They were "children" who had to survive in an adult environment. From the very beginning of the book Huck and Jim are in ecstasy whenever they are safe "for a time." Both are required to use their wit just to continue to exist. Huck and Jim are forever warding off trouble, escaping from trouble, or resting from trouble....
>
> I could not help but draw a comparison between the story written in 1885 and modern day events concerning child abuse, lack of socialization resulting from ineffectual foster care, homelessness, and prejudice.

These passages offer examples of an adult tendency to establish strong personal connections to the reading based on specific experiences. Nothing prevents the reader from jerking the text out of its context to place it within a time more congenial to interpretations based on contemporary events or concerns. While I would often have to lead the discussion away from any number of parenthetical and hypothetical discussions of Twain's reactions to today's issues, all of these students worked with a strong sense of the importance of the story and allowed the tale to dominate their reactions and thoughts. It was important that they use that strong reaction to understand that all worthwhile critical work begins with personal interest and provocative ideas and that their reactions formed the basis for our critical discussion and their analytical writing. Context could come later. Right now, the reading evoked strong feelings shaped by the different experiences of reading the text as a child and as an adult. And those feelings propelled the study.

Here are a few more samples from their brief responses:

> While on the surface this book appears to be an adventure story aimed toward children, *Huckleberry Finn* is also an adult book. The story deals with many relevant issues of the day. Clemens spoke through Huck who hates sham, artificial restraints, and injustice. When the book is closely examined one recognizes the issues of religion, government, slavery, racism, and mob mentality are among the many points satirized by Clemens.
>
> Rereading this book I found myself laughing at Clemens' descriptive vernacular. He was a great humorist. It is much more enjoyable reading this book as an adult.

While this student continued to focus on the humor in Twain throughout the term, others were less taken with the laughter as they looked beneath the surface tale:

> I read this book with mixed emotions; as a child my father kept trying to get me to read it and although I started it once or twice I could never get into it, on the other hand after Labor Management and Presidential Politics, I was looking for a class that would allow me to read novels, even if they were not ones of my choosing. . . .
>
> I intend to read this book again and use a high-lighter to pick out some of my favorite parts. I regret I didn't think to do this when I

read it the first time. Although this was not a book that I couldn't put down, I was anxious to get back to it each and every time.

The next:

> As a sixth grader, I remember reading and enjoying both *Tom Sawyer* and *Huck Finn*. I don't remember which had the most effect on me at the time, but I do remember that I was excited by their adventures and probably influenced too much by their lack of respect for authority. Although I never ran away from home, I did live near the Hudson River and could identify with some of their adventures. I remember that we found an abandoned rowboat on the riverbank and we would row out toward the barges and ride the waves made by the wake of them. I also remember one spring when we built a raft and floated it on a pond near the Oakwood cemetery. This raft was not big enough for more than one person, and would almost capsize when we walked too close to the edge. As I read *Huck Finn* back then, I wondered how they managed to float down the river with so many people on board through storms without sinking.
>
> As I picked up the book again, I remembered a little of the story, but I had forgotten (or never learned the first time) the moral lessons. As I reread the story, I was surprised at the different aspects of the story which affected me. The most important aspect was the realization that Huck was basically a good hearted boy who was struggling to deal with his feelings toward Jim, and the poisoned attitude he had toward negroes and slavery and race. Although he didn't deal with it as well as someone who had been raised in a more tolerant society, he managed to overcome the racial attitude he learned from his society and eventually do the right thing in spite of his feeling that he was doing wrong.

The next:

> My first remembrance of Mark Twain and his work was a movie that I saw as a child. It was the *Adventures of Tom Sawyer*. I enjoyed the story, the action and the characters. It was great suspense for me but left me fearful of Indians, caves, and old aunts. I looked forward to watching it every year but never got over the terrorizing sight of Injun Joe climbing the ledge to get Tom Sawyer. . . .

Reading the *Adventures of Huckleberry Finn* again renews fond memories of what life on the river was like for Huck. The first time I read it, I became part of it. I pictured my self [*sic*] on the raft with Huck and Jim. I was included in the dialogue. I new [*sic*] what would be said next, what Huck was thinking. I felt Jim's pain of being separated from his family. I surrendered to the dialogue, to the river and the life it gave and took away. I felt the poverty and desperation of people trying to survive while living like animals.

I felt more emotion this time around with Huck. The word nigger cut through the walls I build around myself. My heart broke when I think about Jim, lashing out at his deaf and dumb daughter for not closing the door and then how he felt, staring at her, with a half smile still rimming her face, looking for acceptance, loving him regardless. How touching.

This is what I asked myself: Do I feel this way now because I am a parent and have acted in a similar way to my child? Was Twain a father who felt and acted like I had?

And, finally:

The Adventures of Huckleberry Finn strikes a number of emotions with this reader. It is an enjoyable, fun book filled with humorous moments that describe people and their tendencies. Its descriptions, through the eyes of a boy, are instantly vivid and I felt pulled from adventure to adventure. . . .

I believe Twain was attempting to detail a time when slavery, as an institution, as a thought process, was so widely accepted that it could pervert the thinking and actions of children. Through description he spoke to the problem without waving a sword in the air.

Other topics he spoke to with his quiet details were education, religious training, child abuse, alcoholism, and the slow movement of the judicial system. I know that when I read this book as a youngster I only saw the adventures and identified with Huck and Tom. The ugliness was pushed aside in my own childish enthusiasm for fun; much as Huck and Tom pursued the "stylish" adventures of a jailbreak and ignored the danger to Jim.

Invariably, my students brought their own experiences to *Huck*. They brought their experience as children and their experience as adults and parents. Their adult lives provided insight into the relationship between Huck and Tom and Jim. They were unanimous in damning Tom Sawyer as a bully and a sham, but they also understood his hold on both Huck and Jim. They greeted Huck's turn back to "civilization" with sadness rather than anger, a sadness seasoned with the experience of compromises and battles fought and rarely won. Lessons of adult and parental concern drew them most often to a new and unexpected notion of Twain. As the college term progressed, these students faced not Mark Twain the legend, but Sam Clemens the man—the father and husband and citizen—who wrote compelling tales based on human emotion. Their longer papers explored women in Twain's fiction, incidents of alcoholism and abuse, Twain's social criticism, and issues of duality and twins both related to identity and as metaphor for a country split by civil war.

Their experience as parents, however, may have had the most influence. Most were drawn to *Huckleberry Finn* as the predicament of the parentless boy and the childless parent brought together to learn a lesson in the definition of human connection and family. They were energized by Roxy's plight in *Pudd'nhead Wilson*; they were genuinely and deeply upset by Twain's hasty requiem to Jean Clemens, "The Death of Jean." It was an impression reinforced by the tales of Jacobs and Douglass. In fact, one of the dominant themes throughout was the resilience of family—a theme they eventually saw connecting the writing of a white transplanted Southerner and black runaway slaves. That, I think, startled them.

As we moved into the second half of the study and began our reading of Jacobs and Douglass, one student wrote: "I never appreciated how hideous slavery was and how the pain it caused is still felt today. . . . I read the *Life of a Slave Girl* [sic] and found it hard to justify my ignorance of slavery." Again, notions of family seemed to have the most impact as we moved through Jacobs's and Douglass's texts. Several students found Jacobs's tale especially hard-hitting:

> I found myself getting more emotionally involved as I read Jacobs's story. In analyzing why this was the case, I felt that first and foremost being a woman and a mother myself I could put myself in her situation and secondly I felt that a woman was much more vulnerable than a male. What she endured, although at times unbelievable, was absolutely horrible. . . . She was always at a disadvantage

as she had to consider her children and the impact her actions would have on them.

And another:

> I found reading this book to be very difficult. I would have to read some, then put it down, and pick it up later. I could not read it continually. The ordeals that Jacobs survived were painful to read about. I could not begin to imagine her pain and discomfort during her seven years in a crawl space. To have so little control over your life and the lives of those that you love, is a terrible fate. Being abused and having no recourse is inhumane.

Douglass's underlying concern with family was also prominent in the students' writing:

> Douglass' personal experiences and those of others that he witnessed, demonstrate the barbaric side of slavery that is not addressed in the Twain literature that we read. The experience of a slave would be different from that of a free white man, but Twain does not address the issue of cruelty. He says that no slaves were mistreated on his [uncle's] farm, and that he did not see them mistreated by others. I don't believe he was ignorant of these transgressions, he was not personally acquainted with them. . . .
>
> To be loved and cared for, and then to be torn from that love is something that no one, especially a child, should have to experience. Being abandoned by his grandmother, to a new home, not to mention a new life style, was devastating. How terribly frightened and alone he must have been. Yet you cannot blame his grandmother or his mother for abandoning him, for the choice was not theirs to make. The moves that occurred later in his life were less painful, but still heartless in that they were out of his control, as was almost everything in his life.

A lesson in basic literary criticism would attempt to move these students away from the intensely personal reaction—or at least away from the announcement of that reaction in their public writing. These students, however, were finding out how to use writing to come to terms with the emotional and intellectual dissonances they were experiencing. Telling them to remove their "selves" from their writing would have only shut down their search to understand the import of what they were now reading—most for the first time. One student prefaced his paper in reaction to Jacobs with a brief explanation: "As I began to write for this assignment I began to attempt to explain my feelings about the book and other things, but the explanation grew into a much longer paper than I wanted. I went back over it and found that I couldn't cut any of the ideas without leaving a hole. The result is this seven page paper which probably could have been said in the last two." It took me considerably longer to read those seven pages. But my reading and commenting demonstrated that thinking and writing were important.

All of these experiences bring me to my goals as a teacher. Three memories stay with me: one was the general response to literary criticism as a cottage industry and a surprisingly hostile reaction to the close reading that is the hallmark of our trade. This was clearest in the student reactions to David Sloane's handbook. If there was one book that pushed them to the edge of revolt, it was Sloane's. They were not troubled by what he wrote as much as by the notion that people (and I was one of them) made a living tearing apart books and then putting them back together. One student mentioned that her daughter had just finished *Huck* in a college class and had warned her that she would never appreciate literature once I was through with it and with her. She was genuinely concerned that I was going to take something away from her—that I would remove (perhaps with some violence) her ability to enjoy reading. Other students were simply aghast that we read that carefully, that we look so deeply into texts, and that we have chosen to do this as a job and worse, as a form of stimulation. One student (almost) shouted, "Hey, get a life!"

The other two experiences came as we drew closer as a group. The first was the response of the lone African American student. As we approached the issue of Twain's racism and the problems within *Huck*, he was genuinely disturbed. For him, Jim took on a deep and abiding meaning. And the relationship between the escaped slave and the young white boy became important because it presented a vision that he had not had as a child or as an adult. As a child in South Carolina, he had been in class as the teacher read *Huck* as part of rest time. During one of our breaks, he told me how troubled his rest time was: "I looked up to this man," he told me, "and here he was reading this story and using that language. I used to sit at home on the porch and my grandmother would point to trees and tell us stories about beatings and whippings. I didn't always believe her. And then I read these stories and see that this did happen. She told us not to trust white people. That there weren't any good white people." In an addendum to his paper in response to Jacobs, he wrote: "My grandmother would go to great lengths to tell me of the evils of white people. She was exposed to the fiery tongue of racism after slavery was abolished. My days of listening to healthy black men refusing to work for white people is heightened by these books on slavery." Yet he was an active defender of Twain and of Twain's portrayal of Jim. The evasion episode held no traps for him—he asked, "What did you expect Jim to do?"

My third memory is of a student who called me one afternoon in tears. She had just finished reading "The Death of Jean." "I needed to talk to someone," she said. "I couldn't call my husband. He would just laugh and say, 'There you go again.' I just needed to let someone know how terrible this made me feel." Other students had reactions as strong. One wrote:

> The poignant documentary found in the descriptions of his emotional bankruptcy at the death of his daughter is one of the saddest, most moving pieces of literature I have ever read. He spoke to me as a parent; a heartbroken man unable to muster any anger or frustration, capable only of expressing the utter desolation of a parent faced wth the impossible task of burying a child. I felt like an intruder; his grief was so overwhelming and his sadness so compelling that I wanted to stop reading but all I could do was continue, and cry.

Here, I think, is how life experience infuses our reading with an unexpected power. Our shared experience of family and of loss or even the fear of loss leaves us open to all-too-human feelings and failings. Huck and Roxy, Jacobs and Douglass, Jean and (ultimately) Clemens himself are linked more strongly because we interpret their lives and actions and thoughts through the lens of our personal context and experience. Today, both youth and age bring a wealth of experience to their reading. Age, however, brings the distance that sharpens our sense of the pain inherent in human contact. *Huck*, I think, gets better as *we* age.

All of this leads to my final point. It has to do more with how and why we teach than with how and why we teach *Huck*, but it is my experience with *Huck* that has tuned my thinking and made me reflect on my role as a teacher. The lesson is fairly simple. It is also fairly subversive. I did not enter that study group thinking that I was going to turn these students into English majors or even part-time literary critics. They had jobs, and they were not going to drop them and run to literature. But what they did want and need from me at that point was permission—permission to read and think and to let their reading and thinking move along at their pace and for their own purposes. They needed permission to challenge me and my thinking and to make me answer why I thought I was expert enough to sit with them and regulate the conversation as well as to make me meet that challenge whenever we got together. They needed permission to tell me when they thought a book was terrible, or even when a critic's carefully researched and reasoned approach was "bullshit." They needed permission to have their own ideas and reactions. They needed permission to think and act their age.

I like to think that I helped them rediscover reading, and that I assisted them in tuning at least some of the skills they can use to read and explore. I like to think that I moved them toward an appreciation for learning and a willingness to ask questions (as one student wrote: "A lifetime could be spent on dissecting one book so obviously I don't have the answer—but I learned enough [to] raise the question"). Several of them will go on to read more Mark Twain (one even ordered *Personal Recollections of Joan of Arc* for summer reading). One or two will read more slave narratives. Others will consider that there may be more going on in a story than simple plot and action. Brian even chose to take yet another study with me—this one on Defining the American Self. He did not even check to see how much the books were going to cost.

Notes

1 SUNY Empire State College serves students at various locations throughout New York State. The college presently enrolls approximately seven thousand students.

2 ESC requires 128 credits for the baccalaureate, which students may receive through various avenues. Transcripted credit, credits awarded for prior learning, and credits gained by successful completion of learning contracts are the three primary means.

3 Students develop their plan of study in consultation with a faculty mentor who

guides the student through the process of designing a degree program that will meet professional, personal, and institutional demands. Students work with the same mentor throughout their time in the college, although they most often take individual studies with other members of the faculty.

4 The text I chose for the autobiography is *Mark Twain's Own Autobiography: The Chapters from the North American Review,* ed. Michael J. Kiskis, Madison: University of Wisconsin Press, 1990.

5 The entire passage is instructive: "Every culture seems, as it advances toward maturity, to produce its own determining debate over the ideas that preoccupy it: salvation, the order of nature, money, power, sex, the machine, and the like. The debate, indeed, may be said to *be* the culture, at least on its loftiest levels; for a culture achieves identity not so much through the ascendancy of one particular set of convictions as through the emergence of its peculiar and distinctive dialogue. (Similarly, a culture is on the decline when it submits to intellectual martial law, and fresh understanding is denied in a denial of further controversy.) Intellectual history, properly conducted, exposes not only the dominant ideas of a period, or of a nation, but more important, the dominant clashes over ideas. Or to put it more austerely: the historian looks not only for the major terms of discourse, but also for major pairs of opposed terms which, by their very opposition, carry discourse forward. The historian looks, too, for the coloration or discoloration of ideas received from the sometimes bruising contact of opposites" (1–2).

6 I want to thank those students and acknowledge their contribution both to the study group and to this article. My thanks to Joy Chambers, Gerry Charles, Brian Condon, Pat Curtin, Roseann Goodman, Charles Lewis, Thomas McGreevy, Pat Town, Charles Hale, and Linda Isaacs. Their ideas and insights helped me better understand Mark Twain; their sense of humor helped me keep all of our work in clear perspective.

Works Cited

Douglass, Frederick. *My Bondage and My Freedom.* Ed. William L. Andrews. Urbana: University of Illinois Press, 1987.

Jacobs, Harriet A. *Incidents in the Life of a Slave Girl: Written by Herself.* Ed. Jean Fagan Yellin. Cambridge, Mass.: Harvard University Press, 1987.

Leonard, James S., Thomas A. Tenney, and Thadious M. Davis, eds. *Satire or Evasion? Black Perspectives on Huckleberry Finn."* Durham, N.C.: Duke University Press, 1992.

Lewis, R. W. B. *The American Adam: Innocence, Tragedy, and Tradition in the Nineteenth Century.* Chicago: University of Chicago Press, 1955.

Sloane, David E. E. *Adventures of Huckleberry Finn: A Student's Companion to the Novel.* Boston: Twayne, 1988.

Twain, Mark. *Adventures of Huckleberry Finn.* New York: Penguin, 1959.

———. *The Adventures of Tom Sawyer; Tom Sawyer Abroad; Tom Sawyer, Detective.* Berkeley: University of California Press, 1980.

———. *Life on the Mississippi.* New York: Bantam, 1981.

———. *Mark Twain's Own Autobiography: The Chapters from the North American Review.* Ed. Michael J. Kiskis. Madison: University of Wisconsin Press, 1990.

———. *Personal Recollections of Joan of Arc.* Hartford, Conn.: Stowe-Day Foundation, 1980.

———. *Pudd'nhead Wilson.* New York: Penguin, 1964.

Contributors

Joseph A. Alvarez. Instructor of English and Chair of English and Humanities, Central Piedmont Community College. Author of articles and conference papers on various figures in literature and issues in composition pedagogy; coauthor of preparation books for College Board composition (1988) and literature (1990) achievement tests and for the Medical College Admission Test (1991), all published by Research & Education Assn.

Lawrence I. Berkove. Professor of English, University of Michigan at Dearborn. Editor of Dan De Quille's *The Fighting Horse of the Stanislaus: Stories and Essays* (University of Iowa Press, 1990), De Quille's *Dives and Lazarus* (Ardis, 1988), and Ambrose Bierce's *Skepticism and Dissent: Selected Journalism* (UMI Research Press, 1986); author of numerous articles on Twain and other writers of the nineteenth and twentieth centuries.

Anthony J. Berret, S.J. Assistant Professor of English, St. Joseph's University (Philadelphia). Author of *Mark Twain and Shakespeare: A Cultural Legacy* (University Press of America, 1993) and of articles and papers on Twain and on music and literature in the works of F. Scott Fitzgerald and Toni Morrison.

Wesley Britton. Harrisburg Area Community College. Author of articles on Mark Twain in such journals as the *Mark Twain Journal, Mark Twain Circular,* and *South Dakota Review;* contributor to the *Mark Twain Encyclopedia.*

Louis J. Budd. James B. Duke Professor Emeritus, Duke University. Author of *Mark Twain: Social Philosopher* (Indiana University Press, 1962; Kennikat Press, 1973) and *Our Mark Twain: The Making of His Public Personality* (University of Pennsylvania Press, 1983); editor of the two-volume *Mark Twain: Collected Tales, Sketches, Speeches, and Essays* (Library of America, 1992) and numerous essay collections about Twain and about other American authors; formerly editor of *American Literature.*

James E. Caron. Associate Professor of English, University of Hawaii. Coeditor of *Sut Lovingood's Nat'ral Born Yarnspinner: Essays on George Washington Harris* (University of Alabama Press, 1996). Author of articles on the American comic tradition, as well as Mark Twain and Frank Norris, in such journals as *Modern Language Quarterly, Texas Studies in Literature and Language, Studies in American Humor,* and *Nineteenth-Century Fiction.*

Everett Carter. Professor Emeritus of English, University of California, Davis. Author of *Howells and the Age of Realism* (J. B. Lippincott, 1954), and *The American Idea: The Literary Responses to American Optimism* (University of North Carolina Press, 1977).

Jocelyn Chadwick-Joshua. Associate Director, Dallas Center for Humanities and Culture. Author of *The Jim Dilemma: Reading Race in Huckleberry Finn* (University Press of Mississippi, 1998); author of articles and conference papers on Mark Twain and on censorship of books.

Pascal Covici, Jr. (1930–1997). Late E. A. Lilly Professor of English, Southern Methodist University. Author of *Mark Twain's Humor: The Image of a World* (Southern Methodist University Press, 1962), *Humor and Revelation in American Literature: The Puritan Connection* (University of Missouri Press, 1996), and essays on Twain and others; editor of Stephen Crane's *The Red Badge of Courage, and Other Stories* (Penguin, 1991) and *The Portable Steinbeck* (Viking Press, 1971; Penguin, 1978).

Beverly R. David. Professor of Humanities (Retired), Western Michigan University. Author of *Mark Twain and His Illustrators* (Whitston, 1986) and of many articles on the illustrations in Twain's novels.

Victor Doyno. Professor of English, SUNY, Buffalo. Author of *Writing "Huck Finn": Mark Twain's Creative Process* (University of Pennsylvania Press, 1991); editor of *Mark Twain, Selected Writings of an American Skeptic* (Prometheus, 1983) and Barnabe Barnes's *Parthenophil and Parthenophe* (Southern Illinois University Press, 1971); author of foreword and textual addendum for *Adventures of Huckleberry Finn* (comprehensive edition; Random House, 1996).

Dennis W. Eddings. Professor of Humanities, Western Oregon University. Editor of *The Naiad Voice: Essays on Poe's Satiric Hoaxing* (Associated Faculty Press, 1983) and author of articles on Poe and Twain.

Shelley Fisher Fishkin. Professor of American Studies and English, University of Texas at Austin. Author of *Lighting Out for the Territory: Reflections on Mark Twain and American Culture* (Oxford University Press, 1997), *Was Huck Black?: Mark Twain and African-American Voices* (Oxford University Press, 1993), and *From Fact to Fiction: Journalism and Imaginative Writing in America* (Johns Hopkins University Press, 1985; Oxford University Press, 1988); coeditor of *Listening to Silences: New Essays in Feminist Criticism* (Oxford University Press, 1994) and *People of the Book: Thirty Scholars Reflect on Their Jewish Identity* (University of Wisconsin Press, 1996); editor of the 29-volume *Oxford Mark Twain* (Oxford University Press, 1996).

S. D. Kapoor. Professor of English, JN Vyas University (Jodhpur, India). Author of many articles on Mark Twain and African American literature. Editor, *Jodhpur Studies in English.* Currently at work on a comparative study of Dalits and African Americans.

Michael J. Kiskis. Associate Professor of American Literature, Elmira College. Editor of *Mark Twain's Own Autobiography: The Chapters from the North American Review* (University of Wisconsin Press, 1990); editor of *Studies in American Humor: The Journal of the American Humor Studies Association;* author of articles on Twain and on adult nontraditional educational program development.

James S. Leonard. Professor of English, The Citadel. Coauthor of *The Fluent Mundo: Wallace Stevens and the Structure of Reality* (University of Georgia Press, 1988); coeditor of *Satire or Evasion?: Black Perspectives on Huckleberry Finn* (Duke University Press, 1992) and *Author-ity and Textuality: Current Views of Collaborative Writing* (Locust Hill Press, 1994); editor of the quarterly *Mark Twain Circular* (since 1987).

Victoria Thorpe Miller. Associate Professor and Coordinator, Department of English, Alverno College. Coauthor of *Composing with WordStar* (1986) and *Composing with PFS:Write/PFS:Professional Write* (1988); Associate Editor, *Style* (1986–88). Currently at work on a biography of Eleanor Clark [Warren].

Stan Poole. Associate Professor of English, Louisiana College. Author of articles on Mark Twain, published in *Studies in American Fiction* and *The Mark Twain Encyclopedia.*

Tom Reigstad. Professor of English, Buffalo State College. Has written extensively on Twain's period in Buffalo and was a 1989 Research Fellow-in-Residence at the Elmira College Center for Mark Twain Studies.

David E. E. Sloane. Professor of English, University of New Haven. Author of *Adventures of Huckleberry Finn: American Comic Vision* (Twayne, 1988) and *Mark Twain as a Literary Comedian* (Louisiana State University Press, 1979); editor of *American Humor: New Studies, New Directions* (University of Alabama Press, 1998), *Mark Twain's Humor: Critical Essays* (Garland, 1993), *The Literary Humor of the Urban Northeast: 1830–1890* (Louisiana State University Press, 1983), and two other books; editor of the journal *Essays in Arts and Sciences.*

David Tomlinson. Professor of English, U.S. Naval Academy. Author of articles about Twain that have appeared in the *Mark Twain Journal* and *The Mark Twain Encyclopedia.* His work about computer use has been printed in the *Computer Assisted Composition Journal, CHIPS, Computing at USNA,* and other publications. Tomlinson is the creator of two hypertext computer programs, *Exploring the Novel* and *Exploring Drama* and of two web sites, *Poe Perplex* and *Ethics Everywhere.*

Index

Library of Congress Cataloging-in-Publication Data
Making Mark Twain work in the classroom / edited by James S. Leonard.
 p.   cm.
Includes index.
ISBN 0-8223-2278-1 (cloth : alk. paper).
ISBN 0-8223-2297-8 (paper : alk. paper).
 1. Twain, Mark, 1835–1910—Study and teaching.   2. Literature and
society—United States—History—19th century—Study and teaching.
3. Twain, Mark, 1835–1910. Adventures of Huckleberry Finn.
4. Social classes in literature—Study and teaching.   5. Adventure
stories, American—Study and teaching.   6. Sex role in literature—
Study and teaching.   7. Race in literature—Study and teaching.
I. Leonard, James S.
PS1338.M23   1999   818'.409—DC21   98-42358 CIP